Contents

"Reality is merely an illusion, albeit a very persistent one."

— Albert Einstein

1. Embarking on the Quantum Journey: An Invitation

In a universe that sprawls infinitely beyond our comprehension, hidden realms beneath the surface of everyday existence hold secrets that challenge everything we believe to be true. Welcome to the quantum world, a place where particles behave in the peculiar ways that defy conventional logic and reality.

Though the domain of the very small, quantum mechanics has vast implications, influencing everything from the nature of reality to the technology that propels our modern world. Here, electrons and quarks dance in a symphony of probabilities, intertwined with waves and particles in ways that mystify even the most astute minds.

As we delve into "Beneath Reality: The Hidden Quantum World," prepare to embark on a journey that unveils the enigmatic truth beneath the tapestry of the universe. Each chapter offers a new facet, a different lens through which to see the unseen, and better understand the foundational principles governing our world.

Let this book serve as your guide through the labyrinth of quantum mysteries—where conventional laws of physics fall away and a more bizarre, yet extraordinarily intricate reality emerges. Join me, Britney Eileen Kelly, as we unravel the fabric of the cosmos, threading through the known and unknown, until we uncover the very essence of life as we know it.

2. Foundations of Quantum Mechanics

2.1. The Birth of Quantum Theory

The dawn of quantum theory emerged in the late 19th and early 20th centuries, birthed from the ashes of classical physics, which dominated scientific understanding for centuries. At the heart of this revolutionary shift were experiments and discoveries that revealed an unsettling truth: the world is not as straightforward as it appears. Instead of a deterministic universe governed by fixed laws, the quantum world is ruled by uncertainty, probability, and an intricate web of interactions that defy classical intuitions.

The initial sparks of quantum theory were ignited by Max Planck in 1900, who introduced the concept of quantization in the face of the blackbody radiation problem. Classical physics, with its reliance on continuous energy spectra, could not explain why objects heated to incandescence emitted light in discrete frequencies, known as spectral lines. Planck proposed that energy is not continuous but quantized, emitted or absorbed in discrete packets he termed "quanta." This radical idea challenged the very fabric of classical thought and laid the groundwork for the arrival of quantum mechanics.

In the years that followed, the landscape of quantum theory broadened as pioneers like Albert Einstein built upon Planck's ideas. In 1905, Einstein extended the notion of quantization to light itself in his explanation of the photoelectric effect, demonstrating that light could behave as both a wave and a particle. This proposed wave-particle duality would later become a central tenet of quantum mechanics, highlighting the complex nature of reality we once thought to be simple.

As the 1910s gripped the scientific community, the development of atomic theory further propelled the birth of quantum mechanics. Niels Bohr emerged as a pivotal figure, introducing his model of the atom in 1913. Bohr proposed that electrons traverse defined orbits around the nucleus, akin to planets around the sun, but only at certain energy levels. The electron's transition from one orbit to another emitted or absorbed quanta of energy, explaining the spectral lines observed in atomic emissions. Bohr's postulates codified the principles of quantization in atomic physics while also highlighting the limitations of classical approaches.

By the 1920s, the burgeoning field of quantum mechanics found new champions. Werner Heisenberg, born in this era of enlightenment, contributed the matrix formulation of quantum mechanics, emphasizing observable quantities rather than physical trajectories. His uncertainty principle emerged as a critical insight, asserting that the precise position and momentum of a particle could not simultaneously be known. This shattered the deterministic underpinnings of classical physics, ushering in an era bound by probabilities and uncertainties.

In parallel, Erwin Schrödinger introduced his wave equation in 1926, offering an alternative interpretation of quantum phenomena. Schrödinger's wave mechanics computed the behavior of quantum systems through wave functions, cementing the concept that particles possess wave-like properties. The beautiful, swirling mathematics of his equation captured the hearts and minds of scientists, intertwining elegance with the sheer strangeness of the quantum world.

The birth of quantum theory was not without its philosophical ramifications. As theorists grappled with the implications of their findings, the question of what it means to observe and measure came to the forefront. The debate would lead to various interpretations of quantum mechanics, including the Copenhagen interpretation championed by Bohr and his contemporaries, which suggested that physical systems do not possess definite properties until measured.

As quantum theory coalesced into a rigorous scientific framework, early experiments served to validate its principles. Notable experiments such as the double-slit experiment vividly showcased the duality of particles and waves. When individual particles were fired at a barrier with two slits, they created an interference pattern as if they were waves, suggesting that particles can exist in multiple states until observed. This revelation forced humanity to revisit its understanding of reality, challenging perception and encouraging deeper enquiry into the nature of existence itself.

The profound implications of quantum mechanics extended beyond academia; they began to permeate technology, shaping innovations that define modern society. The invention of transistors and semiconductors, which are grounded in quantum principles, revolutionized electronics and computing. Similarly, lasers emerged from understanding quantum mechanics, transforming fields from telecommunications to medicine.

Yet, the birth of quantum theory represents merely the tip of the iceberg. It catalyzed a scientific revolution that has yet to fully unfold. With advanced research, the influx of new technologies, and continued philosophical discussions on the nature of reality, the quantum realm invites us still to further question and explore the relationship between humanity and the universe.

As we move deeper into the intricacies of quantum mechanics, it becomes clear that the foundation laid by early pioneers is not just a chapter in scientific history but a springboard into a new paradigm of thought—one that beckons us to embrace uncertainty, to dance with probabilities, and to recognize that beneath the seemingly mundane surface of reality lies a hidden world filled with wonders and mysteries waiting to be discovered. The birth of quantum theory marks not just the inception of a scientific discipline but an awakening to the fascinating, complex reality that lies beneath our familiar existence.

2.2. Classical Physics vs. Quantum Realities

Classical physics and quantum realities present two distinctly contrasting paradigms that shape our understanding of the universe, both on macroscopic and microscopic levels. These frameworks not only describe physical phenomena but also influence the very way we perceive reality. Classical physics, encapsulated by Newtonian mechanics, Maxwell's equations, and thermodynamics, paints a deterministic and structured picture of nature, while quantum mechanics radically redefines our comprehension, incorporating uncertainty, duality, and superposition into the narrative of existence.

At its core, classical physics operates on principles of cause and effect, where a clear relationship exists between actions and outcomes. This deterministic view suggests that if we possess complete knowledge about a system at any given time—its forces, velocities, and positions—we could predict its future states. However, as scientists began probing the atomic and subatomic realms, it became evident that classical physics was insufficient to account for the peculiar behaviors observed.

One of the most emblematic distinctions between classical physics and quantum mechanics lies in the nature of entities. Classical physics depicts particles as discrete, solid objects that obey well-defined trajectories influenced by forces. In contrast, quantum mechanics reveals that particles such as electrons do not possess fixed positions or paths but exist within a haze of probabilities. This notion culminates in the principle of superposition, where particles can exist in multiple states simultaneously until observed or measured. Such phenomena defy our intuitive understanding of reality, shaking the very foundation of classical assumptions regarding matter and energy.

Additionally, classical physics operates under deterministic laws, expecting stability and predictability in the behavior of physical systems. Yet, quantum mechanics introduces an inherent level of unpredictability through Heisenberg's uncertainty principle, which articulates that certain pairs of physical properties—like position and momentum—cannot be simultaneously known to arbitrary precision. This introduces a fundamental limit to knowledge, diverging dramatically from classical assertions that precise measurements can be obtained.

Furthermore, the concept of wave-particle duality, posited by the groundbreaking work of scientists like Louis de Broglie and later corroborated by experiments such as the double-slit experiment, demonstrates that particles exhibit both wave-like and particle-like properties, depending on the context of observation. This duality can be perplexing: an electron can display interference patterns, characteristic of waves, yet when observed, it collapses into a singular state as a particle. Such behavior challenges the binary categorization of phenomena as merely waves or particles, forcing a re-evaluation of our theoretical frameworks.

As we examine the implications of quantum phenomena, we discover that the boundary between classical and quantum realms is not simply a divergence of methods but also extends into philosophical territories. Quantum mechanics invites questions about the observer effect—whether the act of observation fundamentally alters the state of a system. In classical physics, the observer can remain entirely detached, but in the quantum framework, the observer's role becomes integral, raising profound inquiries about the nature of reality, existence, and consciousness itself.

The technological advancements that arise from quantum phenomena further accentuate these differences. Technologies such as lasers, semiconductors, and quantum computing are predicated on principles that challenge classical physics, enabling the design of devices and systems that exploit quantum behaviors to achieve feats unattainable through classical means. For instance, while classical computing relies on binary states to process information, quantum computing harnesses the unique properties of qubits, which can represent multiple states simultaneously due to superposition, offering enormous potential for computation speed and efficiency.

Despite the conflicts and conundrums posed by quantum mechanics, it is essential to recognize that classical physics retains its relevance in our daily experiences. At larger scales, classical laws often effectively approximate the behavior of systems, with quantum effects remaining negligible. The elegant equations of classical mechanics still govern the trajectories of planets, the motion of vehicles, and the interplay of macroscopic objects.

Yet, by acknowledging both paradigms, we glean a more nuanced understanding of the universe—a tapestry woven from classical truths and quantum mysteries. As we transition from understanding the everyday realities shaped by classical physics into the fascinating intricacies of quantum behavior, we find that both realms are necessary to capture the full essence of the physical universe. The coexistence of these realities invites us to embrace the complexity of existence and ponder questions about nature that allure the curiosity and intellect of humanity.

In summary, the journey from classical to quantum is a profound metamorphosis of thought. This shift not only recasts our conception of the physical world but also culminates in a rich stream of technological innovation, philosophical reflection, and a deeper inquiry into the foundations of reality itself. As we forge ahead into this exploration of quantum phenomena, we must remain mindful of the tensions and harmonies between the classical and the quantum, and how each influences our ongoing quest for knowledge and understanding.

2.3. Key Founders and Their Breakthroughs

The realm of quantum mechanics emerged not merely as an academic endeavor but through the transformative visions and breakthroughs of a handful of pioneering scientists whose courage and creativity reshaped humanity's understanding of nature. These key figures laid the groundwork for the intricate, and often paradoxical, laws that govern the quantum world. Their discoveries compel us to reconsider our definitions of reality and existence itself, serving as the pillars upon which modern physics and technology rest.

Max Planck, often heralded as the father of quantum theory, initiated this scientific revolution in 1900 with his quantum hypothesis. Faced with the unresolved problem of blackbody radiation, Planck proposed that energy is emitted in discrete units, or "quanta," rather than as a continuous flow. This proposition, starkly contrasting the classical view of energy distribution, served as the catalyst for quantum mechanics. Planck's work not only resolved a pressing scientific issue but ignited a philosophical shift that questioned the very nature of energy and its interaction with matter. He famously remarked that his discovery led to a world view grounded in both light and darkness, encapsulating the duality intrinsic to quantum phenomena.

Building upon Planck's groundbreaking ideas, Albert Einstein revolutionized our comprehension of light and energy in 1905 through his explanation of the photoelectric effect. He posited that light could exhibit both wave-like and particle-like characteristics, introducing the concept of "photons." Einstein's assertion that light quanta have discrete properties laid the foundation for wave-particle duality, fundamentally altering the trajectory of physics and compelling future theorists to grapple with the perplexities of dual nature in matter. His work not only expanded the boundaries of quantum mechanics but also paved the way for the further exploration of atomic theory and subatomic particles.

Niels Bohr emerged shortly thereafter, constructing a model of the atom that intertwined earlier quantum concepts with a visualization of atomic structure. In his 1913 model, Bohr proposed that electrons occupy specific, quantized orbits around the nucleus, akin to planets orbiting the sun. This revolutionary model provided explanations for the spectral lines produced by various elements, bridging quantum concepts with observable phenomena. Bohr's insistence on the quantization of angular momentum in atomic systems constituted a monumental advancement, solidifying his place as a key figure in the nascent field of quantum mechanics. His collaborative discussions and intellectual exchanges with contemporaries enabled the formation of the Copenhagen interpretation, asserting cosmic phenomena's probabilistic nature through measurement, an outlook that remains influential today.

Theoretical physicist Werner Heisenberg made indispensable contributions with his formulation of matrix mechanics in 1925 and the introduction of his uncertainty principle a year later. Heisenberg's uncertainty principle established a fundamental limit to our measurements of certain physical properties, denying the possibility of simultaneously pinpointing a particle's position and momentum. This revolutionary insight confronted the deterministic nature of classical physics and ushered in an era where the act of measurement itself emerged as an integral component of quantum mechanics. Heisenberg reframed our understanding of reality itself, suggesting that reality is not a fixed entity but a spectrum shaped by observation.

Simultaneously, Erwin Schrödinger provided an alternative perspective with his formulation of wave mechanics, manifesting in the famed Schrödinger equation. Released in 1926, this equation offered a mathematical description of quantum phenomena, portraying particles as wave functions defined by probability distributions. Schrödinger's work introduced the notion of superposition, wherein particles could exist in multiple states concurrently, fundamentally altering our grasp of causality. His wave function concept became a cornerstone for interpreting quantum systems, merging elegance in mathematics with the underlying strangeness of quantum behavior.

The collective insights of these founders converged to address pivotal questions that challenged existing paradigms. However, as quantum characters integrated into a cohesive framework, dissent arose regarding the philosophical implications of their findings. The debates surrounding the role of the observer—the impact of measurement on quantum states—evoked philosophical inquiries that bridged science and metaphysics. This intellectual battleground fostered discussions that washed over a breadth of interpretations, each seeking to reconcile the apparent contradictions posed by quantum mechanics.

In the decades following their groundbreaking advancements, physicists such as John Bell and David Bohm further propelled the exploration of quantum entanglement, laying the groundwork for our contemporary understanding of nonlocality and communication between entangled particles. Bell's theorem, in particular, proved instrumental by describing the phenomenon where separated entangled particles can influence one another instantaneously, challenging classical intuitions about cause and effect, and provoking philosophical debates about realism versus nonlocal phenomena.

As these early pioneers illustrated through their unwavering commitment to explore uncharted territories, their contributions not only illuminated the intricacies of subatomic behavior but also propelled advancements that would permeate technology and daily life. Their discoveries birthed groundbreaking innovations, from modern electronics to the burgeoning field of quantum computing, showcasing the profound impact of their insights on society.

In examining the trajectory of quantum mechanics, we recognize that the foundational breakthroughs of these key figures signify more than academic triumphs; they encapsulate a paradigm shift that reshaped humanity's perception of reality, existence, and our place in the universe. Each discovery invites us to wander deeper into the fabric of the cosmos, where the mysteries of the quantum world await our probing contemplation. As we appreciate the legacy of these founding thinkers, we simultaneously traverse the ongoing journey of inquiry that continues to challenge our understanding and beckons us to unravel the complexities embedded in the hidden quantum world.

2.4. The Mathematics of Quantum Phenomena

In the intricate tapestry of quantum theory, mathematics serves as both a language and a framework through which we can comprehend the otherwise elusive phenomena that populate the quantum realm. The mathematical formalism of quantum mechanics is not merely a tool for calculation; it reveals deep insights into the underlying principles that govern the behavior of particles and waves at the smallest scales. This language allows physicists to draw predictions about atomic and subatomic behavior, echoing out into applications that define technologies present in our daily lives.

The mathematical foundation of quantum phenomena begins with the wave function, denoted as Ψ (Psi), which provides a comprehensive representation of a quantum system. This complex function encapsulates the probabilities associated with the position and momentum of particles. The square of the absolute value of the wave function, $|\Psi|^2$, indicates the probability density of finding a particle in a given state. The wave function's evolution is governed by

Schrödinger's equation, a differential equation fundamental to quantum mechanics. Schrödinger's equation takes the form:

$$i\hbar \, (\partial \Psi / \partial t) = H\Psi$$

where i is the imaginary unit, $\hbar$ (h-bar) is the reduced Planck's constant, and H is the Hamiltonian operator representing the total energy (kinetic plus potential) of the system. The elegance of this equation lies in its ability to unite the principles of wave phenomena with particle dynamics, fostering our understanding of how quantum systems evolve over time.

However, while Schrödinger's equation provides a deterministic evolution of the wave function itself, the outcomes of measurements are inherently probabilistic. This dichotomy is one of the defining features of quantum mechanics, wherein the act of observation plays a pivotal role. The mathematics reflecting this tension introduces us to concepts such as operators and eigenvalues. In quantum mechanics, observable quantities such as position, momentum, and energy are represented not as static values but as operators acting on the wave function. When a measurement is made, the observable collapses the wave function into one of its eigenstates, corresponding to the eigenvalue associated with that operator. The probability of this collapse occurring in any specific eigenstate is determined by the coefficients in the wave function's representation.

The uncertainty principle, formulated by Werner Heisenberg, reinforces this probabilistic nature with its intrinsic mathematical expression involving the position (x) and momentum (p) of a particle:

$$\Delta x \Delta p \geq \hbar/2$$

This inequality captures the essence of quantum behavior: the more precisely we measure one property, the less precisely we can know the other. The mathematical implications of this principle extend into various realms of physics, leading to revelations that challenge classical interpretations of reality and push the boundaries of what can be known about a system.

In exploring the mathematics of quantum mechanics, we encounter the principle of superposition, which builds on the foundational concept of wave-like behavior. In a quantum context, particles can exist in multiple states simultaneously, represented mathematically as a linear combination of wave functions:

$$\Psi = c_1\Psi_1 + c_2\Psi_2 + \ldots + c_n\Psi_n$$

Here, the coefficients $(c_1, c_2, \ldots, c_n)$ are complex numbers that indicate the likelihood or probability amplitude of each state contributing to the overall wave function. This superpositional capability enables phenomena such as interference patterns, which are starkly observed in experiments like the double-slit, where particles seemingly traverse multiple paths at the same time until measured.

Most profoundly, the mathematics of entanglement—in which two or more particles become interconnected regardless of the distance separating them—exhibits an even deeper layer of complexity. The entangled state of two particles can be expressed mathematically using tensor products, where the overall system is represented by a multi-particle wave function. In this framework, the measurement of one particle instantly influences the state of its counterpart, collapsing its wave function in a manner that appears to defy classical intuitions about locality and causation.

Furthermore, quantum mechanics possesses a remarkable symmetry expressed through group theory, wherein transformations operate across quantum states in congruence with physical conservation laws. The application of group theory allows physicists to classify particles and predict their interactions in a coherent and systematic way, influencing particle physics and leading to the development of the Standard Model.

These mathematical pillars, while abstract, unveil a world that resonates with layers of theoretical and philosophical inquiry. While many practitioners excel in the mathematical formulation, debates surrounding interpretation continue to permeate the field of quantum mechanics. The seeming paradoxes born from equations and their implications invite philosophers and scientists alike to ponder the essence of existence and knowledge within the quantum domain.

In conclusion, the mathematics of quantum phenomena transcends mere calculations; it encapsulates a profound narrative about the nature of reality itself. It provides a window into understanding how particles behave, how probabilities govern their interactions, and how their entangled states challenge our conventional notions of separateness and connection. This numerical tapestry underlines not only the intricacy of the quantum world but also the rich philosophical and technological implications that have stemmed from its exploration. As advancements in quantum theory continue, the mathematical foundations established will unquestionably serve as the bedrock upon which future discoveries will stand, beckoning us deeper into the secrets hidden beneath the surface of reality.

2.5. Early Experiments and Discoveries

Throughout the history of quantum mechanics, a series of early experiments and discoveries propelled the field forward, illuminating our understanding of the atomic and subatomic worlds. These groundbreaking investigations laid the foundation for the peculiar behaviors inherent to quantum systems, revealing properties that contradicted long-held classical perceptions. From the conception of light as quantized to the establishment of complex wave functions, the early empirical efforts advanced the burgeoning field of quantum mechanics, unraveling layers of reality that had remained hidden.

One of the earliest and most consequential experiments was conducted by Max Planck in the late 19th century, addressing the issue of blackbody radiation. Classical physics struggled to explain why the emitted spectrum of light from heated objects didn't align with the predictions based on continuous energy distribution. Planck's resolution came through the assertion that energy is not emitted continuously but in discrete packets (quanta). His proposal fundamentally shifted our understanding of energy and established the groundwork for subsequent quantum theories. This discovery was not merely mathematical; it marked a conceptual leap that echoed through future studies of atomic behavior.

Following Planck, the work of Albert Einstein in 1905 provided another pivotal moment in quantum history. By elucidating the photoelectric effect, Einstein showed that light also behaved as both a wave and a particle, introducing the concept of photons. Einstein's findings demonstrated that light could eject electrons from a material only if their energy exceeded a certain threshold, directly linking the energy of light to its frequency and supporting the notion of quantization. This intersection of light's dual nature sparked ongoing debates while reshaping the foundations of physics.

The so-called wave-particle duality would become integral in subsequent experiments, particularly in the renowned double-slit experiment. When a stream of electrons or photons is fired toward a barrier containing two slits, the resulting pattern on a detecting screen reveals interference—an indication of wave-like behavior. However, when detectors are employed to observe which slit the particles pass through, the interference pattern disappears, demonstrating particle-like behavior. This enigmatic result illustrates the role of observation in quantum mechanics, suggesting that particles exist in a superposition of states until measured. The implications are staggering, challenging our intuitive understanding of causality and the nature of reality itself.

Niels Bohr continued the exploration of atomic structures with his model of the hydrogen atom, developed in 1913. By postulating that electrons occupy quantized orbits around the nucleus, Bohr unified early quantum ideas with observational data, articulating how energy levels could explain the spectral lines of various elements. His model introduced the idea of energy transitions occurring in discrete steps, affirming the principle of quantization and facilitating the synthesis between experimental results and conceptual frameworks.

The subsequent experiments conducted by Werner Heisenberg and Erwin Schrödinger deepened the exploration of quantum behaviors and mathematical formulations. Heisenberg's matrix mechanics, formulated in 1925, diverged from classical physics by emphasizing observable quantities—rather than the trajectories of particles. His uncertainty principle—asserting the fundamental limits of measurement—upended classical determinism and challenged scientists' outlook on the predictability of physical systems.

Similarly, Schrödinger's wave equation, released in 1926, offered a probabilistic representation of quantum states, introducing the wave function Ψ. By assuming that particles could be described as wave-like entities, Schrödinger advanced a radical interpretation of quantum behavior, incorporating the concept of superposition—where particles exist in multiplicities of states until observation compels a singular outcome. His contributions reinforced the mathematical formalism needed to investigate the intricacies of quantum mechanics, establishing a framework that resonates with rigorous precision.

Moreover, experiments validating these theoretical foundations flourished in the subsequent decades. The Stern-Gerlach experiment, for instance, showcased the quantization of angular momentum. When silver atoms passed through a non-uniform magnetic field, they were deflected in discrete directions, evidence for quantized spin states rather than continuous values. This early investigation into atomic behavior elucidated the intrinsic quantum properties that govern fundamental particles, reinforcing the separation between classical and quantum realms.

Other notable experiments, such as the Einstein-Podolsky-Rosen (EPR) experiment, further fueled discussions on entanglement—the phenomenon where particles become interconnected in such a way that the measurement of one instantly affects the state of another, regardless of distance. This exploration of nonlocality unveiled profound philosophical dilemmas regarding determinism and locality, pressing the boundaries of our understanding of reality and testing the limits of classical intuitions.

As this early era of experimentation unfolded, the realization began to dawn that the quantum realm did not conform to the predictable laws derived from classical mechanics. Instead, it revealed a tapestry of uncertainty, distinct probability distributions, and interconnected behaviors that resided beneath a seemingly orderly universe. The implications of these early findings echoed beyond physics, intertwining with philosophy, technology, and our fundamental conception of existence.

In summary, the early experiments and discoveries in quantum mechanics were monumental in revealing the strange and complex nature of reality at microscopic scales. From Planck's introduction of quantization to the rich discussions spurred by wave-particle duality, the journey of inquiry was marked by foundational insights and profound implications. Each experiment served as a stepping stone, progressively unraveling the intricacies of the quantum world and challenging human understanding at its core. As we move deeper into the quantum domain, these early explorations establish the context and complexity of the unseen forces at play beneath our everyday reality, inviting further investigation into the wonders and mysteries that lie beneath the surface of existence.

3. The Quantum Waves

3.1. Wave-Particle Duality: An Introduction

In the exploration of quantum phenomena, one of the most striking revelations is the concept of wave-particle duality — a principle that underscores the seemingly contradictory nature of particles at the quantum level. At its core, wave-particle duality illustrates that sub-atomic entities, such as electrons and photons, possess both wave-like and particle-like characteristics, depending on how they are observed or measured. This duality fundamentally challenges our conventional notions of physics and reality, forcing us to reconsider the very essence of matter and light.

To unpack wave-particle duality, we must first understand its historical origins, beginning with the work of classical physicists who dominated the scientific landscape before the quantum revolution. In classical physics, entities like light were described strictly as waves, characterized by their frequency and amplitude, which could explain many optical phenomena, such as interference and diffraction. However, this wave-centric view could not adequately explain certain observations, particularly the photoelectric effect, where light striking a metal surface would eject electrons. Classical theories failed to account for why light could only release electrons when its frequency reached a specific threshold, regardless of intensity. This paradox required a new conceptual framework.

The breakthrough came when Max Planck introduced the idea of quantization in 1900, asserting that energy is not emitted continuously but in discrete packets of energy called quanta. Planck's revolutionary hypothesis paved the way for Albert Einstein's interpretation of the photoelectric effect in 1905, in which he proposed that light could be thought of as composed of particles, or "photons," each with a quantized amount of energy proportional to its frequency. This dual nature of light—where it behaves as both a wave and a particle —set the stage for a deeper understanding of the quantum world.

The duality of particles was further highlighted through experiments such as the famous double-slit experiment. When light or electrons are sent through two closely spaced slits, they create an interference pattern on a screen, resembling waves interacting with one another. This interference pattern suggests that each particle travels through both slits simultaneously, exhibiting a wave-like behavior. However, when one attempts to measure which slit the particle passes through, this wave interference pattern disappears, and particles behave as distinct entities, reinforcing the notion of wave-particle duality. This experiment exemplifies the strange behavior of quantum systems, giving credence to the idea that the act of measurement alters the state of a particle.

As we delve deeper into the implications of wave-particle duality, we encounter profound philosophical questions. The idea that particles do not possess definite properties, such as position or momentum, until they are measured invites us to ponder the nature of reality itself. It challenges our understanding of determinism and causality while suggesting that the universe operates based on possibilities rather than certainties. In essence, wave-particle duality implies that the fundamental nature of reality may remain unknowable until we engage with it, forever trapped in a web of probabilities.

Additionally, the principle of wave-particle duality leads us to consider the critical role of the observer. The observer effect—where the act of observation influences the behavior of a quantum system—forces us to confront the limits of knowledge and our place within the universe. In classical physics, the observer is merely a passive witness, but in quantum mechanics, the observer becomes an integral part of the narrative, raising questions about subjectivity and the nature of existence.

In practical terms, the implications of wave-particle duality extend beyond theoretical considerations, permeating modern technology. Innovations such as lasers and quantum computing rely on the principles of wave-particle duality to function. For instance, in lasers, photons are emitted in a coherent wave state, showcasing both their wave-like properties and the quantized nature of light. Quantum computers exploit the superposition of qubits—analogous to wave–particle duality—utilizing both states simultaneously to perform complex computations at unprecedented speeds.

As we conclude this introduction to wave-particle duality, we recognize its significance within the broader quest of understanding the quantum realm. This principle not only redefines our conception of light and matter but also reshapes our interpretation of reality itself. Embracing the complexities of wave-particle duality invites us to investigate further the intricate dance between particles and waves, illuminating the hidden quantum world that lies beneath the surface of what we perceive as reality. Wave-particle duality serves as a gateway—a profound and captivating entryway into the fascinating labyrinth of quantum mechanics, where the rules of classical physics dissolve and a more intricate, yet beautifully bewildering understanding of the universe emerges.

3.2. Debating the Nature of Light

The debate surrounding the nature of light has evolved into one of the most profound explorations within the field of quantum mechanics, bringing together centuries of inquiry and discovery. At the center of this discourse lies an intricate tapestry woven from the threads of empirical observation, theoretical innovation, and philosophical contemplation, all seeking to unpack the essence of light itself: is it a wave, a particle, or perhaps something more elusive?

Historically, the journey into the nature of light begins with the wave theory, championed by physicists such as Christiaan Huygens and later bolstered by James Clerk Maxwell's equations in the 19th century. Maxwell proposed that light is an electromagnetic wave propagating through space, defined by oscillating electric and magnetic fields. His equations beautifully unified the existing principles of electricity, magnetism, and optics, providing an elegant framework that described a myriad of optical phenomena, including reflection, refraction, and interference. This wave-centric view positioned light as a continuous entity, akin to ripples on the surface of a pond, capable of exhibiting behaviors that linked directly to its wave qualities.

However, as experimental techniques advanced, the limitations of wave theory in explaining certain phenomena came to the forefront. The photoelectric effect, experimentally verified in the early 20th century, was pivotal to challenging the classical wave perspective. Light striking a metal surface emitted electrons, but classical wave theory failed to elucidate why only light above a threshold frequency would cause this emission, irrespective of intensity. Einstein's revolutionary contribution in 1905 posited that light consists of discrete packets of energy, or photons, each linked to a specific frequency. This marked a significant shift: light was now understood through the lens of quantization, introducing the concept of duality where light exhibits properties of both waves and particles.

This wave-particle duality became a cornerstone of quantum mechanics, encapsulated in the de Broglie hypothesis, which suggested that particles such as electrons also exhibit wave-like characteristics. David Bohm later emphasized this dual functionality through his pilot-wave theory, asserting that all particles have associated wave functions guiding their behavior. This perspective generated rich discussions on the implications of duality—not only challenging classical physics but also inviting philosophical inquiries about the nature of reality itself, the definition of particles, and the underlying fabric of the universe.

The continuing debate sharpened as scientists began to confront the implications of the double-slit experiment, which starkly illustrated the paradoxical behavior of light. When a coherent source of light or particles, like electrons, passes through two narrow slits, an interference pattern emerges on a screen behind, suggesting the wave-like properties of light. Yet, upon measuring which slit the particle traversed, the interference pattern vanishes, as particles behave like discrete entities. This principal observation—a clear divide between the behavior in absence and presence of measurement—catalyzed discussions on the observer's role in quantum mechanics and reality itself. The essence of light thus remained entangled in a web of probabilities until observation compelled a specific outcome, raising questions about determinism, reality, and the limits of human knowledge.

Philosophers and quantum theorists alike grappled with this foundational challenge, discussing whether it is appropriate to speak of light as strictly either wave or particle. Some interpretations posited a more radical stance influenced by the Copenhagen interpretation, which posits that physical systems do not possess definite properties until observed. Here, light exists in a superposition of probabilities, conflicting with the classical determinations of existence. Others, like the philosophers associated with the Many-Worlds interpretation, computationally acknowledged each possible outcome of the measurement as an actualized reality diverging into alternate universes —proposing a broader space of existence where reality proliferates beyond singular observation.

The evolving concepts of light continued to hold practical implications, significantly influencing technological advancements. The quantum principles underlying lasers, optical fibers, and semiconductors illustrate how insights into the nature of light have propelled forward modern technology, yielding devices and systems that function by exploiting these dual characteristics. The exploration of quantum optics further solidified the dual nature of light, fostering innovations that marry theoretical principles with practical applications. For instance, quantum interference effects help design more sensitive measurement devices, particularly in fields such as quantum cryptography and communication.

In addressing the debate on the nature of light, modern physicists and philosophers continue to investigate the ramifications of entanglement and nonlocal correlations between quantum systems. Such considerations extend from the very fabric of light's identity to overarching implications for our understanding of space, causality, and the interconnectedness of the universe—a complex interplay where light serves as both the medium and the message within the quantum domain.

As we reconsider the nature of light, it becomes clear that it is not merely an entity confined to a binary description but rather a profound confluence of possibilities that challenges our conventions, beckoning us to deepen our inquiry into the quantum realm. The legacy of this debate reflects an enduring pursuit of understanding that transcends disciplinary boundaries, unifying physics, philosophy, and the ever-expanding curiosity of humanity in its quest to unravel the intricacies of reality and existence. The ongoing dialogues surrounding the nature of light have become vital threads in the vast fabric of quantum mechanics, encouraging an exploration that bridges the seen and the unseen, illuminating both the mechanics of the universe and the depths of human understanding.

3.3. Solving Schrödinger's Equation

To solve Schrödinger's equation is to embark upon a voyage through the heart of quantum mechanics, a journey that reveals the dynamic interplay of particles and waves. The equation itself, formulated by the Austrian physicist Erwin Schrödinger in 1926, serves as a cornerstone of quantum mechanics, offering profound insights into the behavior of quantum systems. Understanding its implications requires unraveling the intricate concepts entwined within the mathematical framework, grasping the foundational principles governing particle behavior, and appreciating the implications for modern physics and technology.

Schrödinger's equation can be likened to a linguistic expression that details the evolution of a quantum system over time. At its essence, the time-dependent form of the equation is articulated as follows:

$$i\hbar \, (\partial \Psi / \partial t) = H\Psi$$

In this equation, Ψ, the wave function, encapsulates all the information about a quantum system, such as the probability amplitudes for finding a particle in various states. The imaginary unit, i, introduces a mathematical complex nature to the equation, implying that the solutions to the equation will often present themselves as complex numbers. The reduced Planck's constant, ℏ, connects the wave function to the fundamental motions of quantum systems, while H represents the Hamiltonian operator—the total energy of the system expressed in terms of kinetic and potential energy.

Unraveling these variables, we begin to appreciate the significance of the wave function, which is not merely a mathematical abstraction but a direct representation of the probabilities inherent in a quantum system. The wave function acts as a probability amplitude whose magnitude squared, $|\Psi|^2$, provides the probability density of locating the particle within a given region of space. This encapsulates the inherently probabilistic nature of quantum mechanics—an idea that starkly contrasts classical notions of determinism where particles follow defined trajectories.

The mathematical implications of solving Schrödinger's equation yield solutions that exhibit the remarkable feature of superposition, wherein a quantum system can exist in multiple states simultaneously. This central concept fosters the quintessential understanding of phenomena like interference and entanglement, establishing quantum mechanics in stark contrast to classical physics. As solutions to the wave equation, we might encounter steady-state solutions where the wave function resembles standing waves, revealing quantized energy levels analogous to those proposed in Bohr's model of the hydrogen atom. These quantized levels exemplify the delineated orbits where electrons might exist, a direct reflection of the wave nature of particles as they traverse through space.

While the time-dependent equation governs the temporal evolution of systems, the time-independent form proves to be equally significant in practice. Given by the equation:

$$H\Psi = E\Psi$$

the time-independent Schrödinger equation delineates stationary states, where E represents the total energy associated with the system. This form is instrumental in establishing the distinct energy eigenstates available to quantum systems, providing solutions that yield valuable insight into phenomena ranging from atomic and molecular spectra to the behavior of particles in various potentials, including finite and infinite wells.

The rich interplay between the energy eigenvalues and their corresponding eigenfunctions further solidifies the significance of solving Schrödinger's equation. Each eigenstate corresponds to a specific energy level, while the wave functions visualize the probability distributions of particles across space. Through this lens, we can begin to discern how quantum phenomena are woven into the very fabric of nature.

Solving Schrödinger's equation takes on practical importance through the realm of applications and experimental validation. Quantum tunneling, where particles traverse potential barriers energy levels that classical mechanics would deem insurmountable, is rooted in the solutions of the wave function yielding non-zero probabilities even beyond potential barriers. This leads to phenomena such as nuclear fusion in stars, where protons "tunnel" through the Coulomb barrier, facilitating processes that power our universe. Similarly, applications in modern technology such as tunneling microscopy hinge on the principles derived from Schrödinger's equation, enabling us to visualize surfaces at the atomic level.

The impact of these mathematical solutions extends further into theoretical innovations such as quantum field theory, which merges the principles of quantum mechanics with special relativity. The momentum and energy operators derived from Schrödinger's framework evolve alongside the burgeoning field of particle physics, influencing the creation and annihilation operators used to describe fundamental particles.

However, alongside these advancements remain philosophical implications. Not the least of which is the challenge to objectivity and reality posed by the inherent uncertainty associated with wave functions. Schrödinger's equation, although deterministic in its mathematical formulation, fundamentally describes the evolution of a system governed by probabilities, forcing scientists and philosophers alike to grapple with the nature of existence, measurement, and reality at the quantum scale.

In summary, solving Schrödinger's equation reveals a universe brimming with possibilities and complexity. It introduces an inherently probabilistic framework governing the behavior of quantum systems, allowing us to probe deeply into the mysteries of the microscopic world. As we extract answers from the elegance of the wave function, we find ourselves exploring the very nature of existence, armed with the ability to not only understand our universe but also shape technologies that will define our future. Through this mathematical artistry, we unveil a hidden reality beneath the surface, illuminating the intricate dance of particles and waves that constitute our world. The journey towards mastering Schrödinger's equation is not merely an academic pursuit, but a profound expedition into understanding the very essence of the quantum realm.

3.4. The Concept of Superposition

The concept of superposition stands as one of the most defining features of quantum mechanics, offering a profound insight into the nature of quantum states and reality itself. It challenges our classical intuitions and posits that particles can exist in multiple states simultaneously until an observation is made. This notion creates a fertile ground for both scientific inquiry and philosophical contemplation, as it forces us to reconsider what we understand about the fundamental nature of the universe.

At its core, superposition describes the ability of quantum systems to be in a combination of different states at once. When we consider a quantum object—such as an electron—it does not merely occupy a single position or state. Instead, it exists across a range of possibilities, each associated with a certain probability. The mathematical framework that represents this is encapsulated in the wave function, Ψ, which embodies all possible states of the system.

When the wave function is expressed, it often appears as a linear combination of various state functions. For instance, consider two states, $|A\rangle$ and $|B\rangle$. The superposition principle allows for a new state, $|\psi\rangle$, to be formed as follows:

$|\psi\rangle = c_1|A\rangle + c_2|B\rangle$

In this equation, c_1 and c_2 are complex coefficients that signify the probability amplitude of the system being found in state $|A\rangle$ or $|B\rangle$. When a measurement is performed on this state, the superposition collapses, and the system resolves into one of the possible outcomes with a probability given by the squared magnitudes of these coefficients ($|c_1|^2$, $|c_2|^2$).

To illustrate the principle, consider the famous thought experiment known as Schrödinger's cat. This experiment, proposed by Erwin Schrödinger in 1935, presents a scenario where a cat is placed in a sealed box along with a radioactive atom, a Geiger counter, a vial of poison, and a hammer. If the atom decays, the Geiger counter triggers the hammer to smash the vial, releasing the poison and causing the cat to die. However, if the atom does not decay, the cat remains alive. Until an observer opens the box to check on the cat, the system is described by a superposition of states: the cat is simultaneously alive and dead. This thought experiment compellingly illustrates the strangeness of superposition and raises questions about the role of the observer in determining reality.

The implications of superposition extend far beyond esoteric thought experiments; they are foundational to the practical applications of quantum mechanics. For instance, the principle of superposition is crucial to understanding quantum computing. In classical computing, bits can represent either a 0 or a 1. Quantum bits, or qubits, on the other hand, can exist in a superposition of both states. This property allows quantum computers to process information at speeds and efficiencies unattainable by classical systems, as they can explore multiple paths simultaneously.

Additionally, superposition plays an integral role in quantum interference, a phenomenon showcased in the double-slit experiment. When particles such as electrons are directed towards a barrier with two slits, the results observed appear as an interference pattern characteristic of waves. This pattern emerges because each particle travels through both slits and is in a superposition of passing through one slit and the other at the same time. Only upon measurement does this superposition collapse into a defined state, which demonstrates particle-like behavior. Thus, superposition is not merely a mathematical convenience but an essential feature influencing the physical behavior of particles, elucidating the wave-particle duality prevalent in quantum mechanics.

This broader interpretation of reality prompts philosophical inquiries as well, particularly around the nature of existence and knowledge. The idea that a system exists in multiple potential states until measured raises fundamental questions: What does it mean for a particle to "be" in a state? How does the act of observation influence reality? Philosophers and physicists alike have engaged in discussions surrounding the implications of superposition, leading to diverse interpretations of quantum mechanics.

The concept of superposition also invites examinations of determinism and randomness. In classical physics, systems evolve according to deterministic laws, allowing for precise predictions of future states given current conditions. In contrast, quantum mechanics represents a shift where probabilities dictate outcomes, illustrating that while superposition provides a range of possibilities, the actual realization of a state is fundamentally probabilistic. This shift has profound implications not just for physics but for our broader understanding of the universe, engaging with themes of chance, causality, and the limits of human comprehension.

Furthermore, advancements in experimental techniques continuously push the boundaries of our understanding of superposition. Researchers are designing and conducting increasingly sophisticated experiments to create and manipulate quantum superpositions, enhancing our insights into entanglement and coherence. These ongoing investigations affirm the relevance of superposition in the rapidly evolving fields of quantum information science and quantum technology, illuminating pathways to new discoveries.

In summary, the concept of superposition is a cornerstone of quantum mechanics that defines the nature of quantum systems and offers profound implications for our understanding of reality. By allowing particles to exist in multiple states simultaneously, it challenges classical logic and raises significant questions about the nature of measurement, reality, and existence itself. Superposition shapes the theoretical landscape of quantum mechanics while driving innovation in technology. As we deepen our inquiry into the quantum realm, the principles of superposition will remain pivotal in unraveling the mysteries that lie beneath the surface of our observations, guiding us towards an ever-greater understanding of the cosmos and the intricate dance of particles that constitute it.

3.5. The Wave Function and Its Significance

The wave function, a fundamental concept in quantum mechanics, encapsulates the essence of quantum systems and serves as a critical link between the abstract mathematical framework of quantum theory and its physical interpretations. At its core, the wave function, commonly denoted as Ψ (Psi), represents all the possible states of a quantum system. This complex function contains the probabilities associated with the measurement of various observable quantities, such as position and momentum, thereby bringing a key insight into the behavior of particles at the subatomic level.

Understanding the significance of the wave function begins with recognizing its role in describing the probabilistic nature of quantum mechanics. Unlike classical physics, which adheres to deterministic laws where precise predictions can be made given complete knowledge of initial conditions, quantum mechanics engages with a world governed by uncertainty and probabilities. The wave function embodies this uncertainty; the squared magnitude of the wave function, $|\Psi|^2$, provides the probability density of finding a particle in a particular state or position. Thus, the wave function converts the abstract concept of quantum states into a tool for making empirical predictions about the outcomes of measurements.

The historical origins of the wave function intertwine with the evolution of quantum theory itself. Erwin Schrödinger, in his groundbreaking 1926 work, introduced the wave function as part of his efforts to describe the behavior of electrons in atoms. Schrödinger's wave mechanics, articulated through his wave equation, highlighted that particles can exhibit wave-like characteristics, a triumph of synthesis between the corpuscular view of matter and the wave theories of light. This unification offered a new lens through which to understand atomic behavior and paved the way for conceptualizing the fundamentally probabilistic nature of quantum phenomena.

As the wave function gained traction, it became clear that it also posed profound implications for our understanding of reality. In debates about the interpretation of quantum mechanics, the wave function has become synonymous with the philosophical questions surrounding observation, knowledge, and existence itself. The interpretation of the wave function varies among theorists, leading to a spectrum of philosophical perspectives. The Copenhagen interpretation, advocated by figures such as Niels Bohr, posits that quantum systems do not possess definite properties until measured; instead, they exist in superpositions of states defined by the wave function. This leads to the counterintuitive conclusion that observation fundamentally influences the state of a system, blurring the boundaries between objective reality and subjective measurement.

The implications of the wave function extend far beyond theoretical musings; they permeate the practical realm of quantum technology. Quantum computing, for example, leverages the principles of superposition encoded within wave functions. Qubits, the building blocks of quantum computers, exist in multiple states simultaneously, enabling quantum computers to perform complex calculations exponentially faster than classical counterparts. The manipulation of wave functions through quantum gates harnesses the elegant mathematical structure of quantum mechanics, propelling us toward a new age of computational capability.

Moreover, the wave function serves as a linchpin in the phenomena of quantum entanglement and nonlocality. When two or more particles become entangled, their wave functions become intertwined, leading to correlations between their properties irrespective of the distance separating them. This phenomenon defies classical intuitions regarding locality and causality, prompting deep inquiries into the nature of reality and the fabric of the universe. The entangled states describe complex scenarios where the measurement outcome of one particle influences that of another instantly, multiplying the implications of the wave function and challenging our understanding of interaction and separation.

The wave function also plays a critical role in addressing the measurement problem in quantum mechanics, which grapples with how and why a quantum system transitions from a superposition of possibilities to a definitive state upon measurement. This collapse of the wave function during the act of observation remains a topic of intense debate, stirring discussions regarding determinism, free will, and the nature of reality itself. The lingering uncertainty about the process of measurement invites a variety of interpretations, with each approach contributing to the ongoing dialogue shaping the foundation of modern quantum theory.

The developments surrounding the wave function signal not only advancements in science but a paradigm shift in our philosophical understanding of existence. As we explore the wave function's character, we are compelled to confront questions of reality and perception, opening pathways for interdisciplinary studies that merge physics with philosophy and, potentially, consciousness studies. The intricate nexus of mathematics, observation, and reality spark a synthesis that underpins much of modern quantum discourse, encouraging further research and exploration.

In conclusion, the wave function embodies the rich tapestry of quantum mechanics, weaving together the mathematical structures, physical interpretations, and philosophical implications that define this fascinating field of study. It serves as a fundamental bridge between the abstract and the tangible, ushering us into the quantum realm where uncertainty reigns, and reality is not merely observed but actively shaped by the act of observation itself. As we navigate the complexities of the wave function, we venture deeper into the hidden quantum world, unearthing insights that promise to transform our understanding of the universe in profound and astonishing ways. The journey continues as we seek to elucidate the implications of the wave function and unlock the mysteries it holds, heralding a new chapter in the exploration of quantum phenomena that lie beneath the surface of reality.

4. Entanglement and Nonlocality

4.1. Understanding Quantum Entanglement

Quantum entanglement is a phenomenon that exemplifies the strangeness of the quantum world—a realm where the very concepts of space and time, cause and effect, take on an entirely new complexion. At its essence, entanglement describes a peculiar relationship between quantum particles such that the state of one particle is directly linked to the state of another, even when they are separated by vast distances. This interconnectedness operates outside the bounds of classical physics and has profound implications for our understanding of reality.

To grasp the significance of entanglement, it is critical to first understand the characteristics of quantum systems. Unlike classical particles, which maintain a degree of independence and locality, entangled particles become intertwined such that the measurement of one instantaneously dictates the properties of the other, regardless of the distance that separates them. If two particles are entangled, knowing the state of one particle inherently reveals information about the other's state, whether that involves position, momentum, spin, or polarization. This correlation can exist even if the particles are light-years apart, leading to what Einstein famously termed "spooky action at a distance."

The pioneering experiments that illuminated the nature of quantum entanglement began with the work of Albert Einstein, Boris Podolsky, and Nathan Rosen in 1935. In their influential paper, now referred to as the EPR paradox, they formulated arguments questioning whether quantum mechanics could provide a complete description of physical reality. They posited that if quantum mechanics were true, measurements performed on one particle would instantaneously affect the state of another entangled particle, thereby suggesting that some hidden variables must exist to maintain a deterministic framework. In short, the EPR paper laid the groundwork for entanglement's core paradox: does the instantaneous correlation of entangled particles imply that information travels faster than light, or is there an underlying reality that reconciles these apparent contradictions?

The subsequent developments in quantum theory, in particular the formulation of Bell's theorem in the 1960s by physicist John Bell, shifted the landscape of entanglement studies. Bell's theorem provided a way to experimentally test the predictions of quantum mechanics against the proposed hidden variable theories. It showed that no local hidden variable theory could reproduce the correlations predicted by quantum mechanics. The implications of Bell's theorem were staggering: they implied that entangled particles exhibit behaviors that defy classical intuitions about separateness and locality.

The pivotal moment for quantum entanglement came during a series of experiments known as Bell test experiments—conducted in the latter half of the 20th century. These experiments repeatedly confirmed the predictions of quantum mechanics, decisively demonstrating the reality of entanglement and its intrinsic nonlocality. One of the most famous of these tests was performed by Alain Aspect and his team in the early 1980s, which effectively closed loopholes regarding the influence of hidden variables. The results reaffirmed that entangled particles truly exhibit instantaneous correlations, reinforcing the notion that entanglement is a fundamental aspect of quantum reality.

The significance of entanglement extends beyond theoretical intrigue; it serves as a cornerstone for several emerging technologies. In the realm of quantum computing, for instance, entangled qubits can explore multiple computational pathways simultaneously, vastly enhancing processing capabilities. Quantum entanglement is also foundational in quantum cryptography, particularly in quantum key distribution (QKD) systems that leverage entangled states to ensure secure communication. As qubits incorporate the principles of entanglement, they create cryptographic schemes that are inherently secure against eavesdropping, because the act of measuring an entangled state disrupts the overall system and signals an intrusion.

Moreover, entanglement opens doors to exploring new frontiers in quantum teleportation and quantum networks. Quantum teleportation presents a means by which quantum states can be transmitted from one location to another without physical transfer of the particle itself, relying instead on entanglement and classical communication channels. It conjectures a future where classical communication infrastructure may evolve into enhanced quantum networks, facilitating communication and computation on unprecedented scales.

The philosophical implications of quantum entanglement also warrant attention. Einstein, Podolsky, and Rosen believed that the strange interconnectedness evidenced by entangled particles challenged a classical perspective on locality, prompting fundamental questions about the nature of reality, determinism, and the limits of human understanding. This phenomenon stimulates inquiries about the observer's role in collapsing superpositions, redefining our conception of information, causality, and the interconnected fabric of the universe.

In conclusion, quantum entanglement is a fundamental phenomenon that reshapes our conception of reality and underpins much of the modern advancements in quantum technology. Its implications traverse both the physical and philosophical landscapes, challenging our understanding of locality and separateness while paving the way for revolutionary developments in computation and secure communication. As we deepen our comprehension of entanglement and its intricate behaviors, we venture into the hidden realms of quantum mechanics, revealing a level of connectedness in our universe that beckons further exploration and understanding. This captivating aspect of quantum mechanics continues to inspire inquiry, discussion, and innovation as we navigate the mysteries that lie beneath the surface of our reality.

4.2. The EPR Paradox and Its Implications

The EPR Paradox, originating from the seminal paper by Albert Einstein, Boris Podolsky, and Nathan Rosen in 1935, invokes profound questions about the nature of reality and the completeness of quantum mechanics. This paradox explores a radical concept of entangled particles, highlighting how quantum mechanics seemingly contradicts the established tenets of locality and realism. As we delve into the heart of the EPR paradox, we unravel its implications for our understanding of the quantum world and its broader impact on various fields of knowledge.

At the crux of the EPR argument is the notion of entanglement, where two particles become intertwined in such a manner that their physical properties are interdependent, regardless of the distance that separates them. If one measures the state of one particle, the corresponding state of the other particle—even if it is light-years away—immediately becomes defined, embodying what Einstein termed "spooky action at a distance." This instantaneous correlation challenges the classical concept that information cannot travel faster than light, leading to difficulties in reconciling quantum descriptions with classical intuitions.

In traditional physics, a complete theory should provide a comprehensive account of physical reality—one in which every measurable quantity can be determined with precision. The EPR paper contended that if quantum mechanics was indeed complete, it would imply that particles possess properties that are determined at the moment of measurement. However, the entangled nature of quantum systems suggested that these particles might not possess definite properties until observed, raising the question of whether quantum mechanics could ever be a complete theory. If measurements could change the state of a quantum system, this inferred that quantum mechanics was inherently incomplete, lacking the hidden variables required to provide a full picture of reality.

The implications of the EPR paradox reverberate through the fields of physics and philosophy. Philosophers have long grappled with the distinctions between observational reality and the intrinsic properties of particles, drawing attention to crucial ideas about knowledge, measurement, and existence. The EPR paradox challenges the classical conception of a separable, deterministic universe and advocates for a more interconnected reality, where the relationships between particles are central to understanding the fabric of existence.

In the years following the EPR paper, significant developments arose in the realm of quantum theory. John Bell's theorem emerged as a crucial framework to test the implications of the EPR paradox experimentally. Bell formulated a series of mathematical inequalities, now known as Bell inequalities, that presented a way to quantify the degree of correlations between entangled particles and to differentiate between quantum mechanics and local hidden variable theories. Bell's work provided a clear framework to assess whether the predictions of quantum mechanics could be reconciled with classical intuitions about locality and separateness.

The experimental validation of Bell's theorem, realized through a series of experiments in the latter half of the 20th century, has steadfastly supported the predictions of quantum mechanics, confirming the reality of entangled states. The results consistently demonstrated violations of Bell inequalities, reinforcing the notion that entangled particles interact in ways that defy classical explanations. These findings culminated in a paradigm shift, compelling the scientific community to increasingly accept that nature might indeed operate in ways that challenge established conceptions.

At a practical level, the implications of the EPR paradox extend into numerous domains, particularly in the burgeoning field of quantum information science. Quantum entanglement has given birth to transformative technologies such as quantum cryptography and quantum computing. The ability to manipulate entangled states enables secure communication channels that are impervious to eavesdropping, as any attempt to measure an entangled system fundamentally disrupts the communication process and alerts the parties involved. Moreover, quantum computing systems harness the power of entanglement to exponentially enhance computational capabilities, allowing qubits to exist in a phenomenon of superposition and entanglement that classical bits cannot emulate.

The philosophical resonance of the EPR paradox also encourages ongoing discourse surrounding the nature of reality, knowledge, and the observer's role. Researchers and theorists contemplate matters of realism versus anti-realism, where the implications of entanglement prompt reflections on whether quantum mechanics presents a descriptive account of an objective universe or an epistemological framework governed by observer dependency. The intricacies of the EPR paradox stimulate inquiry into how our understanding of information, causality, and existence must be reassessed in light of quantum mechanics.

In summary, the EPR paradox encapsulates fundamental questions regarding the nature of reality, locality, and completeness within quantum mechanics. It serves as a touchstone that bridges quantum phenomena with philosophical inquiry, challenging our intuitions and compelling us to reevaluate our understanding of the universe. Through its continued exploration, the EPR paradox fosters not only advancements in technology but also enriches the ongoing dialogue about the essence of existence and the philosophical underpinnings of our knowledge. The journey into the depths of the EPR paradox remains an invitation to delve deeper into the hidden quantum world, a realm where connections transcend distances and reality morphs into a beautiful tapestry of interdependent states.

4.3. Bell's Theorem: Proving Nonlocality

In its essence, Bell's theorem serves as a pivotal formulation in quantum mechanics, bridging the gap between the esoteric nature of quantum correlations and tangible implications across the realms of philosophy, science, and technology. The theorem stems from John Bell's groundbreaking work in the 1960s, where he sought to test the predictions of quantum mechanics against classical intuitions surrounding locality and realism. This mathematical framework emerged as a response to the profound implications of quantum entanglement, fundamentally challenging our understanding of the interconnectedness of particles in the quantum world.

Bell's theorem postulates that if local hidden variable theories exist —which posit that the properties of particles are determined prior to measurement and, hence, do not exhibit instantaneous correlations over distance—then certain statistical correlations predicted by quantum mechanics would be constrained by specific inequalities (now known as Bell inequalities). In contrast, quantum mechanics predicts correlation values that can exceed these classical bounds, demonstrating a tangible divergence from classical physics.

To elucidate this further, suppose we have two entangled particles —let's consider entangled electrons that can be emitted in opposite directions during a decay process. When these electrons are subjected to measurement, say regarding their spin states (either spin-up or spin-down), the outcomes seem random when observed individually. However, the astonishing aspect lies in their correlation: measuring one electron will instantaneously reveal the measurement outcome of the other electron, regardless of how far they are apart. This instantaneous connection contradicts classical notions of locality—whereby influences can only propagate through space at or below the speed of light.

Bell's inequalities propose that if we could definitively determine the outcomes of measurements based on predetermined local hidden variables, then the correlation between the measurement outcomes would necessarily obey these inequalities. Conversely, quantum mechanics predicts that entangled particles could yield correlations that violate these inequalities, thereby indicating the necessity of quantum mechanics in describing their behavior.

Over the decades, numerous experiments have been conducted to test the validity of Bell's theorem. Notable among these is Alain Aspect's series of experiments in the early 1980s, which addressed significant loopholes that could potentially undermine Bell's conclusions. Aspect's experiments demonstrated consistent violations of Bell's inequalities, corroborating the predictions of quantum mechanics— specifically, the existence of nonlocality that defies classical physical notions. These findings reinforced the idea that entangled particles retain an instantaneous connection, rendering local hidden variable theories inadequate in accounting for the behaviors observed in quantum entanglement.

The implications of Bell's theorem stretch far beyond the confines of theoretical physics. They reverberate through philosophy, invoking profound questions regarding the nature of reality, causation, and the observer's role in the universe. The very fabric of reality is challenged, as the instantaneous correlations implied by quantum entanglement seem to suggest a nonlocal interplay that invites further inquiry into the interconnectedness of all systems at the quantum scale.

Philosophically, the results stemming from Bell's theorem have sparked debate on the nature of objective reality. The violation of Bell inequalities raises poignant inquiries concerning realism—the belief in an objective, observer-independent reality. If entangled particles behave in ways that defy classical locality, what does this imply about the separateness of physical entities? The discussions prompt us to reconsider the foundations of knowledge, pushing boundaries toward epistemological frameworks where the very act of measurement influences not only the observed system but potentially the nature of reality itself.

Moreover, Bell's theorem lays the groundwork for advancements in quantum technologies. The principles of entanglement and nonlocality are integral to the development of quantum information protocols, including quantum cryptography and quantum teleportation. In quantum cryptography, for instance, the entangled states leveraged ensure secure communication channels unbreachable by eavesdroppers—a significant innovation driven by the nonlocal correlations exposed by Bell's interpretation.

In the technological sphere, Bell's theorem enables the creation of quantum networks that harness entangled particles to distribute quantum states without transmitting physical particles through space. These networks can offer groundbreaking capabilities in secure global communication, revolutionizing our capacity for data transmission and privacy.

In summary, Bell's theorem stands as a profound testament to the complexities underlying quantum mechanics. By revealing the limitations of classical theories in explaining entangled particles' behavior, it not only champions the validity of quantum mechanics but also invites us into a realm of inquiry where our philosophical understandings of reality coalesce with empirical science. The interplay between quantum entanglement, nonlocality, and the implications of Bell's theorem drives us to explore the depths of interconnectedness, urging us to reevaluate the very nature of existence at both the quantum and philosophical levels. As we continue to navigate these realms, the insights drawn from Bell's theorem resonate within the ongoing journey to understand the hidden quantum world of which we are an intricate part.

4.4. Experimental Proofs of Entanglement

In the realm of quantum mechanics, experimental proofs of entanglement stand as some of the most astonishing revelations in science, bringing to light phenomena that challenge our understanding of reality itself. These experiments provide concrete evidence of entanglement, a critical aspect of quantum theory that demonstrates the interconnectedness of particles, regardless of the distance separating them. Such experiments have not only validated theoretical physics but also ignited a revolution in the ways we think about the universe and the fundamental laws governing it.

The journey of understanding quantum entanglement began with the theoretical underpinnings laid down by prominent physicists like Einstein, who initially expressed skepticism regarding quantum mechanics due to its non-intuitive nature. The famous EPR paper co-authored with Podolsky and Rosen raised philosophical questions about whether quantum mechanics could be considered a complete theory of reality. It posited that if entangled particles could instantaneously affect each other at a distance—an idea dubbed "spooky action at a distance"—the classical notions of locality should be re-evaluated.

Experimental efforts to prove entanglement gained momentum in the 1960s, sparked by John Bell's groundbreaking theorem. Bell formulated a mathematical framework distinguishing between the predictions of quantum mechanics and those of classical local hidden variable theories. He derived a set of inequalities, known as Bell inequalities, that could be tested through thought experiments and actual laboratory tests. If quantum mechanics were correct, some correlations predicted by it would violate Bell's inequalities, providing a clear experimental criterion for validation.

One of the landmark experiments designed to test Bell's theorem was conducted by Alain Aspect in the early 1980s. In these experiments, pairs of entangled photons were emitted, and their polarization states were measured. By switching measurement settings rapidly, Aspect's team was able to ensure that the choice of measurement on one photon could not influence the other, despite the distance between them. The results were striking: the correlations between the measurements consistently violated Bell's inequalities, providing robust experimental confirmation of quantum entanglement and the nonlocal nature of reality.

These compelling results not only validated the predictions of quantum theory but also raised deeper questions about the nature of reality. The phenomenon of entanglement suggests that the properties of particles are not determined independent of one another; instead, their states are intricately linked, irrespective of their separation in space. This challenges the classical idea that objects have distinct, independent properties, instead implying a profound interconnectedness pervading the quantum realm.

Several pivotal experiments have since reinforced the understanding of entanglement, each contributing to the growing body of evidence affirming its existence. Key among these is the work of researchers who have performed increasingly sophisticated tests aimed at closing potential loopholes in previous experiments. Techniques like 'loophole-free' Bell tests address various experimental concerns, ensuring that results are not influenced by local hidden variables.

In addition to the experimental verification, advancements in technology such as quantum optics and photonics have enabled researchers to create and manipulate entangled states with remarkable precision. As scientists explore more extensive networks of entangled particles, they open the door to practical applications that leverage entanglement, enriching both fundamental science and technological innovation.

The implications of entanglement extend into various domains, shaping the future of quantum computing and quantum communication. In quantum computing, entangled qubits enhance processing power by enabling operations that would be impossible with classical bits alone. In quantum communication, entanglement can provide channels for secure information transfer, fundamentally altering how we approach data security.

Moreover, experimental proofs of entanglement invoke considerable philosophical and epistemological inquiries. They lead us to reflect on the nature of reality, the observer's role in quantum mechanics, and how information is fundamentally interconnected. Entanglement has become a source of fascination not just for physicists but also for philosophers seeking to reconcile quantum mechanics with broader ontological questions about existence, causality, and the structure of the universe.

As experimental technologies advance, researchers continue to explore the realms of entanglement. Future experiments may push beyond current understandings of spatial and temporal limits, potentially revealing deeper insights into the nature of reality itself. With entanglement as a foundation, it becomes evident that our universe operates on a matrix of interconnections that defy classical logic yet speak to a more fundamental, shared existence at the quantum level.

In summary, experimental proofs of entanglement represent a gateway into the extraordinary world of quantum mechanics, illuminating the intricate and often counterintuitive behaviors that govern the behavior of particles. These experiments not only affirm the theoretical predictions of quantum entanglement but also stimulate fresh perspectives on reality, connectivity, and the underlying principles of existence. As we navigate through the complexities of the quantum realm, the story of entanglement invites us to question our understanding of the universe, encouraging ongoing exploration and discovery in an ever-expanding landscape of knowledge.

4.5. Applications of Quantum Entanglement

The ramifications of quantum entanglement stretch across numerous fields, symbolizing a profound shift not only in fundamental physics but also in practical applications that touch upon our daily lives, security, and technological advancements. The notion that particles can become intertwined in ways that render their states interdependent challenges the classical understandings of causality and locality, beckoning us to explore a range of practical implementations derived from this mesmerizing phenomenon.

One of the most immediate and popular applications of quantum entanglement is in the realm of quantum computing. Quantum computers leverage the principles of superposition and entanglement to process vast amounts of data at unparalleled speeds. In traditional computing, information is encoded in bits that are either a 0 or a 1, leading to linear processing speeds based on classical logic. Conversely, quantum bits or qubits utilize entanglement to perform multiple calculations simultaneously. This parallelism allows quantum computers to tackle intricate problems that are currently intractable for classical computers, with potential applications in cryptography, materials science, pharmaceuticals, and complex system modeling. As research continues to refine quantum algorithms, we stand on the edge of a new era in computational capabilities.

Similarly, quantum entanglement plays a critical role in quantum cryptography, providing secure communication channels that are fundamentally more efficient than classical methods. Quantum Key Distribution (QKD) is a prime example, where entangled particles are used to ensure that any attempt to eavesdrop on communication alters the state of the involved particles, alerting the communicating parties to the presence of an intruder. The inherent security of QKD stems from the principles of quantum mechanics themselves—data can only be intercepted at the cost of altering the messages being sent. This innovation is poised to revolutionize how sensitive information is shared across platforms, potentially leading to a future where cyber threats could be mitigated effectively using quantum technologies.

Beyond computing and cryptography, entanglement has significant implications within the broader field of quantum teleportation. Quantum teleportation is a process providing a means to transfer quantum states between particles across distances, using entangled particles as a conduit. This doesn't entail teleporting matter itself but rather the information contained within the quantum state—demonstrating that information can transcend spatial limitations without the accompanying particles moving through space. This could lead to breakthroughs in secure communication networks and distributed quantum computing systems, with the potential for instantaneous transfer of quantum states, reshaping how we understand communication and data integrity.

Entanglement is also vital in the burgeoning field of quantum metrology, where precision measurements are achieved utilizing entangled states. For example, entangled photons can be employed to enhance the sensitivity of sensors far beyond classical limits, allowing for ultra-precise measurements that can be critical in various scientific fields, such as gravitational wave detection, medical imaging, and fundamental physics experiments. Such advancements promise to herald a new age in detection technologies, improving our ability to measure phenomena that were previously obscured by noise or physical constraints.

Furthermore, the exploration of entanglement in biological systems has unveiled new insights into the complex processes underlying life itself. Research has begun to reveal that entanglement might have a role in processes like photosynthesis, navigation in migratory birds, and even the functioning of our senses. These intersections of quantum mechanics with biology propose that quantum effects may be integral to life's fundamental processes, leading to novel applications in bioengineering, drug discovery, and the development of bio-inspired technologies.

As the landscape of quantum entanglement continues to evolve, ethical considerations and societal implications increasingly come into play. As with any powerful technology, the potential for misuse exists. Safeguarding entangled systems and ensuring that our advances are harnessed ethically will require a thoughtful approach to technology governance. Additionally, as these technologies become integrated into societal norms, considerations around equity, access, and privacy will be paramount in steering their adoption in a manner beneficial to all.

The horizon of quantum entanglement applications stretches far and wide, with researchers tirelessly investigating new modalities of implementation in various fields. From the wondrous realms of quantum computing and cryptography to the innovative intersections with biology and practical measurement techniques, the applications of quantum entanglement herald a transformative chapter in technological progress. As our understanding deepens and technologies mature, the implications of harnessing quantum entanglement will resonate throughout society, fundamentally altering the landscape of science and technology as we know it. The journey into this enigmatic quantum realm remains compelling—a thread woven intricately into the fabric of modern science, inviting continual exploration and ingenuity as we strive to unlock the mysteries of the universe.

5. Heisenberg's Uncertainty Principle

5.1. The Challenge to Objectivity

The quest to understand the very nature of reality has been challenged significantly by the profound implications of quantum mechanics, specifically through phenomena such as Heisenberg's uncertainty principle. This principle reveals intrinsic limitations regarding our ability to measure certain pairs of conjugate properties, such as position and momentum, simultaneously with absolute precision. In doing so, it not only challenges our classical understandings of determinism and objectivity but also invites profound philosophical inquiries that resonate throughout the scientific community.

The uncertainty principle states that the more accurately one measures a particle's position, the less accurately one can measure its momentum, and vice versa. Mathematically, this is described by the relation $\Delta x \Delta p \geq \hbar/2$, where Δx represents the uncertainty in position, Δp signifies the uncertainty in momentum, and $\hbar$ is the reduced Planck's constant. This inequality highlights an inevitable limitation imposed by the very fabric of nature, one that is starkly at odds with classical mechanics, where both quantities could be known with arbitrary precision.

The implications of uncertainty fundamentally challenge the notion of objectivity—the idea that the world exists in a specific state independent of observation. In the classical perspective, observers could make measurements without interference in the system under observation. However, in the quantum realm, the act of measurement itself becomes a critical factor. Observers cannot be segregated from the system; their interactions influence the results, leading to states where properties do not possess definitive values until measured.

This realization reshapes our understanding of reality itself. Under the terms of classical physics, the universe appears as a deterministic construct governed by fixed laws, where predictions could be made with certainty given complete information about a system. However, the advent of quantum mechanics, underscored by uncertainties, compels us to embrace a probabilistic worldview—one where fundamental elements exist in states of superposition until observation occurs, collapsing possibilities into specific outcomes.

For scholars in philosophy, these ideas provoke deeper inquiries into the nature of existence, consciousness, and knowledge. If measurement alters the state of what is being observed, then questions arise regarding the role of observers and the extent of subjective experience in defining reality. How much of what we perceive is shaped by our own observations, and how does that influence the objective nature of the universe? Such questions resonate with the philosophical discourse surrounding epistemology—the study of knowledge and justified belief.

Furthermore, the uncertainty principle questions the previously held beliefs of relationships between the observer and the observed. Classical realism posits that objects have properties regardless of whether they are measured. Conversely, quantum mechanics suggests that particles possess properties only in the context of measurement. This philosophical shift encourages reevaluation of foundational principles, leaving scientists and thinkers to reconcile classical views with the realities presented by quantum phenomena.

In the context of particle physics, the uncertainty principle has far-reaching effects on how particles behave and interact. It alters expectations regarding elemental particles and drives inquiries into the behaviors and characteristics of these fundamental building blocks of matter. Particle physicists must navigate this wave of uncertainty to bring clarity to models of particle interactions, quantum fields, and, ultimately, the structures that define the universe itself.

As researchers delve deeper into quantum mechanics and engage in experimental validations of concepts involving uncertainty, they often grapple with the broader implications. The acknowledgment that our knowledge is constrained by uncertainty invites intrigue into areas such as quantum decoherence—the process by which quantum superpositions interact with their environment, leading to apparent classical outcomes and thus integrating uncertainty with observable realities.

Exploration into the philosophical ramifications of the uncertainty principle may lead us to contemplate the nature of free will as well. If the universe operates on probabilistic outcomes at the quantum level, could this open avenues for differing interpretations of freedom and choice? The debate extends into the psychological domain as well, sparking discussions on how human behavior may align with or diverge from deterministic principles.

In conclusion, the challenge to objectivity presented by Heisenberg's uncertainty principle is multifaceted, intertwining the realms of theoretical physics, philosophy, and cognitive science. As we continue to explore the uncertainties and complexities of the quantum world, we are impelled to renegotiate our understanding of reality, knowledge, and existence itself. This tapestry of inquiry is bound to unravel further mysteries, leading us on a journey through the profound depths of the quantum realm, where the interplay between measurement, observer effects, and the very nature of reality beckons us to reconsider our preconceived notions and embrace a more nuanced understanding of the universe. The uncertainty principle stands not as a limitation but as a gateway—inviting us to delve into the vast ocean of possibilities and engage with the most fundamental questions of existence.

5.2. Understanding Uncertainty

Understanding uncertainty in the realm of quantum mechanics unveils profound implications not only for the scientific community but also for our fundamental understanding of reality. At its core, uncertainty intertwines with the fabric of quantum phenomena, guiding the behavior of particles and compelling us to reconsider foundational notions we held regarding determinism, objectivity, and measurement. This chapter seeks to elucidate the various dimensions of uncertainty, exploring its mathematical underpinnings, limitations in measurement, implications for particle physics, and the subsequent philosophical inquiries that arise.

To comprehend uncertainty in quantum mechanics, one must first appreciate its birthplace—the uncertainty principle elucidated by Werner Heisenberg in 1927. This principle asserts that certain pairs of physical properties, such as position and momentum, cannot be measured simultaneously with arbitrary precision. The more accurately we ascertain one property, the less precisely we can know its counterpart. Mathematically expressed as $\Delta x \Delta p \geq \hbar/2$, where Δx represents the uncertainty in position, Δp the uncertainty in momentum, and $\hbar$ is the reduced Planck constant, this inequality encapsulates the foundational limit imposed by quantum mechanics on measurement. Here, uncertainty is not merely a factor of experimental error; it signifies an inherent characteristic of reality itself.

The essence of this principle directly challenges classical intuitions about the nature of knowledge. In classical physics, if one possesses complete information about a system, absolute predictions about its future state can be made. This concept rests on a deterministic view of the universe where laws of motion can be applied with precision. However, the advent of quantum mechanics introduces a probabilistic framework, where uncertainty becomes a guiding principle dictating the behavior of subatomic particles. Events unfold within a spectrum of possibilities rather than certainties, prompting scientists and philosophers alike to grapple with inherent limitations of measurement and prediction.

The limitations imposed by quantum uncertainty extend to experimental physics—where the act of measuring becomes an integral part of the phenomenon being studied. While classical experiments operated under the assumption that measurement does not alter the system, such an assertion fails in the quantum realm. Quantum systems do not possess fixed properties until they are observed, necessitating a deeper inquiry into the relationship between observer and observed. The interplay raises essential questions about how our observations shape the very reality we seek to understand.

Delving deeper, the implications of uncertainty manifest significantly in particle physics. The behavior of fundamental particles—such as electrons, photons, and quarks—mimics the principles outlined in Heisenberg's uncertainty principle. In particle physics, distinguishing between particles' intrinsic properties becomes a complex endeavor; they often exist in superpositions of states until experimentally determined outcomes compel them to resolve into definite states. This interplay complicates the pursuit of a consistent and deterministic model of particle behavior, yielding a realization that our comprehension of elemental interactions is shrouded in layers of probabilistic outcomes.

Moreover, quantum uncertainty intertwines with fundamental discussions about the nature of reality itself. The implications strike at the heart of realism—the philosophical stance that objects possess properties independent of observation. In quantum mechanics, the properties of particles emerge only within the context of measurement, challenging our understanding of the objective reality. The uncertainty principle invokes critical reflections on what constitutes knowledge and encourages a shift in thinking about reality—an invitation to consider the universe as a complex tapestry woven with probabilities, correlations, and interconnectedness, rather than as a deterministic entity.

Philosophically, the uncertainties inherent in quantum mechanics lead to significant arguments regarding free will and determinism. If the fundamental nature of reality is governed by probabilities and uncertainties, can human agency be reconciled within these frameworks? The ripple effects extend into ethics and consciousness studies, where the human experience intertwines with scientific understanding. Philosophers engage with these thoughts, posing questions that probe the limits of knowledge, the nature of existence, and the influence of observation and cognition.

In addition to these philosophical contemplations, the ramifications of uncertainty are evident in contemporary discussions surrounding the nature of information. The concept of information in the quantum realm diverges from classical definitions, which rely on fixed properties. Quantum information theory posits that information is inherently linked to the quantum states of systems, manifesting as a fluid landscape governed by wave functions and entangled states. Understanding how uncertainty influences information allows researchers to explore new horizons in quantum computing and communication, shedding light on the transformative potential of quantum technologies.

As we embrace uncertainty's complexities, ongoing scientific investigations continuously refine our comprehension of the quantum world. Researchers are exploring ways to quantify uncertainty more precisely, leveraging advanced measurement techniques and computational models that navigate the intricate dance of quantum behavior. Within this evolving landscape, we find ourselves at the precipice of further breakthroughs that challenge existing paradigms and unveil new dimensions of understanding.

In conclusion, understanding uncertainty is a gateway to profound insights that reshape our understanding of quantum mechanics, particle behavior, and the very fabric of reality. This exploration leads us to recognize that uncertainty is not merely a limitation of our measurements but rather an integral characteristic of the universe itself. Through a synthesis of scientific inquiry, philosophical discourse, and technological advancements, the journey into the essence of uncertainty enriches our knowledge and fosters a deeper appreciation for the intricate interplay of reality, measurement, and existence in the hidden quantum world. As we venture further, embracing the nuances of uncertainty promises to unlock new dimensions of knowledge, guiding our exploration into the fundamental questions that lie beneath the surface of reality.

5.3. Limitations of Measurement

The limitations of measurement in quantum mechanics constitute a cornerstone of understanding the intricate dynamics of the quantum world. Unlike classical physics, where direct measurements produce clear and reliable outcomes, quantum measurements reveal a landscape steeped in uncertainty and probabilistic behavior. This chapter delves into the multifaceted limitations inherent in quantum measurements, exploring how these constraints shape our comprehension of reality and the implications they carry for both science and philosophy.

At the heart of quantum mechanics lies the principle that particles do not possess definite properties until they are observed. Prior to measurement, particles exist in a state of superposition—each potential state coexisting with others, governed by probability distributions. The act of measurement causes a collapse of this superposition, forcing the quantum system into a singular definitive state. This fundamental shift has deep implications for our understanding of reality; it suggests that particles are not merely existing with predetermined properties but rather embody a spectrum of possibilities that becomes narrowed down upon observation.

This aspect of quantum measurement introduces limitations that starkly challenge classical intuitions. For instance, Heisenberg's uncertainty principle delineates the constraints of measuring conjugate variables—such as position and momentum—simultaneously. The more precisely we attempt to measure a particle's position (Δx), the less precisely we can determine its momentum (Δp), as articulated by the relationship $\Delta x \Delta p \geq \hbar/2$. This inequality encapsulates the intrinsic limitation imposed by quantum mechanics, which reframes our expectations regarding the knowledge we can obtain about particles. Thus, measurement itself becomes an influence on the measured system, disallowing a complete and absolute understanding as long as we abide by classical preconceived notions.

Moreover, the peculiar nature of quantum measurements implies that the observer's role becomes integral to the process. Unlike classical experiments where observers could remain detached, quantum mechanics draws attention to the interaction between observer and system. The observer effect posits that the very act of observation fundamentally alters the state of what is being measured. This raises profound philosophical inquiries about the nature of knowledge and reality, prompting us to confront the question of whether objective reality is accessible or whether it is forever intertwined with subjective perception.

Another significant limitation of measurement in quantum systems arises from the phenomenon of decoherence, which occurs when a quantum system interacts with its environment. In such interactions, the delicate coherence of quantum states is disrupted, leading to apparent classical behavior and making the distinctions between quantum and classical worlds increasingly blurred. Quantum decoherence illustrates not just a limit on measurement outcomes but also the transition from quantum behavior to classical predictability, complicating our understanding of how reality transitions at the macroscopic level.

Limitations of measurement extend into the field of particle physics, where precise measurements govern our understanding of fundamental forces and particles. Quantifying properties such as spin, charge, and energy within the quantum framework demands sophisticated techniques and technologies to mitigate the influence of measurement on particle behavior. The challenge lies in designing experiments that balance the need for accurate measurements while accounting for the inherent uncertainties that accompany quantum systems.

Furthermore, these limitations have ramifications for modern technological applications, particularly in quantum computing, cryptography, and information science. The reliability and accuracy of quantum measurements directly influence the effectiveness of quantum algorithms and cryptographic protocols, pushing researchers to find ways to delineate between measurement uncertainty and the preservation of quantum information.

Ultimately, the limitations of measurement challenge us to rethink traditional notions of knowledge, reality, and our interactions with the universe. As we traverse deeper into the quantum realm, we glean that uncertainties and limitations are not just obstacles but also gateways to understanding the fundamental nature of existence. The fact that the very act of measurement influences what we observe unveils layers of meaning about how we relate to the universe, the interplay of observer and reality, and the intricate tapestry of possibilities shaping our understanding of life itself.

In essence, the limitations of measurement in quantum mechanics serve as a reminder that reality may not be as fixed and comprehensible as our classical intuitions suggest. Embracing these limitations invites us to engage with the mysteries of existence, illuminating the fascinating and perplexing nature of the quantum world beneath the surface of what we see, prompting an ongoing exploration of the realities that lie hidden behind the veil of measurement.

5.4. Impact on Particle Physics

The impact of quantum physics on our understanding of the universe, particularly through particle physics, represents a significant evolution in how we perceive fundamental particles and their interactions. Quantum mechanics invites us to rethink classical assumptions and embrace a new framework wherein particles are not just point-like entities following deterministic paths but manifestations of probabilities and statistical behaviors.

At the core of particle physics lies the Standard Model, a theoretical framework that describes the fundamental particles and forces that govern interactions within the universe. Prior to the quantum revolution, the view of particles was solidly Newtonian; they were viewed as tiny, solid billiard balls, occupying defined spaces with known trajectories. However, quantum mechanics introduced the notion that particles exhibit wave-particle duality, thus existing in superpositions of states. This revelation redefined the particle concept itself, encouraging physicists to shift their focus from rigid categorizations to probabilistic behaviors derived from quantum mechanics.

The role of quantum mechanics in particle physics began to crystallize with groundbreaking experiments that demonstrated the wave-like characteristics of particles, most famously through the double-slit experiment. In this experiment, particles like electrons displayed interference patterns characteristic of waves when not observed, suggesting that they traversed both slits simultaneously. However, upon measurement, the particles ceased to act as waves, collapsing into defined states. This phenomenon illustrated how observation fundamentally influences the behavior of particles, leading to the understanding that the act of measurement brings out the reality of quantum states, allowing them to manifest as discrete particles.

Similarly, the behavior of subatomic particles is fundamentally governed by quantum fields, as articulated in quantum field theory, which postulates that particles are excitations of underlying fields. Each fundamental particle type corresponds to its quantum field— quarks to the quark field, photons to the electromagnetic field, and so forth. When particle interactions occur, such as particle collisions in high-energy accelerators like CERN, those interactions yield a rich tapestry of produced particles, echoing the probabilistic nature of quantum mechanics. Quantum tunneling also plays a critical role in particle interactions, challenging classical barriers and allowing particles to penetrate through potential barriers they classically could not surmount.

The implications of quantum mechanics ripple through various domains within particle physics. For instance, the concept of entanglement birthed from quantum mechanics became fundamentally significant in studying particle behavior. When two particles become entangled, a measurement on one particle instantaneously correlates with the state of the other, regardless of distance. This nonlocal characteristic contradicts classical intuitions and influences how scientists explore interactions within particle physics, unveiling manifestations of intricate relationships between particles that classical physics cannot explain.

Moreover, quantum mechanics introduces uncertainties that necessitate a reevaluation of traditional particle collisions and detections. The Heisenberg uncertainty principle highlights the limits in simultaneously measuring certain properties of particles, necessitating probabilistic models to predict interactions. These uncertainties are not simply inconveniences but are inherent features of the quantum domain, compelling the need for more nuanced approaches in experimental and theoretical frameworks.

The advances in technology fueled by quantum mechanics have propelled particle physics into new realms of discovery. The development of particle accelerators has allowed physicists to probe deeper into the subatomic world, revealing new particles such as the Higgs boson —discovered at CERN in 2012—a monumental finding that affirmed existing theoretical predictions laid out by the Standard Model.

However, despite the successes of the Standard Model, it remains incomplete. The existence of dark matter, dark energy, and the inability of the model to incorporate gravity into the quantum framework highlight the need for further theoretical advancements. Scientists are now exploring beyond the Standard Model, investigating concepts such as supersymmetry, string theory, and quantum gravity—each promising to interweave quantum mechanics and particle physics in richer, more complex patterns.

The impact of quantum mechanics on particle physics extends beyond the analytical realm into philosophical domains. It fuels debates on the nature of reality, determinism, and the concept of an observer-dependent universe. The questions posed by quantum mechanics about the nature of particles as existing in states of probability until observation invites a reconsideration of what constitutes reality itself. Does the universe exist independently of our observations, or do our measurements actively shape the fundamental nature of the cosmos?

In summary, the impact of quantum physics on particle physics represents nothing short of a revolution in understanding the universe. From refashioning our notions of particles and their interactions to propelling technological advancements in experimental methodologies, quantum mechanics serves as a foundational pillar in interpreting the dynamics that govern the subatomic world. As we embrace the intricacies revealed through quantum theory, the interplay between observation, uncertainty, and particle behavior presents a fascinating tapestry awaiting further exploration—one that continues to mold our understanding of the cosmos and redefine our place within it. The synergy between quantum mechanics and particle physics exemplifies the remarkable journey of human inquiry, showcasing an ever-deepening ambition to explore the hidden realities that lie beneath the surface of our perceived existence.

5.5. Philosophical Implications of Uncertainty

In the landscape of scientific inquiry, uncertainty emerges as an inherent characteristic of our comprehension of nature, particularly within the realm of quantum mechanics. At its philosophical core, the implications of uncertainty command a reevaluation of our foundational beliefs about reality, knowledge, and existence itself. As we navigate through the complexities introduced by quantum theory, the very fabric of understanding begins to unravel, compelling us to confront uncomfortable truths about the limitations of the human intellect in grappling with the universe's intricacies.

Heisenberg's uncertainty principle serves as a flagship notion within this discourse, stating that certain pairs of physical properties cannot be precisely measured simultaneously. As articulated in its mathematical expression, $\Delta x \Delta p \geq \hbar/2$, the principle delineates a fundamental boundary that transcends empirical inaccuracies and delves into the nature of existence at its most basic level. Position and momentum, once considered measurable objectives in classical physics, manifest instead as interwoven aspects of a dynamic reality that evades deterministic categorization. This paradigm shift has profound consequences, suggesting a universe governed not by certainties but by probabilities and potentials.

Philosophically, the challenges posed by uncertainty beckon us to question the very notion of objectivity. In classical epistemology, an objective reality exists independent of the observer, allowing for quantitative precision in measurements and predictions of physical states. However, the quantum realm introduces an intricate interplay between observer and observed, where the act of measurement itself shapes the outcomes and character of reality. As practitioners grapple with this interdependence, tensions arise between classical realism —the belief in an independent, observer-free reality—and a quantum perspective highlighting the relational nature of existence. This divergence fosters rich philosophical dialogue on the implications of observation, knowledge acquisition, and the nature of reality itself.

Uncertainty in quantum mechanics challenges not just our perceptions but the core assumptions underpinning scientific inquiry. The pursuit of objective knowledge is invigorated with questions surrounding determinism, free will, and the human experience. As the lines between observer and observed blur, inquiries arise about whether human agency can coexist with the probabilistic nature of quantum events. If the universe is set on a stage of possibilities rather than certainties, does this open avenues for understanding human choice and behavior in a fundamentally different light? Philosophers and scientists alike are drawn into this intricate web, where psychology, cognition, and free will intermingle with quantum principles, compelling a reconceptualization of human agency.

The implications of uncertainty extend into the realm of technology and methodology as well. Derived from the understandings gleaned from quantum mechanics, innovations compute and redesign our tools of observation—from advanced imaging techniques to quantum computing applications that leverage superposition and entanglement to explore complex datasets in ways previously deemed impossible. These technological evolutions further solidify the necessity of integrating uncertainty within the frameworks used to understand the universe, translating theoretical dynamics into practical methodologies that challenge the very constructs of knowledge production.

As scientific exploration continues to evolve, the persistent question lingers: how do we embrace the uncertainties embedded in the quantum landscape? The quest seeks not only to unveil truths about the fundamental nature of matter and energy but also to foster a deeper inquiry into the philosophical ramifications of a universe characterized by uncertainty. Beyond the confines of laboratories and equations, these discussions seep into the fabric of society, nurturing a collective consciousness that grapples with the intricacies of exis-tence, reality, and the quest for knowledge.

In conclusion, the philosophical implications of uncertainty within quantum mechanics extend far beyond the realm of particle physics —they reshape our understanding of reality itself. They challenge us to navigate the delicate balance of knowing and unknowing, a dance between the observer and the observed, amidst the boundless complexities offered by the quantum world. As we continue this journey of inquiry, it is essential to remain open to the mysteries that lie beneath the surface, for the interplay between uncertainty and reality offers an extraordinary landscape waiting to be explored, revealing profound insights about ourselves and the universe we inhabit. Embracing uncertainty invites us to transcend the limitations of our current understanding and recognize that, perhaps, knowledge is not merely a destination but part of a grander tapestry woven from inquiry, experience, and endless possibility.

6. Quantum Tunneling and Beyond

6.1. The Phenomenon of Quantum Tunneling

A striking phenomenon in quantum mechanics, quantum tunneling exemplifies the unusual behavior of particles at the subatomic level, defying classical physics' deterministic boundaries. Essentially, quantum tunneling describes the process by which particles pass through potential energy barriers, despite seemingly lacking the requisite energy to overcome those barriers. This remarkable feature of quantum systems opens up a world of possibilities, challenging our understanding of how particles behave and laying the groundwork for a host of practical applications across numerous scientific and technological domains.

At the heart of quantum tunneling lies the principle of wave-particle duality, encapsulated in the wave function, which represents all potential states of a quantum system. According to quantum mechanics, particles such as electrons do not exist as fixed entities, but rather as probabilities described by their wave functions. These wave functions extend beyond classical definitions, allowing for overlapping states that blur the lines of definitive existence. When faced with a potential barrier, the wave function does not abruptly drop to zero; rather, it diminishes gradually. This mathematical characteristic means that there is a non-zero probability that a particle can "tunnel" through the barrier, despite not having sufficient energy to surmount it classically.

Understanding tunneling begins with an analogy grounded in classical physics. Imagine a ball rolling up a hill. According to classical mechanics, if the ball does not possess enough kinetic energy to reach the top of the hill, it will roll back down. Long-standing belief dictated that particles operated within such definitive parameters. However, within the quantum realm, particles behave less like balls and more like waves, leading to probabilities rather than absolutes. Consequently, even if the ball lacks the energy to scale the hill, it possesses a chance—however small—of appearing on the other side.

The implications of quantum tunneling extend into several fascinating domains, including nuclear fusion, semiconductors, and even biological processes. A prime example of tunneling in nature is found in nuclear fusion, which powers stars, including our Sun. In stars, particles must overcome repulsive forces due to their positive charges to collide at high speeds, allowing for fusion to occur. Classical physics would suggest that these particles do not have enough energy to fuse. However, quantum tunneling permits particles to combine, resulting in immense energy release, a phenomenon foundational to stellar processes.

In the realm of technology, quantum tunneling plays a critical role in the functionality of semiconductor devices, which form the backbone of modern electronics. Tunneling facilitates electron movement across junctions, allowing for control of electrical conductivity. Tunneling diodes, for example, exploit this effect to achieve rapid switching capabilities, driving advancements in logic circuits and digital electronics.

Remarkably, evidence suggests that quantum tunneling may also play a role in biological processes—an area gaining increased attention in recent years. Studies propose that tunneling could be instrumental in photosynthesis, where the transfer of energy via excitons relies on the careful navigation of energy landscapes. The efficiency of this energy transfer may correlate with the tunneling of particles through energy barriers, reshaping our understanding of how life harnesses quantum effects.

While quantum tunneling is well established, researchers continue to explore its frontiers and applications. Understanding the underlying mechanisms governing tunneling processes remains a vibrant area of inquiry. Investigating how tunneling interacts with environmental factors, system coherence, and entropic considerations paves new pathways in quantum research. Examining the principles of quantum tunneling could further lead to advances across a variety of fields, from developing new materials with unique properties to enhancing quantum computing capabilities.

In closing, the phenomenon of quantum tunneling illustrates the enigmatic nature of the quantum world, where particles transcend classical limitations, existing in a realm defined by probabilities and possibilities. The implications of tunneling resonate far and wide, impacting everything from cosmic processes to the latest technological innovations. As researchers continue to delve deeper into this captivating realm, we not only refine our understanding of quantum systems but also unlock new avenues of exploration that redefine our engagement with the universe. The journey into the depths of quantum tunneling is emblematic of the ongoing quest to navigate a world that lies beyond our classical intuitions, inviting us to embrace the intricate dance of particles and waves that shapes the reality we inhabit.

6.2. Barrier Penetration in Quantum Systems

The phenomenon of barrier penetration in quantum systems stems from the fascinating principles underlying quantum mechanics, which fundamentally differ from classical physics. At the heart of this phenomenon lies the concept of quantum tunneling, wherein particles surpass potential energy barriers despite not having sufficient energy to do so according to classical predictions. This process is emblematic of the complex and often counterintuitive nature of particles at the microscopic scale, challenging our conventional understanding of how matter interacts with energy and potential energy landscapes.

To fathom barrier penetration, one must first grasp the core mechanics of quantum mechanics. Unlike classical particles, which are confined to deterministic paths dictated by energy levels, quantum particles are best described by wave functions. These wave functions provide a probabilistic depiction of a particle's position and momentum, rather than definitive values. Crucially, when a quantum particle encounters a potential energy barrier—such as an insulating barrier that it should not be able to cross—classical physics would dictate that it reflect back if its energy is insufficient to surpass the barrier. However, in the quantum realm, the wave function does not merely truncate at the barrier. Instead, it extends into and beyond the barrier, into the classically forbidden zone.

The mathematics that describe this behavior reveals a non-zero probability for the particle to penetrate through the barrier, even if it seemingly lacks the energy required. This tunneling phenomenon highlights that quantum particles do not adhere strictly to classical boundaries; they possess wave-like properties that allow them to "leak" through barriers. The tunneling probability can be calculated using various methods, one common approach being the application of Schrödinger's time-independent equation to solve for the wave function distribution across the potential barrier. The probability of tunneling decreases exponentially with the width and height of the barrier, suggesting that narrower and lower barriers yield higher tunneling probabilities.

This feature of quantum tunneling has profound implications for various fields ranging from nuclear physics to advanced material science and modern technology. In nuclear physics, tunneling is key to nuclear fusion processes in stars, including our Sun. For example, during the fusion of hydrogen nuclei into helium, protons require sufficient kinetic energy to overcome their electrostatic repulsion. Classical physics would suggest that only high-energy collisions would allow for fusion. However, quantum tunneling allows for lower-energy protons to ultimately fuse as they tunnel through the barrier, a vital mechanism that fuels stellar processes, producing the elements necessary for life as we know it.

Barrier penetration also plays a crucial role in the behavior of semiconductors and transistors, where tunneling facilitates electron movement across junctions. In devices like tunnel diodes, electrons can move through thin insulating layers much more efficiently due to tunneling, enhancing performance and speed in electronic components. Such devices leverage the principles of quantum mechanics to achieve higher functional capabilities that transcend what could be accomplished through classical approaches.

Moreover, quantum tunneling has significant implications in phenomena like quantum computing and quantum cryptography. The operations of qubits, the fundamental units of quantum information, often hinge upon tunneling effects and the coherent superposition of states, enabling them to perform calculations at extraordinary speeds and capabilities compared to classical bits. Researchers are exploring quantum algorithms that exploit tunneling effects to accelerate problem-solving within computational domains.

Despite the remarkable nature of quantum tunneling, it also raises questions about our interpretations of causality, locality, and the fundamental structure of reality. How can particles seemingly defy classical constraints to cross barriers? What does this imply regarding our established notions of cause and effect? As physicists continue to probe these inquiries, a richer understanding of the quantum world emerges, challenging long-held beliefs while expanding the boundaries of knowledge.

In conclusion, barrier penetration in quantum systems presents a captivating interplay of probability, wave behavior, and particle dynamics that defines a key feature of quantum phenomena. Quantum tunneling not only underscores the peculiarities of the quantum realm but also influences a wide array of scientific disciplines and technologies. Embracing the complexities associated with barrier penetration invites further exploration into the nature of existence, the mechanics underlying the universe, and the ongoing quest to unravel the mysteries that lie beneath the surface of reality. As researchers and scientists delve deeper into the implications and applications of quantum tunneling, the potential for transformative discoveries broadens, inspiring new innovations that will shape the future of technology and enrich our understanding of the cosmos.

6.3. Applications in Modern Technology

The application of quantum principles in modern technology represents a pinnacle of human ingenuity, combining the rich theoretical underpinnings of quantum mechanics with practical innovations that have far-reaching effects on various aspects of everyday life. As we stand on the threshold of a new technological era driven by quantum advancements, it is crucial to understand how these foundational principles are harnessed to catalyze revolutionary changes across multiple industries.

One of the most significant applications of quantum mechanics is in the field of quantum computing. Quantum computers harness the peculiar properties of quantum bits or qubits, which differ fundamentally from classical bits. While traditional bits can represent either a 0 or a 1, qubits exploit the principle of superposition, allowing them to simultaneously exist in multiple states. This feature enables quantum computers to perform complex calculations that would be practically impossible for classical computers. Additionally, entanglement further enhances computational power, enabling qubits to be correlated in ways that allow for unprecedented parallel processing capabilities. This quantum advantage has profound implications for industries such as cryptography, optimization problems, and complex system simulations, heralding a new era of computational power.

Quantum cryptography, particularly quantum key distribution (QKD), exemplifies another critical application. In a world increasingly reliant on digital security, maintaining the integrity and confidentiality of data is paramount. QKD leverages the principles of quantum mechanics to create unbreakable encryption methods. The security of quantum cryptography relies on the behavior of entangled particles and the fundamental concept that the act of measuring a quantum state affects its state. Any attempt by an eavesdropper to intercept the key will inevitably alter the quantum states, alerting the parties involved to the presence of the intrusion. As a result, quantum cryptography offers a step change in ensuring secure communications over distances that were previously vulnerable to espionage.

In the field of materials science, quantum mechanics has paved the way for innovations in designing new materials with desired properties. For instance, the development of quantum dots—nanoscale semiconductor particles—has revolutionized electronics, optics, and photonics. Quantum dots exhibit unique electronic and optical properties influenced by their size and shape, enabling practical applications in displays, solar cells, and biomedical imaging. The manipulation of quantum states allows engineers and scientists to design materials that optimize energy absorption and improve efficiency, illustrating the profound implications of quantum mechanics across various applications.

Quantum sensing represents yet another frontier where quantum mechanics is applied to enhance measurement capabilities. Quantum sensors exploit the high precision associated with quantum states to detect minute changes in physical environments, allowing for advancements in fields such as geology, navigation, and medical diagnostics. For example, quantum sensors can improve the detection of gravitational waves, facilitating our understanding of cosmic events. The applications in medical technology include advanced imaging techniques, such as magnetoencephalography, which can image neural activity with unparalleled sensitivity and accuracy.

Moreover, the principles of quantum mechanics are also influencing advances in telecommunications and networking. The concept of quantum entanglement forms the basis of quantum networks, which promise secure data transmission and enhanced communication systems. Entanglement-based protocols enable the development of quantum repeaters, which could bridge long distances for quantum communication while preserving entanglement integrity. This transformation has the potential to revolutionize secure communications on a global scale.

The intersection of quantum mechanics with artificial intelligence (AI) is beginning to gain traction as well. Quantum algorithms can optimize machine learning processes, providing faster and more efficient ways to analyze vast amounts of data. By harnessing the unique capabilities of quantum computation, researchers in AI can develop sophisticated models that push the boundaries of what is currently feasible.

At a more speculative level, researchers are investigating the integration of quantum technologies with emerging fields, such as quantum biology, to explore biological processes at the quantum level. This intersection could unlock new understandings of how quantum phenomena play a role in living systems, potentially influencing drug design and therapeutic techniques.

However, these advancements are not without challenges. The successful implementation of quantum technologies requires overcoming issues related to precision control, error mitigation, and practical scalability. As scientists and engineers work to refine these technologies and develop practical applications, ethical considerations around the implications of quantum breakthroughs arise. Issues such as privacy, security, and the societal impact of advanced quantum technologies necessitate ongoing discussions and frameworks to guide responsible development.

In summary, the applications of quantum mechanics in modern technology serve as a testament to the potential of harnessing the peculiarities of the quantum world. From quantum computing and cryptography to novel materials science and sensing capabilities, quantum principles are shaping a future that promises to enhance our understanding of the universe and transform everyday life. As we continue to explore the myriad possibilities offered by these remarkable advancements, we stand on the brink of a quantum revolution, poised to redefine the technological landscape and human experience in profound ways. Embracing the complexities of quantum applications will be pivotal to unlocking the full potential of this extraordinary field, guiding us toward a future enriched by the wonders of the hidden quantum world.

6.4. Tunneling in Nuclear Physics

Tunneling in nuclear physics represents a profound intersection of quantum mechanics and the understanding of nuclear interactions, illuminating how particles navigate potential barriers in ways that defy classical physics' limitations. This phenomenon, integral to numerous processes in the universe, unveils a landscape where probabilities dictate outcomes, ultimately shaping foundational aspects of nuclear reactions, fusion, and even the very stability of atomic nuclei.

At its core, quantum tunneling occurs when a particle traverses a potential energy barrier that it does not possess enough energy to surmount according to classical predictions. In classical physics, a particle with insufficient energy would be reflected back from the barrier, akin to a ball rolling uphill—unable to reach the other side. However, in the quantum realm, the particle's wave-like nature, described by its wave function, allows it to exist in a superposition of states. The mathematical framework governing this behavior permits a non-zero probability of the particle being found on the opposite side of the barrier, thereby tunneling through it.

In the context of nuclear physics, tunneling plays a critical role in facilitating nuclear decay processes such as alpha decay. Here, an unstable atomic nucleus emits an alpha particle—a cluster of two protons and two neutrons—in a process necessitated by the particle tunneling through the potential energy barrier that characterizes the nucleus. The presence of the strong nuclear force binds nucleons together, creating a barrier that particles must overcome. Quantum mechanics provides a detailed description of this tunneling phenomenon, enabling nuclear particles to escape the bounds of instability and ultimately leading to the emission of alpha particles, driving the process of radioactive decay.

This tunneling process underpins the very mechanisms that power stellar fusion, where the extraordinary conditions within stars give rise to immense gravitational forces and high temperatures. In processes like hydrogen fusion into helium, the temperature and pressure inside stars create environments where nuclei are subjected to high kinetic energies. However, classical physics would imply that protons—positively charged and thus repelling one another due to their electromagnetic interactions—should not have sufficient energy to overcome the electrostatic barrier. Yet, through quantum tunneling, protons can still fuse, resulting in the energy released during stellar nuclear fusion. This energy is what powers stars, including our Sun, allowing the endless cycle of thermonuclear reactions that sustain life on Earth.

The influence of tunneling extends beyond nuclear reactions; its implications resonate through various fields such as particle physics, astrophysics, and even biology. Researchers studying particle accelerators exploit quantum tunneling effects to uncover properties of fundamental particles in high-energy collisions. By examining the ways particles interact beneath the surface, physicists gain insights into the very fabric of matter itself, laying the foundations for extensions to the Standard Model.

Moreover, tunneling is not relegated solely to the confines of high-energy physics; its effects manifest in various biological processes as well. Some studies suggest that tunneling may play a part in enzymatic reactions, where quantum effects contribute to the efficiency of chemical conversions that are crucial for life. Tunneling enables particles, such as protons, to traverse potential barriers within molecular structures, thus influencing biochemical pathways and facilitating processes like photosynthesis.

The realm of quantum tunneling does not exist without challenges; researchers continue to investigate the nuances of this phenomenon, seeking greater detail about how it interacts with various environmental factors, temperature variations, and coherence properties within quantum systems. Exploring these questions could unveil deeper insights into not only the behavior of nuclear systems but also the fundamental principles that guide matter and energy interactions throughout the cosmos.

As we move into the future, understanding tunneling in nuclear physics promises to yield transformative insights—providing pathways to advanced technologies in energy production, improving our comprehension of nuclear reactors, and enhancing methods of managing waste. The intricate dance of particles within potential barriers beckons further exploration into the hidden mechanisms that drive both stellar processes and the atomic structures underpinning the universe.

In summary, tunneling in nuclear physics is a monumental phenomenon that embodies the principles of quantum mechanics, reshaping our understanding of nuclear reactions and the behavior of particles. From alpha decay to fusion processes, tunneling enriches the narrative of how particles interact, ultimately revealing a vast interconnected web of possibilities that extends far beyond classical constraints. The continuous study of tunneling in nuclear physics illuminates a path that intertwines theoretical inquiry with practical applications, urging us to delve deeper into the quantum realm where the mysteries of the universe await our exploration. Embracing the complexities and nuances of tunneling not only enhances our understanding of the atomic world but also prepares us for the breakthroughs and advancements that will define the future of science and technology.

6.5. Research Frontiers in Tunneling

The exploration of research frontiers in tunneling underscores a prominent aspect of quantum mechanics that fascinates both scientists and theorists. This field of study not only showcases the perplexing paradoxes that lie within quantum behavior but also delves into tangible applications spanning various scientific landscapes. As we venture into this intricate terrain, we will consider several dimensions, including fundamental principles, cutting-edge research, and the implications of tunneling for both theoretical advancements and practical innovations across disciplines.

Central to the phenomenon of tunneling is the principle that quantum particles do not adhere strictly to classical paths, allowing particles to traverse barriers deemed insurmountable. This departure from classical understanding stems from the wave-like properties that particles exhibit at the quantum scale, encapsulated in their wave functions. The wave function does not simply vanish at barriers; instead, it extends into classically forbidden regions, thereby allowing for a calculable probability of tunneling. Recent investigations into the nuances of tunneling have revealed its myriad implications in fields as diverse as nuclear physics, materials science, and even biology.

In nuclear physics, tunneling plays a critical role in processes such as alpha decay, where the emission of alpha particles from unstable nuclei is facilitated by quantum tunneling through potential energy barriers. The insights gained from research into tunneling phenomena have furthered our understanding of nuclear stability and decay mechanics, inviting deeper discussions on the nature of fundamental forces and interactions at play within atomic structures.

Beyond nuclear physics, tunneling capabilities have profound implications in materials science and engineering. Researchers are investigating ways to design new materials with optimized properties by exploiting quantum tunneling effects. For example, advancements in nanotechnology and quantum dots rely heavily on tunneling principles, leading to innovative electronic devices capable of leveraging quantum behavior for superior performance. The development of faster, smaller, and more efficient electronic components can be traced back to understanding and harnessing tunneling mechanisms.

Additionally, tunneling manifests intriguingly in biological systems, where research indicates that quantum tunneling may contribute to chemical processes such as metabolic reactions. Investigations into enzymatic reactions suggest that tunneling might enhance the efficiency of biochemical pathways, demonstrating how quantum phenomena can play a role in life itself. As studies in quantum biology gain momentum, our understanding of the inherent connections between quantum mechanics and biological functions is poised to expand, promising groundbreaking applications in areas such as medicine and bioengineering.

As we embrace research frontiers in tunneling, it is essential to recognize the technological advancements made possible through a refined understanding of quantum tunneling. This includes innovations like quantum communication systems, where tunneling principles underpin secure methods of data transmission. The applications extend to the realms of quantum computing, where tunneling contributes to qubit operations and overall computational efficiency, paving the way for powerful new technologies that leverage the unique properties of particles.

In light of these developments, researchers are progressively exploring the intersections between tunneling phenomena and emerging technologies such as quantum computing and quantum sensing. The ongoing quest to understand tunneling more graspably has resulted in the formulation of new theories and models that seek to quantify and predict tunneling effects under various conditions, incorporating factors such as temperature, coherence, and external fields. Experimentalists are now working to test these models, seeking to refine our understanding of tunneling and validate theoretical predictions through precise measurements.

Moreover, exploring tunneling leads naturally to philosophical inquiries about determinism, reality, and causality within the quantum realm. If particles can traverse barriers seemingly contrary to classical logic, what does this imply about our foundational understanding of the universe? How do these observations challenge our perceptions of time, space, and the order of events?

In conclusion, the research frontiers in tunneling represent an exhilarating blend of theoretical foundations and practical applications. As we continue to probe the complexities of quantum behavior, the insights gained from studying tunneling phenomena open new pathways not only for advancing scientific knowledge but also for harnessing quantum principles in innovative technologies that transform industry and society. Tunneling challenges our understanding, inspires inquiry, and illustrates the deep connections that exist between the quantum world and the expansive universe around us. Through ongoing research and exploration, we anticipate a future wherein tunneling becomes integral to unlocking the mysteries of the quantum realm and embracing the practical implications for science and technology at large.

7. The Quantum Field Theory Revolution

7.1. Conceptualizing Fields: A Quantum Leap

Conceptualizing quantum fields represents a significant paradigm shift in the domain of modern physics. As scientists strive to bridge the laws of quantum mechanics with the principles of fields and forces—a central theme in both particle physics and cosmology—they embark on a journey that elucidates not just the interactions of particles but the very fabric of reality itself. This exploration is where the notion of fields, intrinsic to the understanding of fundamental forces, illuminates the understanding of particles, interactions, and the universe as a whole.

In classical physics, the concept of fields—such as gravitational and electromagnetic fields—was pivotal in describing forces acting at a distance. Particles could be seen as discrete entities influenced by these fields, representing an amalgamation of interactions grounded in Newton's laws of motion and Maxwell's equations. However, with the advent of quantum mechanics, this view evolved dramatically. Scientists began to conceptualize fields as dynamic, governed by principles that extended beyond fixed particle trajectories to incorporate probabilities, wave functions, and quantum fluctuations.

To comprehend fields within the quantum realm, one must first acknowledge the revolutionary work of significant figures like Richard Feynman and Paul Dirac. Their contributions were instrumental in redefining the relationship between particles and fields. Dirac's formulation of quantum electrodynamics (QED) provided a field-theoretic frame wherein particles, such as electrons and photons, interact via the exchange of virtual particles. This quantum description of electromagnetic interactions not only united particle physics with field theory but also served as a precursor to subsequent developments in quantum field theory (QFT).

Quantum field theory revolutionized particle physics, laying the groundwork for an understanding characterized by a complex interplay of fields and particles. In this framework, particles are considered excitations of their respective quantum fields, representing the fundamental constituents of matter and forces. For instance, electrons arise as excitations of the electron field while photons manifest as excitations of the electromagnetic field. This perspective radically shifts the perspective of particles from isolated entities to dynamic components embedded within the underlying structure of the universe.

As researchers delve deeper, the notion of fields merges with the intricacies of quantum mechanics, producing phenomena that defy classical intuition. Fields fluctuate; they are never static. Quantum field theory captures this principle, incorporating the idea of vacuum fluctuations—temporary changes in the energy of a point in space that produce virtual particles constantly being created and annihilated. This understanding sparks curiosity, as it suggests that the vacuum, previously perceived as empty space, is instead a seething arena of activity hosting myriad processes.

Engagements with these concepts lead to profound implications for cosmology and the ultimate nature of reality. In the context of the early universe, quantum fluctuations in the field may have seeded the structures of galaxies observed today. Concepts like inflation—the exponential expansion of space—coupled with quantum mechanical principles, draw connections between the microcosm and the macrocosm, suggesting that the emergence of cosmic structures may trace back to quantum interactions at the field level.

The development of modern quantum theories further compels inquiry into how these principles are realized experimentally. Advances in collider technologies, such as the Large Hadron Collider at CERN, directly engage with quantum fields, probing the fundamental interactions that govern particles. These experimental platforms serve as laboratories for testing theoretical predictions and exploring unanswered questions about the nature of fields and their interactions.

It is critical to note that conceptualizing fields as dynamic entities invites philosophical considerations. As scientists grapple with the implications of fields in terms of reality, existence, and the nature of knowledge, the boundaries between physics and philosophy blur. What does it mean for a particle to exist as an excitation in a field? Is the reality we perceive merely a manifestation of underlying fields? These inquiries provoke rich discussions that echo throughout both disciplines, inviting broader engagement with the implications of quantum field theory.

In conclusion, conceptualizing fields within the context of quantum mechanics represents a quantum leap—a transformative evolution in understanding the universe and its workings. As we probe these intricate relationships between particles and fields, we unveil layers of complexity that not only challenge classical frameworks but also enrich our comprehension of existence. The interplay of fields transcends mere particle physics, offering a captivating narrative that interweaves quantum theory, cosmology, and profound philosophical questions about the fabric of reality. This ongoing journey into the conceptualization of fields promises to reveal further mysteries beneath the surface of our understanding, guiding us toward an ever-deepening appreciation of the hidden quantum world.

7.2. From Dirac to Feynman: Pioneering Contributions

The evolution of quantum mechanics from its inception to contemporary applications is underscored by the pioneering contributions of remarkable physicists, among whom Paul Dirac and Richard Feynman stand as giants. Their innovative theories and frameworks not only expanded the horizons of quantum physics but also laid the groundwork for quantum field theory, revolutionizing our understanding of particle interactions and fundamentally altering the very fabric of physics as we conceive it.

Paul Dirac, recognized for his profound theoretical insights, played a pivotal role in developing quantum mechanics in combination with relativity. His most famous contributions include the formulation of quantum electrodynamics (QED) and the Dirac equation, which elegantly fused the principles of quantum mechanics with the theory of special relativity. The Dirac equation predicted the existence of antimatter, leading to the discovery of the positron and catalyzing a shift in thinking about particles and antiparticles as fundamental components of the universe. This revolutionary idea challenged the classical notion of particle interactions, embodying the elegance of quantum principles at play within fundamental forces.

Dirac's work laid the foundation for understanding how particles engage with fields, suggesting that particles are excitations or manifestations of their respective fields. This conceptualization shaped the ontology of particle physics and provided impetus for subsequent innovations in quantum field theory. Dirac's influence extends into various domains, linking principles of quantum mechanics to profound implications in cosmology, where understanding matter-antimatter asymmetries remains a crucial area of exploration.

With Richard Feynman, the journey into quantum mechanics took yet another leap. Feynman's approach to physics combined innovation with clarity, culminating in the development of the Feynman diagrams—visual tools for representing particle interactions. These diagrams revolutionized the way physicists visualize complex interactions between particles and fields. They offer a straightforward way to calculate probabilities involving multiple scattering events, and their intuitive nature has become integral to the teaching and understanding of particle physics.

In addition to his diagrams, Feynman was a key figure in developing the path integral formulation of quantum mechanics. His perspective introduced the notion that particles take all possible paths when transitioning from one point to another, weighing these paths with probability amplitudes. This principle not only innovated theoretical approaches to observing particles but also broadly impacted how we formulate and address quantum mechanics' challenges. Feynman's ability to synthesize and communicate complex theoretical ideas contributed significantly to disseminating quantum theory, inspiring generations of physicists to engage deeply with the subject.

Together, Dirac and Feynman cemented the foundations of quantum mechanics, challenging existing frameworks and reshaping our understanding of the quantum world. Their contributions extended beyond mere theoretical formulation; they offered insight into the very nature of reality itself. As we transition from particles to fields, from individual behavior to complex interactions, we find the interplay of ideas catalyzed by these pioneers resonating throughout modern physics.

The revolution initiated by Dirac and Feynman transcended theoretical physics, inviting discourse in philosophical realms that probe the essence of existence itself. Concepts like quantum entanglement, nonlocality, and the probabilistic nature of particles all draw from the legacies of their innovations. The consequences of their contributions reverberate in contemporary physics, providing a lens through which we continue to explore deep questions regarding the relationships between matter, energy, and the forces governing the universe.

Moreover, their work acts as a nexus connecting quantum mechanics with burgeoning technologies such as quantum computing and quantum cryptography. As we explore these realms, their pioneering contributions continue providing pathways for technological innovation—paving the way for a future built on the foundations of quantum understanding.

In conclusion, the transformative contributions of Paul Dirac and Richard Feynman reshaped our understanding of quantum mechanics, quantum field theory, and the underlying principles governing particle interactions. Their legacy persists today, inspiring ongoing exploration into the nature of reality, the complexities of quantum systems, and the possible trajectories of scientific advancement. As we venture further into the depths of the quantum world informed by their insights, we are constantly reminded of the profound implications surrounding the very essence of existence beneath the surface of what we perceive as reality.

7.3. Quantum Electrodynamics: An Overview

Quantum electrodynamics (QED) stands as a cornerstone of modern theoretical physics, providing an intricate and powerful framework for understanding the interactions between light and matter at the quantum level. As the quantum field theory of electrodynamics, QED encompasses a comprehensive description of how charged particles, such as electrons, interact with electromagnetic fields and photons. This subchapter serves as an overview of the key principles, historical development, and ongoing significance of quantum electrodynamics in shaping not only particle physics but also modern technology and our understanding of the universe.

To grasp the essence of QED, one must begin with the foundational ideas of quantum mechanics and special relativity. The synthesis of these two frameworks provided a pathway for scientists to delve into the intricate relationship between particles and forces. QED proposes that electromagnetic interactions arise fundamentally from the exchange of virtual photons—force-carrying particles within the quantum field. This radical shift in perspective marks a departure from classical views of electromagnetism and embodies the probabilistic nature of quantum mechanics, where the behavior of systems is described in terms of probabilities and wave functions.

The historical development of QED traces back to the early 20th century, propelled by the works of several pioneering physicists. The roots can be traced to the groundbreaking contributions of Max Planck, whose quantum hypothesis set the stage for realizing that energy is quantized. Einstein further advanced the field by illustrating that light itself exhibits particle-like properties through his explanation of the photoelectric effect, a phenomenon that could not be reconciled with classical wave theories of light. These contributions laid the groundwork for a more comprehensive understanding of electromagnetic interactions at the quantum level.

Following these early discoveries, innovators such as Niels Bohr and Werner Heisenberg explored the foundations of quantum mechanics. However, the full realization of quantum electrodynamics emerged through the collective efforts of theorists, including Richard Feynman, Julian Schwinger, and Sin-Itiro Tomonaga, who formulated mathematically rigorous approaches to describe charged particles and their interaction with electromagnetic radiation. Their work culminated in the development of Feynman diagrams, a pictorial representation that simplifies calculations of particle interactions, allowing physicists to visualize complex processes and interactions intuitively.

Feynman diagrams illustrate how electrons (or other charged particles) can interact by emitting and absorbing photons, leading to various physical phenomena, from scattering to the creation of particle-antiparticle pairs. These diagrams provide an accessible means to calculate the probabilities of different processes, fostering a deeper understanding of the complexities inherent in particle interactions. The ability to visualize and manipulate these interactions through QED enabled physicists to derive predictions consistent with experimental observations, solidifying its status as one of the most successful theories in physics.

The implications of QED extend beyond theoretical inquiries, influencing a multitude of fields across both fundamental research and applied technology. The predictions made by QED have been confirmed experimentally with extraordinary precision, leading to an understanding of phenomena such as the Lamb shift and the anomalous magnetic moment of the electron. These results exemplify the high level of accuracy inherent in quantum electrodynamics and underscore its predictive power in describing the behavior of particles under varied conditions.

Moreover, QED has paved the way for significant technological advancements that permeate our daily lives. From lasers and transistors to advanced imaging techniques and quantum optics, the principles of quantum electrodynamics underpin critical technologies that shape modern society. The revolutionary impact of lasers, which rely on stimulated emission of photons—a concept rooted in QED—demonstrates how the understanding of quantum interactions has fostered innovations with wide-ranging applications in telecommunications, medicine, and manufacturing.

As we move forward, it is important to appreciate the ongoing inquiries surrounding quantum electrodynamics and its integrative role within the broader framework of quantum field theory. The successful application of QED informs the ongoing quest to develop unified theories encompassing the fundamental forces of the universe, including the strong and weak nuclear forces. Researchers continually investigate the connections between QED and these other fundamental interactions, seeking a deeper understanding of the nature of particle interactions and the underlying principles governing the fabric of reality.

In summary, quantum electrodynamics serves as a profound testament to the intricacies of quantum mechanics and its transformative power within modern physics. By delineating the interactions between charge and electromagnetic fields through the lens of quantum mechanics, QED not only revolutionized theoretical physics but also catalyzed technological advancements that continue to shape society. The journey initiated by the synthesis of electromagnetism and quantum mechanics remains an ongoing exploration, inviting further inquiry into the nature of interactions that define the universe. Quantum electrodynamics exemplifies the elegance of physics —where particles and forces engage in a complex dance, illuminating the hidden quantum world that lies beneath the surface of everyday existence.

7.4. The Intersection with Particle Physics

The evolution of quantum mechanics has led us to unprecedented realms of understanding, particularly reflected in the significant advances in particle physics. As we examine the intersection between these two domains, we discover a deeply intertwined narrative that informs our grasp of the universe. Particle physics, at its core, seeks to elucidate the fundamental building blocks of matter and the forces governing their interactions. Quantum mechanics provides the groundbreaking framework that enlightens how these particles behave, interact, and manifest through both phenomena and theoretical constructs.

Historically, classical physics struggled to fully explain phenomena occurring at atomic and subatomic scales, leaving gaps that needed to be filled. Early quantum theories proposed by visionaries like Max Planck and Albert Einstein shone light on the quantized nature of energy and the wave-particle duality of light. These pioneering concepts laid the groundwork for a more integrated understanding of particles, particularly as it became evident that a dual framework of waves and particles was essential for explaining various behaviors of matter.

As quantum mechanics flourished, it inspired the birth of quantum field theory (QFT), a rigorous theoretical framework that melded the quantum principles with classical field theories. In this new perspective, particles are defined as excitations of underlying fields, suggesting that the universe is fundamentally composed of fields rather than isolated particles—a dramatic shift from previous classical interpretations. Richard Feynman's work in quantum electrodynamics (QED) illustrated this perspective, enabling physicists to visualize and calculate interactions between charged particles and photons using sophisticated Feynman diagrams.

Central to the intersection of quantum mechanics and particle physics is the Standard Model, a theoretical framework that unifies electromagnetic, weak, and strong nuclear forces under a consistent quantum field description. This model delineates a rich tapestry comprising various fundamental particles, such as quarks, leptons, bosons, and their interactions. Notably, the Higgs boson, theorized in the 1960s and finally discovered in 2012 at CERN's Large Hadron Collider, served as a pivotal confirmation of the Standard Model while updating our understanding of mass generation through the Higgs field.

The impasse confronted by physicists surrounding unanswered questions—such as dark matter and dark energy—calls for further examination at the intersection with quantum mechanics. Currently, researchers are exploring extensions beyond the Standard Model, such as string theory and supersymmetry, attempting to reconcile quantum mechanics with the tenets of gravity while adhering to particle interactions. These frontiers exemplify the ongoing quest to blend quantum theory with methodologies for probing subatomic realities, hinting at deeper structures waiting to be unveiled.

Technological advancements driven by understanding quantum properties are now seeping into diverse fields. From quantum computing—with its promise to revolutionize computational speed by leveraging qubits that exploit superposition and entanglement—to quantum cryptography that offers unbreakable encryption through fundamental quantum principles, the practical applications emerging from the intersection are staggering. Engineering increasingly relies on quantum mechanics to refine various devices ranging from semi-conductor technologies to advanced imaging techniques.

Moreover, the philosophical ramifications inherent in the intersection of quantum mechanics and particle physics beckon deeper inquiry. The acceptance of probability and the rejection of determinism challenge long-held beliefs about causation, objectivity, and the very nature of reality. These inquiries compel us to reflect on the foundational aspects of existence, consciousness, and the interpretative frameworks through which we perceive our universe.

In summary, the intersection of quantum mechanics and particle physics represents a dynamic and evolving narrative, continuously reshaping our understanding of the cosmos. Through advancements in theory, technology, and philosophical inquiry, we explore the intricate relationships between particles, fields, forces, and the very essence of existence. As we stand on the precipice of new discoveries, the insights gathered from this intersection illuminate the hidden quantum world beneath the familiar surface, inviting us to venture confidently into the uncharted territories awaiting discovery in the realms of science and beyond.

7.5. Modern Developments in Field Theory

Modern developments in field theory have marked a significant evolution in our understanding of the universe, blending the intricacies of quantum mechanics with the foundational concept of fields. This fusion has not only illuminated the nature of particles and their interactions but has led to profound advancements in both theoretical physics and practical applications across various scientific disciplines.

At the heart of these modern developments is the establishment of quantum field theory (QFT), which fundamentally reshapes our comprehension of particles and forces. In classical physics, particles were often viewed as discrete entities with defined trajectories, influenced by classical fields such as electromagnetism and gravity. However, with the rise of quantum mechanics, the paradigm shifted. Particles emerged not as isolated objects but as excitations of underlying fields permeating the fabric of space-time. Each type of particle corresponds to a specific quantum field, such as the electron field for electrons or the photon field for light. This perspective allows for a more cohesive understanding of nature, where particles and fields are intrinsically linked.

The historical development of quantum field theory can be traced back to prominent theoretical work in the early 20th century. Pioneering physicists such as Richard Feynman, Julian Schwinger, and Steven Weinberg contributed to formalizing QFT, leading to significant milestones such as quantum electrodynamics (QED), which describes electron-photon interactions, and the electroweak theory unifying electromagnetic and weak nuclear forces. Each of these frameworks reinforced the idea that interactions occur through the exchange of virtual particles—transient particles that mediate forces between matter.

The success of QFT has been most evident in the realm of particle physics, particularly at high-energy colliders like the Large Hadron Collider (LHC). Here, physicists have repeatedly validated the predictions of the Standard Model, a comprehensive QFT framework that describes the electromagnetic, weak, and strong nuclear forces. The pivotal discovery of the Higgs boson in 2012 stands as a landmark achievement in particle physics, confirming the existence of the Higgs field, which imparts mass to other particles through the Higgs mechanism. Such breakthroughs underscore the predictive power and robustness of quantum field theory, reaffirming its centrality in contemporary physics.

Modern developments in field theory have also expanded into cosmology, where quantum field theoretic concepts are integral to understanding the early universe. Inflationary theory, which posits a rapid expansion of space-time immediately following the Big Bang, relies on quantum fields to explain the uniformity and structure of the observable universe. Quantum fluctuations in these fields are thought to give rise to the density variations that eventually led to galaxy formation. Thus, field theory elegantly connects quantum mechanics to grand-scale cosmic phenomena, bridging micro and macro realms of physics.

Furthermore, advancements in quantum field theory extend beyond the theoretical domains, influencing technologies that permeate everyday life. Quantum technologies, ranging from quantum computing to quantum sensing, leverage the principles outlined in quantum field theory to achieve capabilities unattainable through classical methods. In quantum computing, qubits, representing superpositions of quantum states, harness quantum field interactions to perform complex computations. Quantum sensors utilize field fluctuations to measure phenomena with unprecedented precision, paving the way for innovations in healthcare, navigation, and environmental monitoring.

The modern developments in field theory also invite a reexamination of the philosophical implications of quantum mechanics. Concepts such as entanglement and nonlocality, central to QFT, challenge classical notions of separateness and locality, prompting deep discussions about the nature of reality and our perception of it. The interplay between particles, fields, and observers calls into question reductive interpretations of physics, suggesting a more interconnected and dynamic universe.

As research continues to delve into the intricacies of field theory, new frontiers emerge. Ongoing inquiries into concepts such as quantum gravity aim to reconcile the principles of quantum mechanics with general relativity, offering the potential for a deeper understanding of the universe's underlying structure. Moreover, exploration of topics like string theory, which extends quantum field theory into higher-dimensional spaces, shows promise in unifying fundamental forces and particles.

In summary, modern developments in field theory signify a profound resurgence in our understanding of reality, integrating quantum mechanics into an expansive framework that elucidates the nature of particles and interactions. Fueled by groundbreaking theoretical insights and experimental validations, quantum field theory continues to shape our understanding of the universe, bridging theoretical physics with practical applications. As advancements unfold, the implications of these developments resonate across disciplines, inviting us to explore the hidden quantum world that underpins the delicate tapestry of existence. Embracing the complexities of modern field theory illuminates pathways for future exploration, redefining our engagement with the universe and expanding the frontiers of human knowledge.

8. Quantum Computing and Information

8.1. The Quest for Quantum Supremacy

The race towards quantum supremacy represents one of the most exhilarating frontiers in contemporary science, as researchers seek to harness the unconventional properties of quantum systems to outperform classical computers in specific tasks. This pursuit not only signifies a paradigm shift in computing but also challenges our traditional notions of what computation entails, as we explore capabilities that transcend classical limitations.

At its core, the quest for quantum supremacy revolves around developing quantum computers that utilize qubits—quantum bits that can exist in superpositions of states—allowing them to process information in ways classical bits cannot. Unlike classical bits, which can be either 0 or 1, qubits can represent both values simultaneously, drastically expanding the computational capacity. This extraordinary characteristic arises from the principles of quantum mechanics, including superposition and entanglement, forming the foundation for quantum algorithms that promise exponential speedup for specific problems.

Pioneering work in this field has illuminated the avenues through which quantum computers can gain supremacy. Notably, Google claimed quantum supremacy in 2019 with its 53-qubit quantum processor, Sycamore, completing a specific problem in 200 seconds that would take classical supercomputers thousands of years to solve. This monumental achievement demonstrated the potential of quantum systems to exceed classical capabilities, igniting a wave of interest and inquiry into the broader implications of quantum computation.

However, the quest for quantum supremacy extends beyond mere performance benchmarks; it invites a reevaluation of algorithms and problem domains where quantum computing can offer a distinct advantage. Noteworthy examples include Shor's algorithm, which proposes an efficient method for factoring large integers at a speed unattainable by classical algorithms, posing potential threats to classical encryption techniques and emphasizing the importance of developing robust quantum cryptography methods alongside quantum computation.

Quantum supremacy also implicates scientific domains such as materials science, drug discovery, and complex system modeling. The ability of quantum computers to simulate quantum systems and molecular interactions at unprecedented levels of complexity can lead to transformative breakthroughs in understanding chemical reactions and developing novel therapies. These capabilities underscore the far-reaching potential of quantum computing to address pressing global challenges, from renewable energy solutions to optimizing complex logistical systems.

As researchers race towards achieving sustained quantum supremacy, they confront formidable challenges, including error rates and decoherence—phenomena where quantum states lose their coherence due to interactions with the environment. Building fault-tolerant quantum computers necessitates the implementation of error correction protocols capable of protecting qubits from noise, ensuring reliable operations over significant computational tasks. Overcoming these hurdles is paramount to realizing practical quantum computers that can effectively tackle real-world problems.

Moreover, the escalating complexity of quantum systems also demands advances in quantum algorithms and software. Researchers must not only design new algorithms tailored to take advantage of quantum properties but also develop tools and programming languages that enable broader engagement with quantum computation. This shift requires interdisciplinary collaboration between physicists, computer scientists, and engineers, fostering an ecosystem conducive to sustained innovation and knowledge exchange.

As we envision the future of quantum supremacy, it becomes evident that its implications reach far beyond computation alone. The race encapsulates philosophical inquiries into the nature of intelligence, computation, and the fundamental understanding of information itself. It beckons us to ponder profound questions surrounding the limits of classical mechanics, the scalability of intelligence, and how these emerging systems redefine our relationship with technology.

In conclusion, the quest for quantum supremacy marks a momentous chapter in the ongoing saga of scientific exploration. By harnessing the unique properties of quantum systems, we stand on the brink of monumental shifts in computing, addressing complex challenges that beset society today. As we forge ahead into the quantum future, our collective ingenuity and determination will ultimately define not just the outcomes of computational capabilities but the very way we understand and interact with the world around us. The interplay of ambition, innovation, and collaboration serves as the guiding light as we navigate the exhilarating frontier of quantum supremacy, unveiling the hidden potential that lies beneath the surface of traditional computation.

8.2. Quantum Bits and Their Properties

Quantum bits, or qubits, represent the fundamental units of quantum information, embodying the principles that set quantum computing apart from classical computing. To understand their properties and implications, it is critical to grasp how they differ from classical bits, how they behave, and the consequential impacts they have on technology and information processing.

At the most basic level, a classical bit can exist in one of two distinct states: 0 or 1. This binary representation forms the foundation of classical computing systems, where information is processed in binary logic. In contrast, a qubit can occupy a state of 0, 1, or any weighted combination of both simultaneously, thanks to the principle of quantum superposition. Mathematically, this state can be represented as:

$$|\psi\rangle = \alpha|0\rangle + \beta|1\rangle$$

Here, $|\psi\rangle$ is the qubit's state, and α and β are complex numbers that denote the probabilities of measuring the qubit in state $|0\rangle$ or $|1\rangle$, respectively. The coefficients fulfill the normalization condition $|\alpha|^2$

+ $|\beta|^2 = 1$, indicating that the sum of probabilities must equal one. This capability allows quantum computers to process vast numbers of possibilities simultaneously, significantly increasing computational speed and efficiency for certain problems.

One of the remarkable properties of qubits is their ability to become entangled. When qubits are entangled, the state of one qubit becomes directly related to the state of another, regardless of the distance separating them. This phenomenon violates classical intuitions about separateness and locality, as measuring one qubit will instantaneously affect the other, even if they are light-years apart. Entanglement enables quantum computers to perform tasks that would be impractical or impossible for classical systems, facilitating developments in quantum algorithms that tap into this interconnectedness.

Another essential property of qubits is that they exhibit interference —an effect of wave-like behavior unique to quantum systems. When multiple qubits interact, their respective states can combine in ways that amplify certain outcomes while canceling others. This principle underlies many quantum algorithms, such as Grover's algorithm, which provides quadratic speedup for searching unstructured databases and Shor's algorithm, which factors large numbers exponentially faster than classical algorithms.

However, working with qubits presents challenges primarily due to their susceptibility to decoherence—a process through which a quantum system loses its quantum properties due to interactions with its environment. Decoherence can disrupt the delicate states of qubits, leading to errors in computation. As such, maintaining coherence over extended periods is crucial for the successful deployment of functional quantum computers. Researchers continuously strive to develop error correction methods that can mitigate these issues, given that practical quantum computing requires robust systems capable of reliably processing information.

Moreover, qubits can be realized through various physical implementations, including superconducting circuits, trapped ions, quantum dots, and photonic systems. Each platform has unique advantages and challenges, contributing to the diverse landscape of quantum technology and research. These advancements enable the rapid exploration of new algorithms and operational capacities that push the boundaries of what quantum computing can achieve.

The implications of qubits extend beyond computation alone; they reach into cryptography, optimization, complex simulations, and the treatment of large datasets across different sectors, including finance, healthcare, and artificial intelligence. Quantum key distribution (QKD), as an application derived from the principles surrounding qubits and entanglement, provides secure communication channels against eavesdropping, showcasing how quantum information encompasses both computation and communication paradigms.

In summary, quantum bits and their properties encapsulate the essence of quantum computing's potential to revolutionize technology and information processing. Through superposition, entanglement, and interference, qubits can encode and manipulate information in ways previously deemed unimaginable, opening new pathways for advancements across disciplines. They represent not merely a technical curiosity but a fundamental shift in our approach to understanding and harnessing the quantum realm, with implications that promise to redefine multiple areas of science, technology, and society as we forge ahead into the future of quantum information science.

8.3. Entanglement in Quantum Information Processing

Entanglement in quantum information processing is a fascinating topic that highlights the unique characteristics of quantum mechanics and the potential applications that arise from these properties. At its core, entanglement describes a phenomenon where two or more quantum systems become intertwined such that the state of one system cannot be described independently of the state of the other, no matter how far apart they are. This peculiar connection, which

Einstein famously referred to as "spooky action at a distance," has significant implications for information theory, computation, and secure communication in the quantum realm.

To understand the role of entanglement in quantum information processing, it is essential to start with the fundamental principles of quantum mechanics, particularly superposition and entanglement itself. Superposition allows quantum particles, such as qubits, to exist in multiple states simultaneously, while entanglement creates correlations between these states that transcend classical limitations. As a result, when measurements are made on entangled particles, the outcomes are statistically correlated in ways that classical physics cannot explain, enabling various applications that exploit this unique linkage.

In quantum information processing, entanglement serves as a resource that enhances the performance of quantum algorithms and protocols. This has led to the design of algorithms that outperform classical counterparts in specific tasks. For example, Shor's algorithm for factoring large integers takes advantage of entangled states to achieve exponential speedup compared to the best-known classical algorithms. Similarly, Grover's algorithm provides quadratic speedup for searching through unstructured databases. These algorithms not only represent the power of entanglement in computation but also illustrate its potential to revolutionize cryptography and data security.

One of the most prominent applications of entanglement in quantum information processing is quantum key distribution (QKD). By using entangled particles to generate shared encryption keys, QKD allows two parties to communicate securely in the presence of potential eavesdroppers. The security of QKD arises from the principles of quantum mechanics; any attempt to measure or intercept the entangled states would disturb them, alerting the legitimate users to the presence of an eavesdropper. This revolutionary method enhances the security of communication systems and addresses vulnerabilities present in classical encryption schemes.

In addition to encryption, entanglement plays a vital role in quantum teleportation, a process by which the quantum state of a particle can be transmitted from one location to another without the physical transfer of the particle itself. By leveraging entanglement and classical communication channels, teleportation enables the transfer of information with remarkable fidelity, which has implications for future quantum networks and communication systems.

Furthermore, advances in quantum computing rely heavily on entangled qubits, allowing quantum systems to perform complex calculations in parallel. Entanglement enables qubits to work together, enhancing computational efficiency and providing results more quickly than classical computers. The ability to manipulate and maintain entangled states over extended periods remains a significant challenge, but researchers are actively developing techniques to address these issues while harnessing the power of entanglement in burgeoning quantum technologies.

Despite these advancements, challenges remain in the practical application of entanglement for quantum information processing. One of the primary obstacles is maintaining coherence in entangled states since they are exceptionally sensitive to environmental interference — a phenomenon known as decoherence. Researchers are exploring various approaches, including error correction codes and fault-tolerant quantum computing, to mitigate these effects and enable robust quantum systems capable of executing entangled-based algorithms effectively.

Additionally, the distribution of entangled states over long distances, essential for practical applications such as global secure communication, raises logistical challenges. Techniques such as quantum repeaters are being developed to facilitate the transmission of entangled states across vast distances, laying the groundwork for future quantum networks.

In summary, entanglement is a cornerstone of quantum information processing, providing powerful advantages in computation, cryptography, and secure communication. As the field of quantum information science continues to evolve, advancements in our understanding of entanglement and its properties will unlock new possibilities that transform our technological landscape. Harnessing entanglement poses substantial challenges, but the pursuit of these developments holds great promise for securing the future of information technology in an increasingly connected, quantum-powered world. The continued exploration of entanglement in quantum information processing exemplifies the beauty and complexity of the quantum realm, inviting us to uncover the limitless potential beneath the surface of our understanding.

8.4. Potential Applications and Challenges

The potential applications of quantum mechanics present a tantalizing glimpse into a future where technology can harness the bizarre and often counterintuitive phenomena intrinsic to the quantum realm. However, along with these opportunities come significant challenges that must be addressed as we advance in our understanding and implementation of quantum principles.

In the field of quantum computing, the promise of performing complex calculations exponentially faster than classical computers is perhaps one of the most widely discussed applications. Potential uses range from solving optimization problems, enhancing machine learning algorithms, to simulating molecular and atomic systems for drug discovery. However, building a scalable and fault-tolerant quantum computer remains one of the most formidable engineering challenges. Qubits are incredibly sensitive to environmental factors, leading to high error rates due to decoherence and noise. Researchers continue to explore error correction methods and new qubit designs to mitigate these issues, which presents a bottleneck to realizing the full potential of quantum computing technologies.

Quantum cryptography, particularly through Quantum Key Distribution (QKD), offers groundbreaking possibilities for secure communication. By utilizing the principles of quantum mechanics, specifically entanglement and superposition, QKD ensures that any attempt to eavesdrop on a communication channel will disturb the quantum states, alerting users to security breaches. Despite the potential, widespread implementation of quantum cryptography in commercial applications is still hindered by the limitations of current technologies, such as distance and infrastructure. Developing practical systems that can operate securely over long distances remains a challenge, requiring advancements in quantum repeaters and communication protocols.

In fields such as quantum sensors, entanglement can also improve measurement precision beyond classical limits. Applications could range from geological mapping to extremely sensitive measurements for medical diagnostics. The challenge, however, lies in isolating quantum systems from environmental influences that can lead to loss of coherence. This requires continuous innovations in materials science and techniques for managing decoherence.

Quantum networks represent another promising application, creating interconnected systems that leverage entanglement for secure information exchange. However, challenges pertaining to the scalability of quantum networks and the effective distribution of entangled states over considerable distances require the development of new technologies, such as quantum repeaters and novel communication protocols. Building reliable and efficient quantum networks poses technical difficulties, and researchers must devise methods to manage both the quantum states and the classical data streams essential for effective communication.

Philosophical challenges also accompany the potential applications of quantum mechanics. Concepts such as entanglement, superposition, and the measurement problem raise questions about the nature of reality and human perception. As quantum mechanics increasingly influences technology, issues regarding privacy, security, and the implications for societal dynamics emerge, necessitating interdisciplinary dialogue among scientists, ethicists, and policymakers.

Additionally, public understanding and perception of quantum science represent another challenge. With its abstract concepts and counterintuitive nature, quantum mechanics can often evoke skepticism or misunderstanding among the public, complicating efforts to garner support for research funding or technological adoption. Education initiatives aimed at demystifying quantum principles and raising awareness about its practical applications could pave the way for more informed discourse.

As we look to the future of quantum mechanics, the potential applications offer an exhilarating glimpse into unprecedented advancements in technology, medicine, communication, and more. Yet, significant challenges persist that require continued research, collaboration, and innovation. By addressing these dual facets—both the promise of quantum applications and the intricacies of the challenges at hand —we can work towards a future where the hidden quantum world is fully realized, fundamentally transforming our technological landscape and our understanding of reality itself. The journey forward invites curiosity, exploration, and effort, as we seek to unlock the mysteries and possibilities embedded in the quantum realm that lies beneath the fabric of our everyday lives.

8.5. The Future of Quantum Information Science

In the transformative landscape of scientific inquiry, the future of quantum information science holds immense promise, serving as a nexus where innovation, technology, and understanding intersect. As researchers continue to unveil the subtleties of quantum mechanics and its implications for information processing, we stand on the brink of advancements that will redefine our perspectives on reality, computation, and communication.

The trajectory of quantum information science is marked by the ambition to harness the unique properties of quantum systems— principally superposition, entanglement, and quantum interference —to develop technologies that surpass classical limits. At the forefront of this burgeoning field is quantum computing, which leverages qubits to perform operations that enhance computational speed and capacity beyond what is currently attainable. This development not only promises dramatic improvements in problem-solving capabilities, such as in optimization, material science, and cryptography but also challenges our conventional approaches to computation and data processing.

Within quantum computing, efforts to achieve quantum supremacy —a point where quantum devices outperform classical ones in specifically defined tasks—are gaining momentum. Noteworthy milestones, such as Google's declaration of achieving quantum supremacy in 2019, highlight the strides made in realizing practical quantum systems. Researchers continue to explore new architectures and algorithms that optimize qubit interaction and coherence, ensuring that the path toward scalable quantum computers remains an exhilarating focus of investigation.

The implications of quantum information science extend profoundly into the realm of secure communications through quantum cryptography, specifically in Quantum Key Distribution (QKD). By utilizing the principles of quantum mechanics, QKD allows for the generation of secure keys between parties, impervious to eavesdropping due to the observer effect. As concerns over data security heighten in our increasingly digital world, the adoption of quantum cryptographic techniques is poised to provide solutions that uphold the integrity of sensitive communications.

As we reflect on the expansive domain of quantum information science, we also confront challenges that must be addressed to fully realize its potential. The susceptibility of quantum systems to decoherence demands robust error correction methods that ensure reliable operations in quantum computing and information processing. Researchers are actively exploring solutions such as topologically protected qubits and novel materials that can withstand environmental perturbations, along with algorithms that can gracefully manage noise in quantum operations.

In addition, the burgeoning field of quantum networks, which seeks to enable secure and reliable communication over long distances, calls for continuous advancement in quantum repeater technologies. These systems will enhance the distribution of entangled states necessary for quantum communication, paving the way for a globally interconnected quantum internet that would transform how information is shared.

The intersection of quantum information science with artificial intelligence (AI) represents an exciting frontier for future exploration. Quantum algorithms could empower machine learning systems, enhancing their capabilities to analyze vast and complex datasets more effectively than classical approaches. This potential synergy between quantum computing and AI may catalyze advancements across industries, leading to breakthroughs in areas such as healthcare, finance, and logistics.

As we envision the future of quantum information science, we must also consider its broader socioeconomic implications. The rise of quantum technologies necessitates nurturing a skilled workforce equipped to navigate the complexities of this evolving landscape. Educational initiatives must adapt to include quantum literacy, empowering individuals with the knowledge to engage critically with quantum principles and technologies.

Moreover, ethical considerations surrounding quantum technologies must be thoroughly examined. As quantum systems transition from the laboratory to practical implementations, issues related to privacy, security, and societal impact will require transparent discussions involving policymakers, researchers, and the public. Collaborative engagements that sensitize communities to quantum advancements can foster a more informed discourse about their implications and ensure equitable access to the benefits they offer.

In closing, the future of quantum information science is laden with transformative possibilities and challenges yet to be fully realized. As researchers, technologists, and thinkers continue to probe the intricacies of quantum systems, we can anticipate a landscape where quantum capabilities reshape computation, communication, and our understanding of the universe itself. The commitment to navigating the complexities of quantum information science will serve not only as a pursuit of knowledge but as a vital endeavor toward harnessing the hidden potential that lies beneath the surface of our reality. Embracing this frontier invites us to expand the boundaries of what is possible, as we usher in a new epoch defined by the wonders of the quantum world.

9. Quantum Cryptography: Secure Communications

9.1. Basics of Quantum Cryptography

Basics of Quantum Cryptography

Quantum cryptography represents an innovative leap in securing information, leveraging the principles of quantum mechanics to create fundamentally secure communication systems that stand resilient against classical eavesdropping techniques. Central to this evolution is the connection between cryptography—the art and science of secure communication—and quantum physics, which governs the behavior of particles at the atomic and subatomic levels.

At its core, quantum cryptography utilizes the unique properties of quantum states to achieve security. The cornerstone of this technology is Quantum Key Distribution (QKD), a protocol enabling two parties to generate a shared, secret key used for encrypted communication. Unlike classical cryptographic methods, which may rely on the mathematical complexity of certain problems (such as factoring large integers for RSA encryption), QKD fundamentally hinges on the laws of quantum mechanics, particularly the principles of superposition and entanglement.

One of the key concepts underpinning QKD is the uncertainty principle articulated by Werner Heisenberg, which implies that any attempt to measure a quantum state inevitably alters that state. Consequently, in a QKD protocol, any interference or interception by an eavesdropper would disturb the quantum states being exchanged between the legitimate communicators. This disturbance can be detected, allowing the parties to ascertain whether the communication is secure or compromised.

The first legitimate QKD protocol proposed was the BB84 protocol, introduced by Charles Bennett and Gilles Brassard in 1984. The BB84 method employs the polarization states of photons to encode bits of information. For instance, a photon can be polarized vertically or horizontally to represent a bit value of 0 or 1, respectively. Meanwhile, diagonal polarization states could signify the other bit values. When the sender (often called Alice) and receiver (Bob) transmit and compare the polarization of photons, they establish a shared key.

To ensure security, the protocol defines a series of steps. Alice sends a sequence of photons to Bob, each photon being randomly polarized according to one of the states from a defined set. Bob then measures the received photons, selecting polarization states randomly. After the transmission, Alice and Bob communicate over a classical channel to discuss which states they used for their measurements to determine the bits of the shared key. Importantly, they discard any bits where their polarization choices do not match.

If an eavesdropper (commonly referred to as Eve) attempts to intercept the communication, any measurement performed on the photons will inevitably disturb their polarization states. This disturbance can be detected when Alice and Bob compare a subset of their results. If the error rate exceeds a certain threshold, the pair knows that the key has been compromised, allowing them to abandon the attempt and start anew.

The potential applications of quantum cryptography extend far beyond simple key exchange. Its inherent security features make it highly suitable for securing sensitive communications across various sectors that value data confidentiality, including government operations, financial institutions, and healthcare systems. Furthermore, as society increasingly shifts toward digital communication, the integration of quantum cryptography stands to address the growing concerns surrounding data security and privacy in the information age.

Despite its numerous advantages, several challenges remain to be addressed to ensure widespread implementation and practical usability. The technological demands associated with generating, transmitting, and measuring quantum states require sophisticated and expensive infrastructure, limiting the initial rollout to specific environments, such as financial institutions or government applications. Additionally, issues related to the distance over which QKD can be reliably implemented pose further constraints; effective long-distance implementation necessitates the development of quantum repeaters that can extend the range of entangled states.

The field of quantum cryptography continues to evolve, with researchers exploring new methods, enhancing existing protocols, and adapting them to various platforms and technologies, including satellite-based systems that promise to cover vast geographical areas and enhance connectivity. The quest for robust, scalable, and user-friendly solutions remains a driving factor as developments in quantum cryptography continue in tandem with advancements in quantum mechanics and technology.

In summary, quantum cryptography, built upon the principles of quantum mechanics, represents a revolutionary shift toward secure communication in the digital age. By leveraging the characteristics of quantum states to ensure the integrity and confidentiality of exchanged keys, quantum cryptography provides a glimpse into the future of information security—a future where communication is inherently protected by the laws governing the quantum realm. As we advance deeper into this field, the continued exploration and refinement of quantum cryptographic protocols promise exciting opportunities and breakthroughs, ushering in a new era of secure communications that stand resilient against the evolving challenges of modern society.

9.2. Quantum Key Distribution Methods

The landscape of quantum key distribution (QKD) epitomizes the application of quantum mechanics in achieving secure communication methods, fundamentally altering the way we conceptually approach security in data transmission. As digital communication becomes increasingly vital in today's interconnected world, ensuring the confidentiality and integrity of transmitted information is paramount. QKD leverages the unique properties of quantum mechanics, particularly superposition and entanglement, to create cryptographic keys that are theoretically unbreakable.

Quantum key distribution operates on the principle that any interception or measurement made on the quantum states transferring the key will inherently disturb those states. This quality arises from Heisenberg's uncertainty principle, which states that the act of measuring a quantum system affects the system itself. In practical terms, this means that if an eavesdropper attempts to access the communication, their presence would manifest as detectable errors in the transmitted key. This detection capability provides a built-in security feature that classical cryptographic systems lack.

The most well-known QKD protocol is the BB84 protocol, proposed by Charles Bennett and Gilles Brassard in 1984. In this protocol, polarizations of single photons are used to encode information. Each photon is polarized randomly in one of two bases (rectilinear or diagonal), and the receiver subsequently measures the photons to generate a shared secret key. After transmission, the sender and receiver compare their measurement bases over a classical channel to distill the bits that remained consistent. Any discrepancies from potential eavesdropping can be detected, allowing the parties to discard compromised keys and use secure ones.

Real-world implementations of QKD have already seen success in various domains, including secure banking transactions, governmental communication, and corporate data transfers. Efforts to expand QKD technology include integrating it with existing telecommunications infrastructure to enable practical applications over extensive distances. Nevertheless, challenges remain in ensuring the efficiency and scalability of QKD systems.

One significant barrier to widespread adaptation is the limited distance over which quantum states can be reliably transmitted. Quantum states are susceptible to loss and degradation, leading to potential vulnerabilities in key generation. To tackle this, researchers are investigating quantum repeaters that can effectively transmit entangled states over long distances, enabling the extension of secure quantum communication networks.

Furthermore, the threat landscape evolves alongside quantum technology. While QKD is designed to provide immune security, potential adversaries continuously explore new methods to compromise communication systems. This necessitates the ongoing advancement of quantum cryptography techniques. A range of solutions, including device-independent QKD that eliminates reliance on the trustworthiness of devices and the search for new protocols that extend beyond the limitations of BB84, is under active investigation.

Simultaneously, the emergence of quantum computers presents both opportunities and threats. Quantum algorithms have the potential to break certain classical encryption methods, compelling a reevaluation of current cryptographic practices. Hence, the field of post-quantum cryptography, which aims to develop new cryptographic algorithms that can withstand attacks from quantum computers, serves as a critical area of research.

As we look ahead, the trajectory of quantum key distribution signifies just the beginning of a burgeoning field that challenges traditional security paradigms. The integration of quantum mechanics into communication technology heralds new frontiers in confidentiality, integrity, and authenticity. The collaborative efforts of researchers, technologists, engineers, and policymakers will be pivotal in navigating this landscape, ensuring that the promise of quantum security extends not just into research labs but into the everyday lives of individuals and organizations seeking reliable communication solutions in an increasingly digital world.

In conclusion, quantum key distribution represents a revolutionary shift in securing communications, offering insights grounded in the intriguing nature of quantum phenomena. With rigorous development and implementation, it holds the potential to redefine our approaches to security in an era where digital threats continue to evolve. As research and application of quantum cryptography advance, the shifting paradigm will undoubtedly unlock new pathways for secure communication in the modern world, reinforcing the critical importance of safeguarding information in our interconnected society.

9.3. Real-World Applications and Security

In the evolving landscape of quantum mechanics, the intersection of practical applications and the foundational principles of security offers a glimpse into the future of how quantum technologies will shape our lives. Real-world applications of quantum mechanics are being developed across multiple industries, driven by advancements in encryption, communication, computing, and sensing technologies. As we venture into this new frontier, it is imperative to address the implications these innovations carry for security, privacy, and legal frameworks while recognizing the complex challenges that characterize the integration of quantum technologies into our daily lives.

One of the most significant arenas where quantum mechanics exerts influence is quantum cryptography, particularly through Quantum Key Distribution (QKD). QKD harnesses quantum principles to create secure communication channels that are theoretically invulnerable to eavesdropping. Utilizing the peculiar properties of entangled particles, QKD allows parties to generate shared secrets while ensuring that any attempt to intercept the key results in detectable anomalies. The security afforded by quantum cryptography is not merely heuristic but is backed by the robustness of quantum mechanics itself. This has profound implications for various sectors, from government and military communications to corporate data protection and personal privacy in the digital age.

Yet, the implementation of quantum cryptography is not devoid of challenges. As the technology matures, addressing the practicalities of long-distance communication becomes paramount. Quantum states tend to degrade over distance due to attenuation and noise, necessitating advancements in quantum repeaters and network infrastructure. Moreover, the integration of quantum protocols into existing communication systems requires careful consideration of interoperability, regulatory frameworks, and adherence to privacy standards. Developing effective methodologies for transitioning to a quantum-secured world remains a key focus area for researchers and policymakers alike.

Another significant aspect of the real-world application of quantum mechanics is in the realm of quantum computing. Quantum computers are poised to revolutionize problem-solving capabilities across various fields, including healthcare, finance, and logistics. Their potential to process complex data sets in ways classical computers cannot creates opportunities for significant advancements in areas such as drug discovery, optimization of supply chains, and financial modeling.

Nevertheless, the landscape of quantum computing is equally laden with hurdles. Early-stage quantum systems are prone to errors arising from decoherence and operational noise. Achieving fault-tolerant quantum computation is vital for delivering reliable results, and continued investment in research to enhance quantum error correction techniques and scalable architectures is paramount. Furthermore, as quantum computing advances, the specter of quantum attacks looms large over classical encryption algorithms, driving the urgent need for the development of post-quantum cryptographic methods that can withstand the computational prowess of quantum systems.

The realm of quantum sensing offers another avenue for real-world applications that hold immense promise. Quantum sensors leverage quantum interference and entanglement to achieve measurement precision far exceeding that of classical sensors. Applications span diverse fields, including environmental monitoring, navigation, medical diagnostics, and fundamental physics experimentation. However, the deployment of such technologies requires overcoming maintainability, noise management, and environmental shielding challenges to ensure effective operation outside laboratory settings.

As we explore the multifaceted implications of harnessing quantum technologies, ethical considerations surrounding these advancements are paramount. Privacy concerns, security implications, and the risk of digital disenfranchisement from underprivileged communities pose critical questions that society must navigate. Additionally, the unpredictable impact of advancing technologies on labor markets and economic structures compels us to engage in broad discussions about governance, regulation, and equity in access to quantum technologies.

The road ahead for quantum applications will likely see collaborative efforts among governments, academia, industry, and civil society. The melding of scientific inquiry with social awareness fosters a holistic understanding of how quantum advancements can contribute positively to societal welfare while addressing concerns related to security and privacy.

In summary, the real-world applications of quantum mechanics are vast, with technologies poised to redefine secure communication, computing, and measurement systems. While the potential benefits are transformative, significant challenges must be addressed to ensure these advancements are both practical and equitable. As we move forward, our collective responsibility includes navigating the ethical implications while fostering the continued exploration of the quantum realm's realities, ensuring that the potentials and promises unfold in ways that enhance the fabric of society itself. As quantum mechanics continues to penetrate the seams of modern life, the intersection of security and advancement will remain at the forefront of this captivating journey into the hidden depths of reality.

9.4. Threats and Advances in Cryptography

The rapid advances in cryptography, propelled by developments in quantum mechanics, have the potential to reshape the landscape of secure communications profoundly. The application of quantum principles to cryptographic systems introduces techniques that promise higher security than ever before, particularly in the face of emerging threats posed by quantum computing. However, as we harness these groundbreaking technologies, it is equally crucial to be cognizant of the challenges and vulnerabilities that accompany them.

At the forefront of advancements in cryptography is Quantum Key Distribution (QKD), a method that employs the principles of quantum mechanics to establish secure communication channels. The security of QKD systems derives from the very nature of quantum states, where any attempt to observe or measure a quantum key would disturb the key and alert the legitimate users to an intrusion. This built-in security feature sets QKD apart from traditional cryptographic methods, which depend on the complexity of mathematical problems and could be compromised by powerful quantum algorithms.

Current QKD protocols, such as the BB84 protocol, utilize the properties of polarized photons to create and share secure keys between parties. Through the exchange of photons that represent binary values and the reformation of keys based on matching measurement bases, users can generate random keys securely. Notably, protocols employing entanglement, like the Ekert protocol, leverage the correlations established between entangled particles to ensure the confidentiality of the key distribution process.

However, despite the promise of quantum cryptography, several challenges restrict its implementation and scalability. One of the most pressing issues is the efficiency of existing quantum communication channels. Quantum states are vulnerable to loss and noise, limiting the distance over which QKD can operate effectively. Researchers are actively developing quantum repeaters, which are devices designed to extend the range of quantum communication by effectively generating pairs of entangled photons across long distances, thereby creating a quantum internet ultimately capable of facilitating global secure communications.

Additionally, as quantum computing advances, the potential threats it poses to classical encryption systems necessitate that we rethink existing security frameworks. Quantum computers are expected to efficiently execute algorithms like Shor's algorithm, which can factor large integers in polynomial time. This threat underscores the urgency for quantum-resistant alternatives or algorithms that could withstand quantum attacks while ensuring the security of data.

In response to these advances in quantum computing, the field of post-quantum cryptography has emerged, focusing on the development of cryptographic systems secure against both classical and quantum attacks. It encompasses a range of approaches rooted in classical hard problems that are not readily solvable by quantum computers. Such systems aim to safeguard sensitive information even as we transition toward a future with robust quantum computing capabilities.

Moreover, as quantum technologies threaten to disrupt standard security practices, attention must also be directed toward standards, regulations, and industry norms that govern their deployment. Policymakers and regulatory bodies will need to work alongside technologists to develop frameworks that address vulnerabilities, ensure interoperability, and promote ethical practices in the development and use of quantum cryptographic systems.

Lastly, research into the societal implications of quantum cryptography and its integration into everyday communications requires a thoughtful approach. As we adopt new technologies, potential issues surrounding privacy, access, and equity come into play. It is essential to engage in discussions that consider how quantum cryptography can enhance security without compromising personal freedoms and societal values.

In summary, the threats and advances in cryptography, particularly in the context of quantum mechanics, mark a pivotal moment in the pursuit of secure communication. As quantum technologies continue to evolve, they present unprecedented opportunities alongside evolving challenges that must be carefully managed. By addressing these complexities, engaging in robust research, and fostering interdisciplinary collaboration, we can navigate the intricacies of quantum cryptography and work toward a future where secure communication remains a cornerstone of our technological interactions—a future where the principles of quantum mechanics help safeguard the very fabric of our interconnected society.

9.5. The Road Ahead for Quantum Security

The landscape of quantum security is at a pivotal juncture, marked by rapid advancements in quantum computing, communication, and cryptographic protocols. As researchers and technologists push the boundaries of what is possible with quantum mechanics, the implications for information security and data integrity become increasingly profound. The future of quantum security not only embodies the potential for revolutionary advancements but also the grappling with distinct challenges that accompany the integration of quantum principles into our communication and computational infrastructures.

As quantum computers become more sophisticated, the ability to break traditional encryption methods poses significant threats to data security across multiple sectors. Classical encryption, which underpins most secure communications today, inherently relies on the difficulty of certain mathematical problems—such as factoring large integers and computing discrete logarithms. However, quantum algorithms like Shor's algorithm have the potential to solve these problems exponentially faster than classical counterparts, necessitating a re-evaluation of existing security frameworks. Organizations must begin to prepare for a future where data security could be compromised by adversarial quantum computing architectures capable of breaching modern cryptographic protections.

To counteract these threats, the field of quantum cryptography presents groundbreaking solutions. Quantum Key Distribution (QKD) represents one of the most promising applications of quantum mechanics, providing a method through which two parties can securely exchange encryption keys without the risk of eavesdropping. By using the principles of quantum superposition and entanglement, QKD ensures that any attempt to intercept the key will distort the quantum state, alerting the communicating parties to potential breaches. Ongoing research seeks to develop QKD systems that can be deployed over greater distances and scaled for widespread use, expanding the reach of quantum-secured communications.

Building a robust quantum security infrastructure will also involve fostering collaborations between researchers, industry leaders, and policymakers. Addressing the multifaceted challenges posed by quantum threats requires a cohesive strategy that encompasses not only advancements in technology but also regulations, standards, and ethical considerations. Policymakers and regulatory bodies must work in tandem with technologists to establish frameworks that govern the deployment of quantum security solutions, ensuring their efficacy while safeguarding individual privacy and civil liberties.

Additionally, the future landscape of quantum security will benefit from the integration of quantum-resistant algorithms within the purview of post-quantum cryptography. Developing cryptographic schemes based on problems resistant to quantum attacks is essential to preserving information security in the quantum era. As research continues to identify and evaluate post-quantum algorithms, the transition to quantum-resistant cryptographic methods must be executed seamlessly alongside advancements in QKD and other quantum technologies.

In academia, as well, education must evolve to prepare the next generation of scientists and technologists for the quantum age. Embedding quantum information science into curricula ensures an informed workforce capable of addressing the complexities of quantum technologies. Fundamental research combined with educational programs will accelerate advancements in quantum security technologies while cultivating public awareness and understanding of the challenges and opportunities presented by these innovations.

As we contemplate the road ahead for quantum security, the potential applications and advances span various sectors, including healthcare, finance, telecommunications, and national security. The truths inherent in quantum mechanics compel us to address the vulnerabilities while simultaneously capitalizing on the benefits that quantum technologies offer. This equilibrium will be vital in maximizing the potential of quantum security initiatives, ensuring that society harnesses the power of the quantum realm as a shield for confidentiality, integrity, and trust in an increasingly digitalized world.

In conclusion, the road ahead for quantum security represents both a remarkable frontier and a complex landscape filled with challenges and opportunities. The interplay of quantum technology, cryptography, and public policy will be instrumental in shaping the future of secure communication, safeguarding information systems against emerging threats, and forging a path toward a new era defined by the principles of quantum mechanics. As we navigate this exhilarating journey, the collective effort to integrate quantum advances into our infrastructures will define the security of the digital age, paving the way for a resilient and safe connected world.

10. Interpretations of Quantum Mechanics

10.1. Copenhagen Interpretation and Its Influence

In the arena of quantum mechanics, the Copenhagen interpretation stands as one of the most influential frameworks, shaping our understanding of quantum phenomena and our relationship with the nature of reality itself. Developed by Niels Bohr and Werner Heisenberg in the early 20th century, the Copenhagen interpretation seeks to reconcile the peculiar aspects of quantum mechanics with our observations of the physical world. At its core, this interpretation emphasizes the role of measurement and the inherent limitations of our knowledge regarding the states of quantum systems.

The Copenhagen interpretation proposes that quantum systems do not possess definite properties until they are measured. Prior to measurement, particles exist in a superposition of probabilities, represented mathematically by their wave functions. This means that a quantum system can be in multiple states at once, and the act of measurement collapses this superposition into one specific outcome. This idea challenges classical intuitions that suggest a reality exists independent of observation, positing instead that measurement plays a critical role in determining the state of a system.

Furthermore, the concept of complementarity is integral to the Copenhagen interpretation. This principle asserts that different experimental setups reveal different aspects of a quantum system, such as wave-like or particle-like behavior. For example, in the double-slit experiment, electrons exhibit wave-like interference patterns when not observed, but behave as particles when measurements to determine their paths are made. Complementarity thus encapsulates the idea that quantum entities can display contradictory properties depending on the context of observation, supporting the notion that reality is contingent upon the measurement process.

The Copenhagen interpretation has shaped various fields beyond physics, notably influencing philosophy, technology, and the understanding of consciousness. Its implications raise profound questions about the nature of reality, prompting discussions surrounding determinism, realism, and the observer's role in shaping outcomes. Philosophers have engaged with these ideas, debating whether quantum mechanics implies a fundamentally subjective reality or if there exists an objective state independent of observation.

In the realm of technology, the Copenhagen interpretation guides the development of quantum devices and experiments, informing approaches in quantum computing, cryptography, and quantum optics. The very techniques employed in quantum technologies hinge on the principles outlined by the Copenhagen interpretation, confirming its relevance in both theoretical and practical domains.

Despite its enduring influence, the Copenhagen interpretation has faced various critiques and alternative theories. Some researchers advocate for the Many-Worlds Interpretation, which suggests that all possible outcomes of quantum measurements coexist in parallel universes, eliminating the need for wave function collapse. Others champion de Broglie-Bohm theory, which introduces hidden variables to provide a deterministic account of quantum phenomena. This ongoing debate illustrates the richness of interpretations within quantum mechanics, underscoring the complexity and sometimes counterintuitive nature of quantum reality.

In summary, the Copenhagen interpretation has profoundly influenced our understanding of quantum mechanics and its implications for reality. By asserting that quantum systems do not possess objective properties until measured, it challenges classical notions of existence and invites inquiry into the very fabric of reality itself. As our technological capabilities advance and alternate interpretations emerge, the legacy of the Copenhagen interpretation remains vital in navigating the hidden quantum world. It continues to provoke thought and discussion, guiding our exploration into the mysteries that lie beneath the surface of observed existence and shaping the future trajectory of quantum science and philosophy.

10.2. Many-Worlds Theory: An Exploration

As we journey into the fascinating realm of Many-Worlds Theory, we uncover a profound interpretation of quantum mechanics that holds significant implications for our understanding of reality. Proposed by physicist Hugh Everett III in 1957, Many-Worlds Theory offers a radical perspective on the nature of measurement, observation, and the evolution of quantum systems. Unlike traditional interpretations, which posit the collapse of the wave function upon measurement, the Many-Worlds interpretation rejects this notion altogether, suggesting instead that all possible outcomes of a quantum event occur in a vast multiverse of simultaneously existing realities.

At the core of Many-Worlds Theory is the assertion that the universe continuously bifurcates into multiple branches with each quantum event. When a measurement is made, rather than a single outcome manifesting while others vanish, all potential outcomes coexist in a branching structure, leading to a multitude of parallel universes. According to this interpretation, if an observer measures a quantum system, such as a particle existing in a superposition of states, the universe forks into separate branches: one where the observer measures one outcome and another where they measure an alternate result. This branching character encapsulates the idea that every possible history or reality manifests and diverges from every quantum interaction.

The implications of Many-Worlds Theory extend beyond mere theoretical musings, inviting critical reflections on the nature of reality itself. If we accept the idea that all possible outcomes occur in their respective branches, it raises profound questions about the nature of consciousness, perception, and experience. Are the various outcomes of our decisions equally real? What does it mean for our sense of identity if every choice leads us onto a different trajectory? These inquiries tread into the philosophical territory, challenging our understanding of free will, deterministic versus nondeterministic perspectives, and the framework within which we interpret our existence.

Another layer of complexity within Many-Worlds Theory is its implications for the concept of probability. In traditional quantum mechanics, probabilities arise from the inherent uncertainty associated with wave functions. However, in a multiverse governed by Many-Worlds, probabilities could be construed differently; if every outcome is realized, how do we interpret the likelihood of specific events? This question has spurred discussions among physicists and philosophers alike, prompting them to reevaluate the fundamental principles of probability theory in the context of a branching reality.

Despite the rich theoretical foundation and intriguing philosophical implications, Many-Worlds Theory also encounters criticisms and challenges. Critics argue that the theory leads to an extravagant ontological commitment—claiming the existence of countless unobservable universes raises questions about scientific parsimony and testability. Skeptics point out that without empirical evidence for the multiverse, Many-Worlds remains a speculative interpretation that lacks the predictive power we associate with scientific theories.

Moreover, the radical departure from classical intuitions presents challenges in integration with existing frameworks. Many physicists favor interpretations like the Copenhagen interpretation or pilot-wave theory, believing they offer a more intuitive grasp of quantum mechanics without necessitating the vast complexities of multiple universes. The debate over the most accurate interpretation of quantum mechanics remains a lively and unresolved topic in contemporary physics, with Many-Worlds standing as a formidable—and often controversial—contender.

In recent years, advancements in quantum technology have reignited interest in Many-Worlds Theory, particularly in relation to quantum computing. As researchers explore potential computing architectures that leverage the properties of superposition and entanglement, questions about the implications of parallel processing and computation across multiple branches of reality have emerged. Could the Many-Worlds interpretation provide insights into new quantum algorithms or the mechanics of quantum error correction? Such explorations demonstrate the continuing relevance of Many-Worlds in contemporary research, bridging foundational theory with cutting-edge developments.

In summary, Many-Worlds Theory offers a thought-provoking interpretation of quantum mechanics that challenges conventional notions of reality, measurement, and the nature of existence. By proposing a multiverse where all outcomes coexist, it invites us to reconsider our understanding of identity, choice, and probability. Despite criticisms and unresolved questions, Many-Worlds remains a compelling framework for exploring the complexities inherent in quantum mechanics and continues to inform contemporary inquiries in both theoretical and experimental contexts. As we delve deeper into the mysteries of the quantum realm, the implications of Many-Worlds Theory beckon us to contemplate the hidden worlds that lie beneath the surface of our observed reality, enriching our quest for knowledge and understanding in the unfolding narrative of the cosmos.

10.3. Pilot-Wave Theory: Ideas and Criticisms

Pilot-wave theory, also known as de Broglie-Bohm theory, provides a compelling alternative interpretation of quantum mechanics, aiming to restore determinism and realism to the quantum realm. Proposed initially by Louis de Broglie in the 1920s and later developed by David Bohm in the 1950s, this interpretation introduces the concept of "hidden variables" to account for the apparent randomness inherent in quantum measurements, as dictated by the conventional Copenhagen interpretation. In essence, pilot-wave theory posits that particles have definite trajectories guided by a wave function, which encodes information about the particle's state and evolves according to the Schrödinger equation.

At the heart of pilot-wave theory lies the idea that particles possess well-defined positions and velocities at all times, contrary to the probabilistic nature of wave functions emphasized by traditional quantum mechanics. The wave function still plays a crucial role in determining the behavior of particles; however, it is not merely a probabilistic tool. Instead, it propagates through space, guiding particles along deterministic paths, akin to a pilot guiding a plane. This concept encourages the view that reality encompasses both wave and particle aspects, allowing for a more intuitive understanding of quantum phenomena through the lens of classical mechanics.

One of the strengths of pilot-wave theory is that it yields the same experimental predictions as standard quantum mechanics while addressing several foundational issues. For instance, the theory provides a clearer interpretation of quantum nonlocality. In pilot-wave theory, all particles are interconnected through their respective wave functions, enabling instantaneously correlated measurements that preserve the essence of Bell's theorem. This distinctive nonlocal characteristic prompts discussions about the implications for causality and the fabric of reality, offering a sense of continuity between quantum mechanics and classical intuitions.

Furthermore, pilot-wave theory successfully addresses certain paradoxes present in quantum mechanics, such as the measurement problem and the concept of superposition. By positing that particles exist in a state of definite location, albeit influenced by the broader wave function, pilot-wave theory allows for a seamless interpretation of measurement. When a measurement occurs, the wave function instantaneously reacts to the interaction, resulting in the observed outcomes without invoking the collapse of the wave function, as the Copenhagen interpretation requires. This framework preserves a sense of objectivity and realism, inviting renewed reflections on our understanding of reality.

Despite its advantages, pilot-wave theory has faced criticism. Detractors argue that it introduces unnecessary complexity to quantum mechanics by requiring additional hidden variables, undermining the simplicity that the Copenhagen interpretation offers. Furthermore, pilot-wave theory often lacks the widespread acceptance of conventional quantum mechanics, partly due to its non-local implications and the challenge of deriving empirical predictions distinct from those yielded by standard quantum theories. Critics assert that the theory's reliance on unobservable hidden variables raises concerns about falsifiability, as these hidden aspects may elude experimental verification.

Another notable criticism arises from the question of determinism and whether fundamental randomness can truly be eliminated from quantum mechanics. The initial motivation for the pilot-wave interpretation was rooted in the desire for realism; however, opponents argue that the retroactive guidance of hidden variables might still present challenges in reconciling the fundamentally probabilistic nature of quantum measurements. The tension between determinism and the inherent uncertainty of quantum mechanics remains a key point of contention among physicists and philosophers alike.

Pilot-wave theory has recently garnered renewed interest as discussions surrounding interpretations of quantum mechanics have intensified. As advances in technology continue to bridge experimental inquiry with theoretical exploration, pilot-wave interpretations must contend with contemporary advancements that put its principles to the test. Recent developments in quantum technologies and experiments may provide opportunities to explore the applicability of pilot-wave theory in new contexts, encouraging deeper investigations into the richness of quantum interpretations.

In summary, pilot-wave theory stands as a distinctive and thought-provoking interpretation of quantum mechanics that reintroduces determinism and realism. By conceptualizing particles as guided by wave functions, it reinterprets complex phenomena while addressing fundamental issues such as measurement and locality. While the theory has faced challenges, ongoing discussions surrounding its premises and implications foster a profound dialogue about the nature of reality, reinforcing the idea that interpretative frameworks in quantum mechanics invite continued exploration and contemplation. As we progress deeper into the quantum domain, pilot-wave theory helps illuminate the hidden world beneath classical barriers, enriching our understanding of the intricate tapestry that defines our universe.

10.4. Relational Quantum Mechanics: A New Perspective

Relational Quantum Mechanics (RQM) offers a fresh perspective on the enigmatic nature of quantum systems, challenging traditional interpretations of quantum mechanics through its emphasis on the relational aspect of quantum states. Developed primarily by physicist Carlo Rovelli in the 1990s, RQM posits that the properties of quantum systems do not exist in isolation but are meaningful only in relation to other systems. This interpretation shifts the focus from an objective reality independent of observation to one where the relationships themselves define the context of what we perceive.

At its foundation, RQM asserts that information in quantum mechanics is relative to the observer. Different observers can make measurements on a quantum system, and each will experience outcomes that depend on the interaction between the observer and the system being observed. For example, consider two observers measuring the position of a particle. Each observer may arrive at different conclusions based on their respective measurement apparatus and the interactions they impose. However, the scenario does not imply a lack of objectivity; rather, it highlights that objectivity is contingent upon the relationships established during measurement processes.

One influential aspect of RQM is its treatment of the wave function. Instead of viewing the wave function as an objective entity prescribing a system's state, RQM interprets it as a tool for calculating the probabilities of different outcomes, dependent on the observer's interaction and history. This conceptualization aligns with the relational nature we see in everyday interactions, where entities acquire their properties through relationships with one another. RQM thus reframes quantum mechanics through an epistemological lens, suggesting our knowledge and understanding of the quantum world is inherently relational, rather than absolute.

The implications of RQM ripple through various debates within quantum mechanics. It offers a response to the measurement problem, traditionally a vexing conundrum in quantum physics. In RQM, wave function collapse ceases to exist as a standalone problem—measurements and collapses occur within a relational framework. When observers measure a quantum system, each interacts with it according to their context. Consequently, the aggregate of these relational states helps construct a coherent narrative that describes the observed phenomena without recourse to an absolute reality driving the outcomes.

RQM also fosters rich philosophical inquiries about the nature of reality and existence itself. While illuminating the relational characteristics of quantum systems, RQM prompts discussions about objectivity, knowledge, and the implications of a fundamentally interconnected universe. The philosophical ramifications extend far beyond quantum physics, engaging questions about how we understand reality, our place within it, and the relationship between observers and the observed.

Despite its compelling propositions, RQM faces criticism and challenges. One notable contention arises from the interpretative nature of its framework—how do we reconcile the apparent reality dictated by external observers versus the relational stances defined in RQM? Critics assert that RQM may lead to relativism, where objective truths become elusive, potentially undermining the search for a coherent understanding of the universe. Others highlight challenges in experimentally testing or verifying predictions made solely within a relational context, as existing measurement apparatus are often rooted in classical intuitions.

Yet, RQM has spurred significant research, including practical implications in quantum technologies such as quantum computing and cryptography. By embracing relations and interactions, researchers find novel pathways for developing quantum systems that can more effectively harness quantum attributes. As quantum technologies evolve, the relational understanding of quantum states offers insights into designing systems that can dynamically interact while maintaining coherence across bound states.

In summary, Relational Quantum Mechanics provides a promising and innovative perspective on the nature of quantum systems while emphasizing the interdependence of relationships and knowledge. By reframing reality as inherently relational, RQM guides us toward a deeper understanding of quantum phenomena, intertwining physical inquiry with philosophical aspects of existence. As this interpretation continues to evolve, it holds the potential to reshape the discourse surrounding quantum mechanics and inform advancements in quantum technologies, revealing the complex fabric underlying our reality and its interplay with our perceptions. Embracing RQM invites us to explore the intricacies of the hidden quantum world, allowing us to perceive reality as an interconnected web rather than a collection of isolated entities.

10.5. Comparing Interpretations: A Synthesis

In the endeavor to unravel the complexities of quantum mechanics, interpretations play a pivotal role, offering frameworks through which physicists can conceptualize the perplexing behaviors observed at the quantum level. Among these interpretations, the Copenhagen Interpretation and Many-Worlds Theory stand out, each presenting its distinctive understanding of reality and measurement in quantum systems.

The Copenhagen Interpretation, championed by physicists like Niels Bohr and Werner Heisenberg, posits that a quantum system does not have definite properties until it is observed. The act of measurement causes the "collapse" of a wave function, resulting in a specific outcome from a set of possibilities, effectively implying that observation plays a crucial role in determining the state of a quantum system. This interpretation emphasizes the role of the observer, leading to philosophical inquiries about the nature of reality and the limits of human knowledge. Critics of the Copenhagen view argue that it invokes an unsettling dualism, where reality exists only when observed, raising questions about the objective existence of particles outside human engagement.

Conversely, the Many-Worlds Theory, proposed by Hugh Everett III, argues against the collapse of the wave function. Instead, it suggests that all possible outcomes of a quantum event occur, and each measurement leads to a branching of realities, resulting in an infinite multiverse of concurrent outcomes. This interpretation raises intriguing possibilities regarding the nature of existence, probability, and free will, challenging traditional assumptions about determinism. It has garnered both acclaim and criticism, sparking debates on the implications of a reality that continually bifurcates into countless parallel worlds.

In synthesizing these interpretations, we recognize the common threads woven through the fabric of quantum mechanics: the intricate relationship between the observer and the observed, the role of measurement in defining reality, and the philosophical ramifications of embracing probabilistic frameworks. The dialogue between proponents of the Copenhagen Interpretation and advocates of Many-Worlds Theory signifies the richness of quantum discourse, wherein each perspective enriches the ongoing inquiry into the nature of existence.

Furthermore, we find that modern developments in quantum mechanics seek to bridge these interpretations with empirical research, exploring emerging questions about consciousness, free will, and the boundaries of human understanding. As researchers delve deeper into quantum information science, they increasingly engage with aspects of these interpretations, utilizing quantum phenomena to develop technologies that transform communication, computation, and understanding.

The challenge to reconcile the contrasting views presented by various interpretations of quantum mechanics highlights an ongoing evolution of thought within the scientific community. As advancements unfold, the interplay between interpretations fosters a vibrant exchange of ideas, propelling inquiries into the very essence of reality while challenging our understanding of knowledge, perception, and existence.

In summation, the exploration of interpretations like the Copenhagen Interpretation and Many-Worlds Theory offers a lens through which to ponder the mysteries of the quantum realm. Their synthesis reveals a dynamic discourse that facilitates a deeper appreciation of reality's complexity, instigating a collective pursuit to understand the hidden processes that govern our universe. This ongoing intellectual journey beckons us to embrace both the peculiarities and wonders embedded in quantum mechanics, continuously enriching the narrative of existence as we strive to grasp the fabric of our quantum reality. As we bridge philosophical inquiries with empirical research, we pave the way for a more nuanced understanding of what it means to observe, measure, and exist in a quantum-dominated world.

11. Quantum Mechanics and Philosophy

11.1. Reality and Perception in the Quantum Realm

In the quantum realm, perceptions of reality become an intricate interplay of observation, measurement, and the very fabric of existence itself. The peculiarities of quantum mechanics challenge our traditional understandings, prompting us to rethink what we perceive as reality. Unlike the neatly deterministic universe of classical physics, the quantum world is often marked by probabilistic outcomes, reinforcing the notion that our observations actively shape our understanding of reality.

As we delve into the implications of quantum mechanics, it becomes clear that the act of observing a quantum system has a significant effect on its state. Prior to measurement, particles exist in superposition, embodying multiple potential states simultaneously. When a measurement occurs, this superposition collapses, manifesting a singular outcome. This phenomenon raises profound questions about the nature of reality: does the universe exist in a definite state independent of our observation, or is our perception intimately tied to the measurement itself? The quantum world suggests that the observer plays an intrinsic role in defining what is real, as measurement results can vary based on the context and nature of interaction between the observer and the system.

This observer effect extends to discussions regarding consciousness and the mind, inviting philosophical inquiries into the relationship between quantum mechanics and human perception. If reality is shaped by observation, how do our cognitive processes engage with the underlying quantum world? Philosophers of mind have postulated various theories suggesting that consciousness itself could influence quantum events, a notion that has sparked considerable debate. While speculative, exploring these intersections may reveal a greater understanding of consciousness in the context of quantum mechanics, where the boundaries of physics and philosophy begin to blur.

Moreover, concepts of free will and determinism are called into question within the framework of quantum mechanics. The indeterminate nature of quantum events introduces an element of randomness that challenges classical notions of a perfectly deterministic universe, where every action and reaction could be precisely predicted given the initial conditions. The implications are substantial; if the universe operates on probabilistic foundations, could the existence of free will be reconciled with quantum mechanics? What does it mean for our decision-making processes if quantum randomness plays a role in the unfolding of events? These considerations invite rich discussions in philosophical circles, probing the essence of autonomy and human experience amid the complexities of the quantum realm.

The exploration of reality and perception in the quantum realm necessitates a multidisciplinary approach, intertwining physics, philosophy, and cognitive science. While empirical research in quantum mechanics provides insights into the nature of particles and interactions, the philosophical implications extend beyond the confines of laboratory experiments. These discussions challenge us to reconsider foundational assumptions about existence, the role of the observer, and the implications of quantum discoveries on our understanding of reality.

As we navigate these uncharted waters, engaging with the philosophical implications of quantum mechanics will be crucial in shaping the trajectory of future research. Quantum science's ongoing evolution invites us to remain open to new ideas and interpretations, fostering discussions that empower deeper inquiries into the hidden aspects of reality. By embracing the complexities inherent in the quantum realm, we are propelled toward a richer understanding of existence—one where the boundaries of perception and reality dissolve, inviting a captivating exploration beneath the surface of the visible universe.

As we delve further into the tapestry of quantum mechanics, we recognize that awareness of our perceptions, decision-making processes, and the universe's underlying structure fosters a deeper connection to the profound mysteries surrounding our existence. This journey showcases the dynamic interplay between science and philosophy, guiding us into an expanding horizon where the nuances of both realms converge, revealing the astonishing truths that lie beneath our observed reality.

11.2. The Observer's Role: Philosophy Meets Science

In the context of Quantum Mechanics and its broader implications, the observer's role has emerged as a pivotal consideration that intertwines philosophy with scientific inquiry. The nuances of observation in quantum physics challenge conventional perceptions of reality, further complicating our understanding of existence itself. This chapter aims to explore how the observer's influence shapes quantum events, and the implications this relationship has on our philosophical interpretations of reality.

Traditionally, in classical physics, the observer is seen as a passive entity—one that merely measures and records phenomena without affecting the outcomes of those measurements. This deterministic framework aligns with the view that the universe operates in a predictable manner, governed by fixed laws. However, as we venture into the quantum realm, we encounter a radically different narrative. Here, the act of observation is not just a passive endeavor; it is an active process that fundamentally alters the state of what is being observed.

The intricacies of the observer's role become especially evident when examining the concept of wave function collapse. In quantum mechanics, particles exist in a superposition of states—a manifestation of their intrinsic probabilistic nature—until a measurement is performed. Upon observation, the wave function collapses, resulting in a specific state being realized. This phenomenon implies that the very act of measurement impacts the outcome, raising significant questions about objectivity. Is the observer simply a witness to reality, or is their perception ingrained within the very fabric of occurrence?

This inherent interconnectedness between the observer and the observed dovetails with philosophical inquiries surrounding the nature of reality. Several interpretations of quantum mechanics engage with the implications of this relationship. The Copenhagen Interpretation emphasizes the significance of measurement in determining the properties of quantum systems, suggesting that reality cannot be decoupled from the act of observation. In contrast, Many-Worlds Theory posits that every potential outcome of a quantum event coexists in parallel universes, fundamentally altering how we conceive reality as a branching continuum of possibilities. Each interpretation invites deep reflections on the essence of existence, knowledge, and the interplay between consciousness and the universe.

The implications of the observer's role extend not only into philosophically rich inquiries but also into technological applications. Quantum technologies such as Quantum Key Distribution (QKD) function intrinsically through the principles of measurement and observation, potentially revolutionizing secure communication methods. As we increasingly integrate quantum principles into practical applications, understanding the observer's influence will be essential in cultivating systems that leverage these fundamental properties to their fullest extent.

Philosophically, the implications surrounding the observer's role forge pathways toward discussions about consciousness itself. What does it mean for consciousness to exist in a universe governed by quantum indeterminacy? Do our thoughts and observations have tangible, quantum-based consequences that shape reality? These questions propel us into the realm of epistemology—the study of knowledge—prompting us to ponder the relationship between perception and existence in a quantum-dominated world.

Moreover, ethical considerations surrounding the observer's role and the nature of reality beckon attention as technology continues to evolve. From the implications of developing quantum systems to the responsibility of harnessing quantum insights for societal benefit, we must engage in thoughtful discourse about how these advances theoretically and practically affect our understanding of life, consciousness, and interconnections.

In summary, the observer's role in quantum mechanics blurs the boundaries between science and philosophy, challenging conventional perceptions of reality. As we delve deeper into the quantum realm, recognizing the active participation of the observer prompts a reevaluation of our understanding of existence, knowledge, and the interrelationships that underpin our universe. This exploration invites further inquiry into the nature of reality as we seek to understand the profound implications of quantum mechanics for both our scientific and philosophical odysseys. As we continue to unravel the intricate tapestry of quantum phenomena, we find ourselves at the intersection of science and philosophy—an exciting frontier that promises to deepen our comprehension of the hidden quantum world beneath the surface of our observed reality.

11.3. Free Will Versus Determinism: Quantum Insights

Free will versus determinism is a philosophical debate that assumes a new dimension within the context of quantum mechanics, particularly as it relates to the intricacies of human decision-making and the nature of reality itself. The discourse navigates through the foundational principles of quantum mechanics and their implications for agency, choice, and the deterministic laws that govern the universe as we perceive it.

In classical deterministic frameworks, every event or state can theoretically be predicted with precise knowledge of initial conditions and governing laws. This perspective suggests that human actions are predetermined, rooted in the strict causality upheld by classical physics. If every event follows a chain of causation, the argument for free will becomes tenuous, leading to philosophical tensions concerning agency. However, quantum mechanics revolutionizes this understanding by introducing an inherent level of unpredictability and randomness through phenomena like wave function collapse and superposition.

At the heart of this debate is the behavior of quantum particles, which appear not to follow deterministic rules but rather operate under probabilistic frameworks. When a quantum system is observed —a process that causes the wave function to collapse—the potential outcomes manifest in a singular state defined only at the moment of measurement. This realization prompts questions about whether the act of observation implies a degree of agency that transcends predetermined pathways. In essence, the observer plays a critical role, blurring the line between determinism and the potential for agency.

The implications of quantum mechanics on our understanding of free will extend into discussions about consciousness—how aware individuals are of their choices and the impact of their decisions. The role of consciousness in measurements raises profound inquiries about whether human cognition itself could influence quantum events or if individuals are merely passive observers in a predetermined universe. This intersection of consciousness and quantum physics invites further examination, as various theories, including quantum consciousness, propose that the human mind may harness quantum processes in decision-making.

Importantly, the challenge to deterministic views in light of quantum mechanics does not result in a universal advocacy for free will. Instead, it forces a reconsideration of what free will means within the context of a probabilistic universe. The unpredictability inherent in quantum mechanics introduces a nuanced understanding of choice —one that reconciles degrees of freedom alongside probabilistic outcomes. Rather than seeing free will as an absolute construct, it may be viewed through the lens of possibilities intertwined with the unpredictable nature of quantum events.

As we contemplate the ongoing dialogue surrounding free will and determinism informed by quantum insights, it becomes evident that interdisciplinary collaboration is vital. Philosophers, physicists, cognitive scientists, and ethicists can come together to explore these themes, aiding in the creation of holistic frameworks that embrace both quantum theories and the deeper questions of what it means to choose, act, and exist.

In summary, the intersection of quantum mechanics with the discourse on free will and determinism offers a rich tapestry of inquiry and discussion. Quantum mechanics reshapes our understanding of agency and choice, presenting a reality defined not solely by deterministic chains but enriched by probabilities and interconnectedness. By delving into these profound dynamics, we open ourselves to new interpretations of existence and the ongoing exploration of human agency within the ever-complex quantum landscape. Embracing this complexity invites deeper reflections into the nature of reality, knowledge, and the essence of being in a world governed by quantum principles and phenomena.

11.4. Mind, Consciousness, and Quantum Theory

In the context of 'Mind, Consciousness, and Quantum Theory,' we delve into the profound relationship between the principles of quantum mechanics and emerging understandings of consciousness, exploring how these realms intersect and what implications this has for our perception of reality.

The intrigue begins with the fundamental concepts of quantum mechanics, where the boundaries of observer and observed become blurred. Quantum theory posits that particles can exist in multiple states simultaneously due to superposition until they are measured. This act of measurement is what causes the wave function to collapse, thereby forcing a quantum state into a definite condition. Intriguingly, this observational dependence raises questions about the role of consciousness in defining reality. If quantum mechanics suggests that the act of observing impacts the state of a system, does that mean consciousness somehow plays a crucial role in shaping the universe we experience?

Philosophers and physicists alike have engaged in extensive dialogue about the implications of this relationship. Some theorists have proposed that conscious observers are necessary to create or "actualize" reality, suggesting that consciousness itself engages with quantum systems in ways we do not yet fully understand. This proposition invites us to reconsider the nature of our own minds and how we fit within the ambit of the universe.

Moreover, the concept of entanglement further complicates our understanding of consciousness within the quantum realm. Entangled particles share a connection that transcends classical notions of distance and separation; measuring one particle instantly influences the other, regardless of space. This peculiar feature awakens questions about collective consciousness or a universal mind that transcends individual observation—areas ripe for philosophical inquiry.

Additionally, we must consider the implications of quantum mechanics for free will and determinism. In a quantum framework where outcomes can be probabilistic, the certainty of predetermined paths gives way to a more nuanced understanding of decision-making and agency. If outcomes are influenced by inherent uncertainties in quantum systems, does this introduce a space for free will to exist? The interplay between uncertainty in quantum events and the conscious decisions we make fosters rich discussions about the nature of human agency, challenging deterministic views that have traditionally dominated our understanding of the universe.

Moreover, research into cognitive processes and their relationship to quantum mechanics raises stimulating questions about potential quantum aspects of the brain. Some theorists posit that consciousness could arise from quantum effects occurring in neural processes, leading to frameworks that merge cognitive science with quantum theory. This notion, while still speculative, leads to intriguing possibilities for understanding human consciousness as a phenomenon with quantum underpinnings.

Yet, despite the allure of such connections, the adoption of quantum mechanics in understanding consciousness faces skepticism from the scientific community, emphasizing the need for empirical investigation. Many researchers maintain that while quantum effects may play a role in facilitated cognitive processes, the brain operates more effectively under classical principles at larger scales, reflecting the current understanding of biological systems. Rigorous experimentation must guide this exploration, grounding claims in verifiable hypotheses.

In summary, the interplay between mind, consciousness, and quantum theory opens avenues for profound inquiries about reality, perception, and human experience. The observer's role in collapsing quantum states prompts questions regarding consciousness and agency in shaping the universe. The relationship between entangled particles and collective consciousness invites deeper philosophical reflection. While the path forward remains studded with uncertainties and challenges, continued exploration into the intersections of quantum mechanics and consciousness has the potential to reveal insights that transform our understanding of existence itself. As we probe these intricate connections, we are beckoned to explore the mysteries of the quantum mind—the unknown realms that lie beneath the surface of our conscious experience.

The journey ahead is one of speculation and inquiry, marrying the disciplines of physics and philosophy in a quest to unravel the fabric of reality, consciousness, and the profound intricacies of the universe we inhabit. The unfolding narrative challenges us to rethink our understanding of mind and matter, inviting a broader examination that encompasses the astonishing subtleties of existence as illuminated by the lens of quantum mechanics.

11.5. Ethical Considerations of Quantum Discoveries

As advancements in quantum mechanics continue to unfold, there emerges a pressing need to consider the ethical ramifications that accompany groundbreaking discoveries in this intricate field. The implications of quantum discoveries transcend mere scientific inquiry, entering realms of societal concern, data security, environmental impact, and the philosophical considerations surrounding consciousness and existence.

Quantum mechanics fundamentally alters our understanding of reality. With concepts such as superposition, entanglement, and the observer effect, we face questions about the nature of existence itself. These principles challenge classical determinism, suggesting that reality is not a fixed entity but an intricate tapestry woven from probabilities and observations. Such a perspective can lead to philosophical dilemmas concerning free will, personal agency, and the implications of human interaction with the quantum realm. As we grapple with these ideas, it is vital to assess the ethical responsibilities that come with harnessing such powerful knowledge.

The application of quantum technologies, particularly in fields such as quantum computing and quantum cryptography, introduces distinct ethical considerations surrounding privacy, security, and the potential for misuse. Quantum computing's rise poses a threat to classical encryption methods currently governing digital security. The rapid development of quantum algorithms capable of breaking conventional cryptographic protocols creates urgency within cybersecurity discussions, urging the need for quantum-resistant algorithms. This necessitates a robust understanding of the ethical responsibilities held by researchers and technologists in ensuring the secure deployment of quantum technologies, particularly for applications involving sensitive data and personal privacy.

Moreover, as quantum discoveries yield new technologies, there are broader societal implications to consider. These include the accessibility of quantum technologies, which may exacerbate existing socio-economic divides. As advancements in quantum computing and communication systems materialize, ensuring equitable access to these technologies is critical to preventing inequality in who benefits from quantum advancements. The potential for creating disparities between those who can access quantum technologies and those who cannot poses questions about social justice and ethical priorities—an area where equity must remain at the forefront of discussions.

Furthermore, the environmental impact of quantum technologies is another ethical concern. While advancements in quantum computing, such as energy-efficient processing and resource-efficient designs, hold the potential to reduce energy consumption, the increased demand for computing power could also lead to negative environmental repercussions. It is crucial for researchers and industry leaders to adopt sustainable practices and consider the ecological footprint of implementing quantum technologies, balancing innovation with environmental stewardship.

The philosophical basis of quantum mechanics also introduces complexities regarding ethical considerations associated with consciousness and the nature of reality. As we explore the relationship between quantum phenomena and consciousness, questions arise about whether advancements in understanding could influence perceptions of mental health, cognitive processes, and the essence of being. Researchers must navigate the implications of asserting that consciousness interacts with quantum states, ensuring that scientific claims are grounded in empirical evidence, particularly when discussing topics as sensitive as mental health.

Moreover, the advent of quantum technologies brings to light the importance of ethical discourse in scientific research. Establishing clear ethical guidelines and frameworks for conducting research across quantum disciplines is essential to the responsible development of quantum technologies. Researchers must establish interdisciplinary dialogue that considers socially acceptable applications, transparency, informed consent, and potential societal repercussions.

In conclusion, as we journey through the expanding realms of quantum discoveries, ethical considerations must be woven into the fabric of scientific inquiry and technological advancement. The need to balance innovation with societal impact, equity, and sustainability is paramount as we navigate the complexities of the quantum world. Engaging stakeholders, researchers, and the public in robust discussions about the implications of quantum technologies will pave the way for a future that responsibly harnesses the promise of quantum mechanics while honoring society's ethical principles. The transformative potential of quantum discoveries is immense; thus, it is our collective responsibility to ensure that this potential is realized equitably, conscientiously, and sustainably, as we explore the hidden quantum world that lies beneath our observed reality.

12. Quantum Cosmology and the Universe

12.1. Origin of the Universe: A Quantum Perspective

In the vast expanse of the cosmos, the origin of the universe remains one of the most profound mysteries humanity seeks to unravel. From the perspective of quantum mechanics, this quest becomes even more intriguing, as it challenges our understanding of time, space, and the very nature of existence. The interplay between quantum phenomena and cosmological theories offers a unique lens through which to explore the beginnings of our universe, inviting us to contemplate concepts that are as bewildering as they are enlightening.

At the heart of quantum cosmology lies the idea that the early universe was governed by quantum laws. The prevailing cosmological model, the Big Bang theory, posits that the universe originated from an extremely hot and dense state approximately 13.8 billion years ago. However, the moments leading up to and immediately following this event remain elusive to direct observation. Enter quantum mechanics, which provides a framework that can illuminate these early stages and introduce phenomena that challenge classical notions of causality.

Inflation theory is one such framework that gives insight into the early universe's expansion. Proposed by Alan Guth and others, this theory suggests that a brief period of exponential expansion occurred just after the Big Bang, driven by a scalar field known as the inflaton. The fluctuations in this field during inflation, described through quantum fluctuations, could have seeded the large-scale structures observed in the current universe. These quantum fluctuations are vital as they provide the initial density perturbations that, through gravitational attraction, led to the formation of galaxies and other cosmic structures.

The role of quantum mechanics in cosmology extends beyond just explaining the early universe. As we delve deeper, we encounter the concept of quantum gravity—the search for a theory that unites quantum mechanics with general relativity. While general relativity describes gravity as the curvature of space-time, quantum mechanics introduces a probabilistic framework for understanding small-scale phenomena. Bridging these two realms presents a formidable challenge, but it holds the promise of offering profound insights into the nature of black holes, singularities, and the behavior of matter and energy in extreme conditions.

Black holes serve as a fascinating intersection between quantum mechanics and cosmology. Traditionally viewed as regions of space from which nothing can escape, their relationship with quantum phenomena prompts intriguing questions. Theoretical work, particularly by physicists like Stephen Hawking, has led to the idea that black holes could emit radiation—known as Hawking radiation—due to quantum effects near their event horizons. This concept suggests that black holes may not be entirely immortal, leading to discussions about the ultimate fate of information and matter that falls into them, raising critical questions about the foundations of quantum mechanics and the conservation of information.

Quantum cosmology, therefore, explores the universe's origins with the understanding that quantum effects played a critical role in shaping our reality. As researchers continue to investigate the interplay between quantum mechanics and cosmology, they aim to resolve fundamental questions about the universe's beginning, the forces driving its expansion, and the ultimate fate of all matter and energy. This field, positioned at the cutting edge of theoretical physics, seeks to weave a comprehensive tapestry that connects the microcosm of quantum behavior with the macrocosm of cosmic phenomena, outlining a narrative that beckons further inquiry into the hidden dynamics of our universe.

In summary, the exploration of the universe's origin from a quantum perspective invites us to reconsider foundational concepts concerning time, space, and existence. The confluence of inflation theory, quantum fluctuations, and quantum gravity presents a formidable framework through which scientists are actively investigating the cosmos's birth and evolution. As we peel back the layers of complexity surrounding these ideas, we find ourselves exploring profound mysteries that lie beneath the surface, expanding our understanding of reality and the very essence of the universe itself. The quest to uncover these truths reflects not just a pursuit of knowledge but an enduring human aspiration to make sense of our place within the grand tapestry of existence.

12.2. Inflation Theory and Quantum Fluctuations

In the cosmos, the relationship between inflation theory and quantum fluctuations offers profound insights into the origins and evolution of our universe. Inflation theory suggests that the universe underwent rapid expansion (inflation) shortly after the Big Bang, transforming from a minuscule, primordial state into the vast cosmos we observe today. This theory addresses several fundamental questions, including the uniformity of the cosmic microwave background radiation and the large-scale structure of the universe. Embedding quantum mechanics into this cosmological framework allows us to better understand how the very fluctuations that arose during this exponential expansion seeded the cosmic landscape.

At the heart of inflationary theory lies the understanding that quantum mechanics governs the behavior of subatomic particles and fields. During the inflationary period, it is suggested that a scalar field known as the "inflaton" dominated the energy density of the universe. As the inflaton field evolved, quantum fluctuations within this field manifested as variations in energy density. These tiny fluctuations, imprinted during the inflationary phase, ultimately led to the density perturbations that would give rise to galaxies and cosmic structures in the ever-expanding universe.

Quantum fluctuations can be precisely described by the principles of quantum field theory, which posits that fields encompass the fundamental forces and particles of the universe. During inflation, as regions of space expanded exponentially, the quantum fluctuations present momentarily became "frozen" as classical perturbations, leading to a universe that transitioned from a homogeneous state to one marked by slight density variations. This transition is crucial to understanding why the universe exhibits large-scale structures, as the initial quantum fluctuations manifest as gravitational potentials that draw matter together, forming galaxies and clusters.

The interplay of quantum mechanics and inflationary cosmology thus represents a fascinating synthesis of two fundamental theories. The conceptual framework parallels the elegant mathematics of quantum field theory while addressing critical observations in astrophysics. Moreover, it provides a coherent narrative for understanding the uniformity observed in the cosmic microwave background radiation— an indirect consequence of expansion wherein quantum fluctuations evolved into the density perturbations that eventually accumulated into the familiar structures of the universe.

Experimental evidence supporting inflation theory has been garnered through various means, notably cosmic microwave background measurements by missions like the Wilkinson Microwave Anisotropy Probe (WMAP) and the Planck satellite. These measurements have confirmed the imprint of quantum fluctuations, as the resulting anisotropies directly correlate with theoretical predictions arising from inflationary models. The study of gravitational waves produced by inflationary processes also provides exciting avenues for validating the concept of quantum fluctuations during the infancy of the universe.

Yet, as we engage with the implications of inflation theory and quantum fluctuations, questions about the multiverse arise. Some interpretations suggest that inflation could lead to an infinite array of bubble universes, each with varying physical laws and constants —a concept that reignites discussions about the nature of reality and the potential existence of parallel worlds. These speculations provoke philosophical and scientific debates about fine-tuning, the nature of natural laws, and the limits of our understanding.

In summary, the synergy between inflation theory and quantum fluctuations represents a pivotal relationship that elucidates the origins and evolution of our universe. The embedding of quantum mechanics within the context of cosmology invites us to explore how the tiniest fluctuations can give rise to the grand tapestry of cosmic structure we observe today—which can profoundly alter our understanding of existence itself. By advancing our inquiries through empirical research and theoretical exploration, the journey through inflation and quantum fluctuations promises to deepen our insights into the mysteries of the universe, ultimately shaping the future trajectory of cosmological research in the unfolding narrative of quantum and astrophysical science. This dialogue between cosmology and quantum understanding invites us to reflect on the hidden quantum world lying beneath the surface of our observed reality, beckoning us to traverse the frontiers of knowledge that connect the beginning of the cosmos to the very fabric of existence.

12.3. The Role of Quantum Mechanics in Cosmology

The exploration of the role of quantum mechanics in cosmology provides insights into the foundational aspects of the universe, where the quantum realm intertwines with cosmic phenomena. The implications of quantum mechanics on our understanding of the cosmos challenge classical concepts, prompting a reevaluation of the origins of the universe, the nature of cosmic structures, and the underpinnings of fundamental forces.

At the heart of quantum cosmology lies the acknowledgment that the very fabric of the universe may be influenced by quantum phenomena. The Big Bang theory, which posits that our universe began as a singularity, is complemented by quantum considerations, especially in the context of the universe's inception. Quantum fluctuations in the early universe are hypothesized to have seeded the large-scale structures we observe today. This concept aligns with inflationary theory, which suggests a rapid expansion of space occurring just after the Big Bang, driven by a scalar field—the inflaton. This inflationary phase inherently relies on quantum mechanics to explain how initial perturbations evolved into the galaxies and cosmic structures we see in the present.

The relationship between quantum mechanics and cosmology also extends to black holes—regions where traditional concepts of space and time are radically altered. Quantum mechanics plays a crucial role in understanding black hole behavior, particularly in the context of Hawking radiation. Proposed by Stephen Hawking, this phenomenon suggests that black holes can emit radiation due to quantum effects near the event horizon, leading to thought-provoking questions regarding information theory and the preservation of data in the face of extreme gravity.

Quantum mechanics further invites discussions on the boundaries of our understanding of the universe. Concepts such as the multiverse arise, where different regions of space may host their own distinct laws of physics stemming from quantum fluctuations. These ideas provoke profound philosophical inquiries about the nature of reality and the limits of human perception. In essence, if quantum mechanics suggests a universe replete with possibilities and branching realities, what does that mean for our understanding of existence and our place within the cosmos?

Another exciting area in which quantum mechanics and cosmology intersect is the search for a coherent understanding of quantum gravity. Attempting to unify general relativity, which successfully describes gravity, with the principles of quantum mechanics poses a significant challenge. Researchers exploring quantum gravity theories, including string theory and loop quantum gravity, aim to elucidate how fundamental forces operate at the intersection of quantum and cosmic scales, hoping to achieve a deeper understanding of the universe's structure and behavior.

The implications of quantum mechanics on cosmology also open avenues for technological advancements. Instruments designed to detect cosmic phenomena, such as gravitational waves and cosmic microwave background radiation, may benefit from insights rooted in quantum principles. The integration of quantum effects into observational techniques could amplify our ability to discern subtle signals from the early universe, thereby advancing our comprehension of cosmic origins and evolution.

In summary, the role of quantum mechanics in cosmology unveils a realm of profound interconnectedness between the smallest scales of reality and the vastness of the universe. The interplay of quantum fluctuations, inflationary theory, black hole dynamics, and quantum gravity presents a tapestry of ideas that continues to challenge our understanding of existence. As researchers navigate these complex relationships, they stand at the forefront of an evolving dialogue that unites physics and philosophy, inviting exploration into the hidden mysteries that lie beneath the visible façade of the cosmos. In doing so, we embark on a quest to decipher the intricacies of our universe, continually shaped by the elements and dynamics of the quantum world.

12.4. Black Holes and Quantum Phenomena

In the mysterious interplay between black holes and quantum phenomena, we confront some of the most bewildering aspects of theoretical physics. Here, the intersection of general relativity—the framework governing the macroscopic structure of space-time—and quantum mechanics, which governs the behavior of particles at the microscopic level, reveals a tapestry of contradictions and prompts compelling inquiries about the nature of the universe itself. Understanding black holes through the lens of quantum mechanics not only challenges our perceptions of reality but also propels us toward the quest for a unified theory that harmonizes the two realms.

At the forefront of this exploration lies Hawking radiation—a groundbreaking proposal by physicist Stephen Hawking in 1974 that merges quantum mechanics with black hole physics. According to this theory, the event horizon of a black hole is not an impenetrable barrier but instead a seething boundary influenced by quantum fluctuations. In essence, particle-antiparticle pairs constantly emerge from the vacuum due to quantum fluctuations. When these pairs occur near the event horizon, it is possible for one particle to be absorbed by the black hole while the other escapes, resulting in the black hole emitting radiation. This phenomenon signifies that black holes can lose mass and energy, ultimately leading to their potential evaporation over vast timescales. The implications of Hawking radiation are profound, suggesting that black holes are dynamic entities rather than simply cosmic sinkholes.

The study of black holes further unveils a philosophical discourse surrounding the nature of information and the implications of its preservation. Quantum mechanics posits that information cannot be destroyed, leading to the famous black hole information paradox: if black holes can evaporate, what happens to the information contained within them? This dilemma invites rich discussions about the fabric of reality and how we conceive information within the universe. Many physicists propose that information may be encoded on the black hole's event horizon in a manner akin to holography—an idea that continues to garner attention in theoretical research.

Entanglement also plays a pivotal role in the dynamics of black holes. The correlations established between particles can offer insights into how black holes interact with their surroundings. Some researchers posit that entangled particles might provide clues about the nonlocal nature of black holes and deeper connections between quantum systems. The entanglement phenomenon challenges classical intuitions about separateness, urging us to reconsider our understanding of interactions at cosmic scales.

As we progress further into the mysteries of black holes, quantum mechanics allows us to revisit the fundamental questions surrounding the formation and evolution of these enigmatic objects. Gravitational collapse, the process by which massive stars may yield black holes, presents a fertile ground for examining how quantum behaviors, such as superposition and entanglement, intermingle with gravitational effects. For instance, recent research posits that quantum information could play a role in shaping the fabric of space-time itself, suggesting potential avenues that unify quantum mechanics and general relativity.

Moreover, the study of black holes may hold keys to unlocking new frontiers in theoretical physics, including explorations of quantum gravity. Many physicists advocate for theories such as string theory and loop quantum gravity, which aim to reconcile classical gravitational descriptions of black holes with quantum mechanics. This ambition signifies a pursuit for deeper knowledge of the fundamental forces that govern the universe and could pave the way for significant breakthroughs in our understanding of both black holes and the underlying principles of nature.

As we continue to unlock the mysteries of black holes and their quantum underpinnings, new experiments may emerge that test the predictions of these theories. Whether through advancements in observational astronomy, exploring the extraordinary conditions around black holes, or harnessing high-energy collisions in particle accelerators, the quest to better understand black holes intertwines with the frontier of quantum mechanics—each illuminating the other.

In summary, the interplay between black holes and quantum phenomena offers a fascinating journey into the unknown, challenging our perceptions of reality and compelling us to engage with the fundamental questions that define existence. As theories evolve and our understanding deepens, we remain at the precipice of discovering the secrets that lie within black holes, the enigmatic giants of our universe, tirelessly working to reconcile the macroscopic with the microscopic, the gravitational with the quantum. The insights gleaned from this exploration promise not only to reshape our comprehension of the cosmos but also to illuminate the hidden truths that resonate throughout the fabric of reality.

12.5. Quantum Cosmology: The Cutting Edge

The intersection of quantum mechanics and cosmology represents a cutting edge of scientific inquiry that promises to deepen our understanding of the universe and uncover the fundamental principles governing existence. As researchers explore how quantum phenomena influence the cosmos, they confront questions that challenge traditional views, reshaping our notions of time, space, causality, and the very fabric of reality.

One of the central themes in this exploration is the ability of quantum mechanics to illuminate the earliest moments of the universe's history. During the Big Bang, the universe began in an extremely hot and dense state, and understanding the precise conditions at that moment is crucial for comprehending the cosmos's subsequent evolution. Quantum field theory offers a framework for theorizing about the mechanisms that could have governed the early universe, where quantum fluctuations in scalar fields led to the density perturbations that would later develop into galaxies and large-scale structures.

Inflation theory, which posits a period of rapid expansion shortly after the Big Bang, aligns beautifully with quantum mechanics, offering explanations for the observed uniformity of the cosmic microwave background radiation. By embedding quantum fluctuations within the inflationary model, researchers can connect the earliest quantum events to the structure of the universe we observe today. The intricacies of quantum field fluctuations during inflation provide insights into the distribution of matter and energy, leading to current phenomena.

In addition to the exploration of cosmic origins, quantum mechanics invites us to reconsider the behavior of black holes and their enigmatic properties. The study of black hole thermodynamics and quantum effects catalyzes discussions about information loss, entanglement, and the relationship between quantum mechanics and gravity. Stephen Hawking's groundbreaking work on black hole radiation exemplifies this intersection, leading to profound implications for our conception of these cosmic behemoths and the broader fabric of reality. The interplay between gravitational physics and quantum mechanics exemplifies the complexities of the universe, urging us toward a unified understanding of fundamental forces.

Furthermore, the role of quantum mechanics in cosmology evokes philosophical inquiries surrounding the concepts of causality and determinism. If quantum events can influence cosmic structures and processes, what implications does that have for our understanding of time? Are we to interpret the universe as a deterministic entity driven by classical laws, or is it a probabilistic tapestry woven from countless quantum interactions? These reflections bring philosophy into the forefront, prompting us to engage with critical questions regarding existence, reality, and knowledge itself.

Quantum cosmology also introduces the infinite potential of multi-verses—universes that may exist parallel to our own with different physical laws and constants. The implications of such theories foster profound philosophical interrogations about the nature of existence and the parameters defining our unique universe. As researchers continue to explore the links between inflation, quantum fluctuations, and cosmic events, discussions about parallel realities are no longer relegated to the realm of science fiction but are considered plausible avenues of inquiry.

To investigate these dimensions of quantum mechanics, scientists employ sophisticated observational techniques aimed at testing predictions and probing fundamental questions. Observations of gravitational waves and high-energy phenomena in cosmic events may provide insights into the workings of black holes and the early universe. Collaborations across disciplines—combining astrophysics, particle physics, quantum mechanics, and philosophy—play a crucial role in expanding our comprehension of the universe and its inherent mysteries.

In summary, quantum cosmology stands at the frontier of scientific exploration, merging the principles of quantum mechanics with cosmological inquiry. The interplay between quantum mechanics and cosmic phenomena garners insights into the origins, structure, and fate of the universe, challenging classical perceptions of reality and inspiring philosophical reflections on existence. As scientists continue to probe the depths of both quantum mechanics and cosmology, they embark on a journey that promises to reshape our understanding of nature, revealing the intricate relationships connecting the microcosm to the macrocosm and unraveling the hidden truths of the cosmos that lie beneath our observed reality.

13. Quantum Biology: The Secret Life of Cells

13.1. Life at the Quantum Level

As science continually advances, the exploration of life at the quantum level reveals a hidden but intricate dimension of biology that challenges our understanding of fundamental processes. At this scale, biological systems do not operate solely under the classical physics paradigm; rather, they exhibit behaviors that are fundamentally quantum mechanical in nature. Investigating these phenomena not only gives us insights into the mechanics of life but also invites consideration of the profound implications for our understanding of consciousness, evolution, and the interconnectedness of all living systems.

One of the key areas of interest in quantum biology is the role of quantum entanglement within biological processes. Entanglement, a phenomenon where particles become interconnected in such a way that the state of one instantly influences the state of another regardless of distance, suggests that quantum mechanics may facilitate communication and coordination within biological systems. In photosynthetic organisms, for instance, studies have shown that entangled excitons—elementary particles related to energy transfer—may exist in mechanisms that enhance the efficiency of energy absorption and transfer. This raises the possibility that quantum effects enable organisms to optimize their energy processes in ways that classical understanding cannot fully explain.

Furthermore, the notion of molecular machines operating through quantum mechanics further complicates our understanding of biological behavior. Molecular machines, such as those involved in ATP synthesis or cellular motility, exhibit dynamic actions that can be viewed through the lens of quantum principles. For instance, certain enzymes can employ tunneling effects that enable electrons or protons to traverse potential energy barriers, facilitating chemical reactions at unprecedented speeds. This insight not only reveals the intricacies of enzymatic function but also underscores the transformative potential of quantum coherence within cellular processes.

Quantum sensing represents yet another fascinating aspect of life at the quantum level. Organisms, particularly migratory species like birds, are believed to utilize quantum entanglement and coherence for navigation. Research suggests that birds possess specialized proteins in their retinas sensitive to Earth's magnetic field, allowing them to perceive direction by engaging quantum processes. This quantum-based navigation mechanism exemplifies nature's ability to leverage quantum phenomena for practical purposes, challenging classical interpretations of biological function and adaptation.

The innovation inspired by quantum biology paves the way for groundbreaking technologies. As researchers glean insights into the mechanisms by which biological systems harness quantum mechanics, they seek to apply these principles to develop new materials, enhanced energy capture systems, and methods of information transfer. Understanding these processes may lead to innovations in biophysics, medicine, and sustainable energy production, revolutionizing how we approach various industries.

However, the exploration of life at the quantum level is not without challenges. The inherent complexity of biological systems, combined with the delicate nature of quantum states, presents formidable hurdles. Developing reliable experimental techniques to observe and measure quantum effects within living organisms necessitates precision and coherence under conditions that are often fraught with noise and environmental interference. These challenges require advancements in technology and methodology to ensure that quantum biological phenomena can be effectively studied and utilized.

As we venture deeper into the quantum dimensions of life, awareness of ethical considerations surrounding quantum biology becomes paramount. Enhanced understanding of biological processes at the quantum level raises questions about the implications of manipulating these systems for human benefit. The integration of quantum insights into synthetic biology, genetic engineering, and environmental applications necessitates thoughtful ethical frameworks that prioritize responsible innovation and equitable access to advancements.

In summary, the exploration of life at the quantum level unearths a hidden world rich with complexity, challenging our classical understanding of biology and inviting new inquiries into the nature of existence itself. Quantum entanglement, molecular machines, and quantum sensing exemplify the profound interconnections between quantum mechanics and biological processes, offering innovative pathways for research and technology. As we continue to investigate the quantum world woven into the fabric of life, it is essential to balance scientific inquiry with ethical considerations, forging a dynamic understanding of how these hidden dimensions influence the living systems that inhabit our planet. The journey into quantum biology is an intriguing one, beckoning us to consider the hidden frameworks underlying life itself, as we explore the delicate dance of particles and waves that defines the essence of existence.

13.2. Quantum Entanglement in Biological Systems

The concept of quantum entanglement in biological systems emerges as a fascinating intersection of quantum mechanics and biology, signaling a revolutionary exploration into how quantum principles may influence life at its most fundamental level. This inquiry dives into the heart of what distinguishes living systems from mere mechanical processes and opens the door to understanding intricate biological phenomena through the lens of quantum mechanics.

Quantum entanglement describes a scenario where two or more quantum particles become interconnected such that the state of one particle can instantaneously affect the state of another, no matter the distance separating them. This phenomenon has long been seen as an exotic feature of quantum mechanics, typically reserved for discussions about subatomic particles and the bizarre behavior they exhibit. However, recent research proposes that similar entanglement-like behaviors might occur in biological systems, influencing processes like energy transfer in photosynthesis, navigation in certain migratory species, and enzyme reactions.

One compelling illustration of quantum entanglement in biological systems is found in the process of photosynthesis. Studies have suggested that photosynthetic organisms such as plants, algae, and certain bacteria utilize quantum coherence to enhance energy capture during light harvesting. In these systems, the energy from photons is absorbed by pigments in complexes known as light-harvesting complexes (LHCs). Quantum coherence enables the excitations produced during light absorption to explore multiple pathways through an entangled state, optimizing the transfer of energy to reaction centers with minimal loss. This phenomenon not only enhances efficiency but also demonstrates how quantum effects can play a functional role in biological systems.

Quantum entanglement has also been hypothesized in the context of animal navigation. Certain migratory birds are believed to utilize quantum mechanisms, specifically quantum entanglement and tunneling, to sense Earth's magnetic field for navigation. The intricate chemical reactions in specialized proteins in their eyes that are sensitive to photonic interactions may result in entangled electron states, allowing these birds to accurately detect and interpret magnetic fields. This interplay of biology and quantum physics raises questions about the evolutionary advantages offered by such quantum strategies, guiding long-distance migratory patterns with remarkable precision.

Furthermore, quantum mechanics extends its influence into enzyme reactions through the phenomenon of quantum tunneling. Enzymes are biological catalysts that facilitate chemical reactions with extraordinary speed and specificity. Recent studies indicate that enzymes may utilize quantum tunneling to enable the efficient transfer of protons or electrons across barriers that would be surmountable only at much higher energy levels. This efficient mechanism not only underscores the significance of quantum effects in biochemistry but also illustrates how quantum mechanics contributes to life-sustaining biochemical processes.

Despite the compelling evidence suggesting the role of quantum phenomena in biological systems, the research in this area is still burgeoning, and much remains to be uncovered. A primary challenge lies in bridging the gap between quantum effects, typically observed in isolated systems, and the complex, noisy environments characteristic of biological systems. Experimental methodologies that effectively probe biological processes and the intricate dynamics of quantum interactions within living organisms must be developed to validate current hypotheses and explore deeper questions surrounding life's foundations.

The implications of quantum entanglement in biological systems invite rich discussions about consciousness, identity, and the underlying principles of life itself. If quantum effects significantly impact living processes, what does this suggest about the consciousness that emerges from biological complexity? Can the inner workings of life be fully understood without considering the quantum realm? These philosophical inquiries extend beyond biology and compel deeper reflections on the nature of existence.

As we navigate through this exciting frontier where quantum mechanics and biology converge, innovative technologies inspired by quantum principles may arise. Quantum biology holds the promise of facilitating advancements in medicine, biotechnology, and material science that leverage the unique properties of quantum systems. Such developments may provide insights into novel therapeutic approaches, enhance energy capture systems, and foster sustainable practices in various industries.

In summary, the exploration of quantum entanglement in biological systems presents an intriguing narrative that invites us to rethink our understanding of life at its most fundamental level. By elucidating the connections between quantum principles and biological processes, we bridge the gap between physics and biology, offering profound insights into the nature of existence and the intricate mechanisms governing living systems. As research in this area continues to develop, the potential for revolutionary advancements looms, promising to expand our comprehension of life while unearthing the hidden dimensions of the quantum world that underpin biological phenomena.

13.3. Molecular Machines and Quantum Mechanics

Molecular machines represent one of the most fascinating and pivotal areas where quantum mechanics intersects with the intricacies of biological systems. At the smallest scales, the behavior of molecules —each of which can be thought of as a complex machine—can often be explained through quantum principles. These molecular machines perform essential functions that drive biochemical processes within living organisms, relying on phenomena such as quantum tunneling, coherence, and entanglement to facilitate actions that sustain life.

The fundamental building blocks of molecular machines are molecules composed of atoms bonded together by quantum forces. Their operation often resembles macroscopic machines, yet their mechanisms are governed by quantum mechanics. Take for instance, ATP synthase, a vital enzyme responsible for synthesizing ATP (adenosine triphosphate), the energy currency of the cell. ATP synthase operates by harnessing the electrochemical gradient generated across membranes, utilizing rotational motion to drive the production of ATP from ADP and inorganic phosphate. This process involves quantum effects, where tunneling allows for the efficient transfer of protons across membranes, showcasing the connection between molecular machinery and quantum principles.

Moreover, in molecular machines such as kinesin and dynein—motor proteins responsible for transporting cellular cargo—demonstrable aspects of quantum mechanics come into play as well. These proteins traverse cellular pathways by converting chemical energy from ATP into mechanical work, utilizing conformational changes influenced by quantum effects. The entangled states of particles within these proteins may enhance their efficiency by enabling them to "choose" paths through complex cellular environments, much like navigators determine routes during travel.

Additionally, molecular machines often engage in quantum coherence, which can enhance the productivity and efficiency of energy transfer during biochemical processes. In systems like photosynthetic complexes, quantum coherence allows excitons—energy carriers in the light-harvesting process—to explore multiple pathways simultaneously, improving energy retention and transfer over the complex molecular structures that lead to photosynthesis. This coherence operates on principles of superposition, providing insights into how life can capitalize on quantum mechanics to achieve remarkable efficiency in energy capture.

The innovations inspired by quantum mechanics expand the applicability of molecular machines in technology and materials science. Researchers are now exploring how to design synthetic molecular machines that mimic these quantum characteristics to deliver breakthroughs in nano-scale robotics, targeted drug delivery systems, and environmentally responsive materials. This burgeoning field of nanotechnology harnesses insights from quantum mechanics to engineer molecular devices capable of precision operations, revolutionizing applications in medicine, manufacturing, and energy.

Nonetheless, engaging with the quantum properties of molecular machines presents unique challenges. Investigating quantum effects in biological systems necessitates advanced experimental techniques capable of probing delicate interactions and maintaining coherence in biological environments. Researchers must navigate these complexities to ensure that insights gleaned from quantum mechanics yield practical applications in biotechnology and materials science.

Furthermore, as we delve into the connections between molecular biology and quantum mechanics, philosophical questions arise. If quantum features are integral to the processes defining life, how should we understand consciousness and its relationship to biological systems? In navigating these inquiries, we extend the boundaries of knowledge into realms where biology, quantum mechanics, and philosophy converge.

To summarize, molecular machines represent a fascinating convergence of biology and quantum mechanics, revealing a hidden world where quantum effects underpin the processes essential to life. By exploring the operational principles of these molecular entities, we can harness insights into how they function, paving the way for innovations and applications that capitalize on quantum mechanics. As we continue to research these intersections, we stand to uncover deeper truths about the nature of life, the structure of existence, and the dynamic interplay between the microscopic and macroscopic realms. The exploration of molecular machines and quantum mechanics highlights the beauty and complexity of biological systems, illuminating pathways toward transformative advancements nestled within the quantum realm that lies beneath the surface of our understanding.

13.4. Quantum Sensing in Nature

In the natural world, quantum sensing plays a pivotal role in enabling organisms to interact with their environment, facilitating critical processes such as navigation, prey detection, and survival. Nature's capacity to employ quantum phenomena enhances our understanding of biological systems, revealing intricate mechanisms that are intricately woven with quantum principles. This chapter explores the various instances of quantum sensing in nature, shedding light on how these capabilities have evolved and the implications they hold for both biology and technology.

One of the most compelling examples of quantum sensing is found in the migratory navigation of certain avian species. Research indicates that some birds possess specialized proteins in their eyes that are sensitive to magnetic fields, allowing them to detect the Earth's geomagnetic information for navigation. These proteins, referred to as cryptochromes, may operate using quantum entanglement, enabling the birds to perceive magnetic directions with remarkable accuracy. The specific reaction to blue light activates these proteins, leading to the formation of radical pairs—molecules whose states are entangled —giving rise to measurable effects that birds can interpret as navigational cues. This remarkable phenomenon illustrates the profound ways in which quantum mechanics can shape behavior and enhance survival strategies in the animal kingdom.

Additionally, quantum sensing capabilities extend into the realm of bioluminescent organisms, such as certain species of jellyfish and fireflies. For these organisms, quantum coherence plays a role in efficiently transferring photons generated by biochemical reactions. The ensemble of excitons within these systems allows for the precise coordination of photon emission, ultimately serving purposes like communication, attracting mates, or luring prey. The ability to manipulate quantum states effectively augments the biological utility of light in ways that classical systems could not achieve.

Quantum sensing also influences biochemical processes at microscopic scales. For example, enzymes may utilize quantum tunneling to facilitate reactions efficiently, allowing for proton or electron transfer that would typically require significantly higher energy inputs under classical conditions. This phenomenon emphasizes the intricate relationship between quantum mechanics and biological activity, highlighting the degree to which quantum properties can enhance the functionality of life-sustaining processes.

Furthermore, researchers are beginning to explore the implications of quantum sensing in human-made technologies. Scientific advancements inspired by natural systems could lead to innovations in quantum sensors designed to detect subtle changes in magnetic fields, temperature, and biological signals. Such sensors could have widespread applications in fields such as healthcare, environmental monitoring, and navigation. Understanding the quantum sensing strategies employed by organisms in nature may pave the way for developing ultra-sensitive instrumentation that can monitor subtle phenomena, leading to improved diagnostic tools and innovative environmental solutions.

Despite the promise of quantum sensing in nature and technology, various challenges remain. Researchers must navigate the complexities associated with preserving and manipulating quantum states, particularly in the presence of noise and environmental degradation. Developing advanced experimental techniques that effectively isolate and manage these states is essential for harnessing quantum phenomena to their fullest potential.

Moreover, the study of quantum sensing prompts philosophical reflections regarding the nature of performance and adaptability in living systems. As we uncover the mechanisms underlying biological entities that leverage quantum principles, we confront deeper inquiries into the interplay between consciousness, perception, and the environment. Exploring these themes invites fresh dialogues about the interconnectedness of life and the quantum world, urging us to contemplate the hidden dimensions of existence.

In summary, quantum sensing in nature exemplifies the remarkable ways in which quantum mechanics intertwines with biological processes. From avian navigation to enzymatic efficiency, the utilization of quantum phenomena bolsters survival and enhances interactions with the environment. As research progresses, the lessons gleaned from nature's quantum sensors might inspire transformative technological innovations, facilitating novel approaches to measurement and monitoring in diverse fields. The journey into the realm of quantum sensing invites us to reflect on the complexities and intricacies of life itself, urging us to recognize the hidden quantum world that enriches our understanding of existence in fundamental ways. As we explore these dimensions, we continue to enhance our grasp of the universe's profound mysteries that lie beneath the surface of our observed realities.

13.5. Innovations Inspired by Quantum Biology

Innovations inspired by quantum biology mark an exciting frontier in scientific research and technological development, bridging the gap between the fundamental principles of quantum mechanics and the intricate systems of biological organisms. As we uncover how quantum effects influence biological processes, we gain insights that could lead to groundbreaking advancements in various fields, from medicine to materials science, and even artificial intelligence.

At the core of quantum biology is the realization that many biological processes seem to depend on quantum mechanics. One significant area of interest is photosynthesis, where plants, algae, and some bacteria transform sunlight into chemical energy. Recent studies reveal that quantum coherence plays a crucial role in this process, allowing for the efficient transfer of energy by enabling excitons—energy-carrying particles—to explore multiple paths simultaneously. The ability of these organisms to utilize quantum phenomena raises profound questions about the efficiency and optimization strategies inherent in nature. Understanding these mechanisms could lead to the development of artificial photosynthetic systems that mimic this efficiency, enhancing solar energy capture methodologies and contributing to sustainable energy solutions.

Additionally, research into avian navigation has highlighted potential quantum applications. Certain migratory birds possess specialized proteins in their eyes, known as cryptochromes, that are sensitive to magnetic fields. Qualitative studies indicate that these proteins may operate based on quantum entanglement, allowing birds to perceive magnetic orientation with remarkable accuracy. If researchers can further unravel this quantum sensing mechanism, valuable insights could emerge regarding navigation technologies, enabling enhanced satellite systems or more efficient navigation methods for drones and autonomous vehicles.

The field of quantum biology is also being explored to advance medicinal practices. Enzyme catalysis in biochemical reactions can benefit from quantum tunneling effects, which allow reactions to occur with much lower energy requirements than classical predictions would suggest. By harnessing these quantum principles, pharmaceutical researchers could design drugs that act more efficiently or target specific molecular pathways with precision, advancing personalized medicine approaches.

Moreover, as we advance our understanding of molecular machines within cells, the implications of quantum effects become increasingly evident. Pathways that employ molecular motors—like kinesin or myosin—that transport cellular cargo may utilize quantum tunneling and coherence to enhance their efficiency. Generating synthetic analogs of these molecular machines could lead to bioengineering applications, the development of smart materials, or nanoscale devices that mimic biological systems to perform complex tasks efficiently.

Despite the exciting potential of quantum-inspired innovations, challenges persist in fully translating quantum biology findings into practical applications. The delicate nature of quantum states requires precision experimental techniques, and further research is needed to ensure that these findings can be reliably harnessed under real-world conditions. Additionally, the ethical implications of manipulating biological systems at the quantum level demand careful consideration, as advancements may provoke debates surrounding safety, environmental impact, and long-term consequences.

The journey of innovations inspired by quantum biology invites collaboration across interdisciplinary domains, including physics, biology, engineering, and ethics. Educating and training a new generation of scientists capable of integrating these disciplines will be essential for maximizing the potential of quantum insights.

In summary, innovations inspired by quantum biology illuminate a hidden world that transcends traditional scientific boundaries, inviting us to explore the extraordinary interconnections between quantum phenomena and biological processes. As we endeavor to leverage these insights for technology and sustainable practices, we unlock transformative possibilities that promise to reshape our understanding of life and the universe. Embracing the elegance and complexity of quantum biology will forge pathways to future innovations, guiding our quest to harness the hidden quantum forces that underpin existence itself. Through continual investigation and interdisciplinary collaboration, we stand on the precipice of a new era defined by the remarkable marriage of quantum mechanics and the life sciences, where the latent potential of quantum biology can reshape medicine, technology, and our understanding of life itself.

14. Quantum Mechanics in Technology

14.1. Semiconductors and Quantum Mechanics

Semiconductors are integral to the technological advancements of today, forming the backbone of modern electronics, telecommunications, and computing systems. Their operation is deeply intertwined with the principles of quantum mechanics—principles that illuminate how materials behave at atomic and subatomic levels. Understanding this relationship not only enhances our grasp of semiconductors but also sheds light on the exciting possibilities within the realm of quantum technology.

At the most fundamental level, semiconductors are materials whose electrical conductivity falls between that of conductors and insulators. This unique behavior arises from the arrangement and interaction of atoms within these materials. The properties of semiconductors can be manipulated through doping—introducing small amounts of impurities to create either excess electrons (n-type) or holes (p-type). This process exploits quantum mechanical principles, particularly the concepts of energy bands.

In quantum mechanics, electrons occupy discrete energy levels within an atom. In solids, these levels form energy bands due to the close proximity of atoms, with the conduction band representing higher energy states where electrons can move freely, and the valence band representing lower energy states. The bandgap—the energy difference between these two bands—determines a semiconductor's conductivity. Doping modifies the band structure, allowing for greater control over electrical properties. These behaviors are fundamentally rooted in quantum mechanics, which governs electron configurations and transitions between states.

Additionally, the quantum phenomenon of tunneling plays a pivotal role in semiconductor devices. Tunneling allows particles to pass through energy barriers they would not ordinarily surmount, and this behavior is exploited in devices like tunnel diodes, where electrons can move through thin barriers at low voltages. The ability to design and fabricate semiconductor devices that leverage tunneling and other quantum effects drives innovation, leading to faster, more efficient electronic components.

The intersection of semiconductors and quantum mechanics also manifests in the development of quantum dots—nanoscale semiconductor particles that exhibit quantized energy levels. Quantum dots can confine excitons (electron-hole pairs) and allow for enhanced photonic properties, making them ideal for applications in fluorescence imaging, solar cells, and LEDs. The tunability of their electronic properties based on size highlights the quantum principles of confinement and energy quantization, presenting exciting avenues for both research and commercial applications.

Moreover, the role of quantum mechanics extends into the design and functionality of transistors, which serve as the building blocks of integrated circuits. Modern transistors, particularly those operating at the nanoscale, rely on quantum effects to achieve high performance and energy efficiency. Techniques such as quantum well transistors and quantum dot transistors enable the construction of smaller, faster, and more power-efficient devices, paving the way for advancements in computing technologies.

As society advances into the era of quantum computing and information processing, semiconductors will play an increasingly crucial role. Quantum computers leverage quantum bits (qubits), which rely on processes rooted in quantum mechanics, including superposition and entanglement. Innovations in semiconductor technology will drive forward the implementations of qubits, facilitating the development of scalable quantum computers that can tackle problems far beyond the reach of classical systems.

However, while the potential of semiconductors in quantum technology is immense, researchers face challenges related to material properties, coherence times, and error rates in quantum computing applications. The quest for materials that can maintain quantum coherence while integrating seamlessly into existing electronic infrastructures remains at the forefront of research.

As we consider the future of semiconductors in the quantum landscape, the intersection of quantum mechanics and semiconductor technology will undoubtedly foster new innovations that transcend the limitations of classical systems. The journey ahead is one filled with opportunities, inviting interdisciplinary collaboration to harness the principles of quantum mechanics and unlock the myriad potentials that lie within these remarkable materials. The exploration of semiconductors and quantum mechanics reveals a fascinating narrative within modern science, unearthing profound insights into the hidden fabric of our technological reality.

14.2. Quantum Dots and Their Applications

Quantum dots are nanometer-sized semiconductor particles that exhibit a phenomenon known as quantum confinement, where the electronic and optical properties are determined by their size and shape. As we delve into the realm of quantum dots and their applications, it becomes increasingly clear that these minute structures serve as a bridge between quantum physics and practical technologies capable of impacting our daily lives substantially.

At the atomic level, quantum dots behave like artificial atoms, with discrete energy levels that lead to size-dependent properties. This size-tunable characteristic arises because, when quantum dots are sufficiently small, they confine electrons and holes in three dimensions. Consequently, moving from larger particles to smaller quantum dots leads to noticeable shifts in their energy levels, a property known as the quantum size effect. This tunability makes quantum dots particularly appealing for applications requiring precise control over electronic and optical behavior.

The initial discovery and research into quantum dots were aimed at fully understanding their semiconductor properties. However, as advancements in synthesis techniques emerged, researchers recognized their potential across a breadth of applications, ranging from electronics to medical technologies, photonics to renewable energy solutions.

One of the most well-recognized applications of quantum dots is in display technology, notably in quantum dot televisions (QLED). By utilizing quantum dots to enhance the display color gamut and efficiency, these displays provide improved color accuracy and brightness compared to traditional liquid crystal displays (LCDs). The ability of quantum dots to emit specific colors upon excitation has positioned them at the forefront of display innovation, paving the way for next-generation visual technologies.

Moreover, in the field of photovoltaics, quantum dots have shown promise as materials for solar cells. Their size-tuned properties can enhance light absorption at various wavelengths, potentially increasing the overall efficiency of solar energy conversion. Quantum dot solar cells can be engineered to absorb both visible and infrared light, which would enable the practical implementation of more efficient solar devices capable of harnessing a broader spectrum of sunlight.

In biomedical applications, quantum dots have emerged as powerful tools for imaging and diagnostics. Their unique optical properties allow for highly sensitive biological labeling, which can significantly enhance the capabilities of fluorescent imaging techniques. Quantum dots can be conjugated with biomolecules to target specific cells or tissues, facilitating real-time imaging of cellular processes with high resolution. This capability could revolutionize medical diagnostics and monitoring, leading to better understanding and treatment of diseases.

Furthermore, quantum dots have garnered attention in the realm of quantum computing. As qubits—essential units of quantum information—quantum dots serve as viable candidates due to their capacity to maintain quantum coherence for relatively extended periods. The prospect of utilizing quantum dots in quantum circuits presents exciting opportunities for the development of scalable and efficient quantum computing architectures.

Despite the many advantages of quantum dots, challenges remain in harnessing their capabilities fully. One primary concern is the potential toxicity of heavy metal-based quantum dots, such as cadmium selenide (CdSe). The advancement of biocompatible quantum dots made from earth-abundant and less toxic materials is necessary to expand their safe use in biomedical applications. Furthermore, ongoing research aims to refine the synthesis processes to improve the uniformity and scalability of quantum dot production while enhancing performance consistency across various applications.

As we look toward the future, the integration of quantum dots into a multitude of technologies reflects the vibrant interplay between fundamental physics and applied science. The advancements driven by quantum dots promise to enhance our capabilities in various fields, from energy efficiency and medical diagnostics to novel computing paradigms. Our comprehension of quantum dots and their multifaceted applications will be pivotal in shaping innovations that impact technology, healthcare, and sustainability, continuing to probe the hidden quantum world that lies beneath the surface of our everyday existence.

In conclusion, quantum dots are not only a product of groundbreaking research in quantum mechanics but also a promising frontier in the application of quantum principles to tangible technologies. As we advance our understanding and technological capabilities, quantum dots epitomize the fusion of science, innovation, and the potential for transformative impact across disciplines, illuminating pathways toward a future where quantum technologies become integral components of our lives.

14.3. Lasers: The Quantum Technology

Lasers, as a revolutionized quantum technology, serve as a vivid testament to the power of quantum mechanics - a field characterized by its abstract yet tangible realities. Originating from the principles of quantum mechanics, lasers have transformed a multitude of applications, ranging from telecommunications to medicine, and continue to pave the way for innovations in various domains. At the core of laser technology lies the concept of stimulated emission - a uniquely quantum process that allows for the generation of coherent light, fundamentally differing from traditional light sources.

The journey of lasers begins with the foundational principles of quantum mechanics. In a laser, atoms or molecules are excited by an external energy source, typically referred to as a pump. This energy input raises the particles to a higher energy state, thus facilitating a process known as population inversion, where a greater number of particles occupy an excited state than a lower energy state. At this stage, three crucial components come into play: the gain medium, the excitation source, and the optical cavity.

The gain medium serves as the substrate for laser operation, and can be composed of gases, liquids or solids, each imparting unique properties to the laser beam. In the optical cavity, mirrors reflect photons back and forth through the gain medium, increasing the probability that photons will stimulate the emission of more photons as they pass through the medium. The result is a cascading effect of stimulated emission, producing a coherent beam of light with uniform phase, frequency, and direction, characteristics that distinguish lasers from ordinary light sources.

This coherence is paramount; the emitted photons are in-phase, resulting in highly focused light beams that can travel long distances with minimal divergence. This principle directly underpins many of the technological applications we rely on today. For instance, in telecommunications, lasers form the backbone of high-speed data transmission over fiber optic networks, encapsulating vast amounts of information into beams of light that can traverse long distances without significant loss.

In medicine, lasers have emerged as invaluable tools in fields such as surgery and diagnostics. From laser eye surgeries like LASIK to targeted therapies for tumors, lasers enable precise interventions while minimizing damage to surrounding tissues, ultimately leading to enhanced patient outcomes. The ability to focus laser beams with high accuracy highlights both the technological advancements driven by quantum mechanics and the profound effects these developments have on human health and well-being.

As lasers continue to evolve, innovations inspired by quantum mechanics open new avenues in technology. The advent of quantum dots, which produce laser light at specific wavelengths based on particle size, exemplifies the intersection of quantum physics and laser technology. These quantum dot lasers hold promise for applications in electronics, display technologies, and energy-efficient devices, expanding the potential uses of lasers even further.

However, the intertwining of lasers and quantum mechanics does not come without challenges. The complexity of controlling and maintaining the excited states necessary for laser operation requires ongoing research and innovation. Additionally, exploring the limits of laser technology requires collaboration across disciplines, including physics, engineering, and material science. It is crucial for researchers to understand how quantum principles can be applied to refine existing laser technologies while developing new paradigms that push the boundaries of what's possible.

In conclusion, lasers exemplify the extraordinary advancements made possible through the principles derived from quantum mechanics. By harnessing stimulated emission and the coherence of light, lasers have revolutionized various fields and continue to foster progress across industries. As we venture deeper into the quantum realm, the role of lasers serves as a vivid reminder of the incredible potential contained within the hidden intricacies of the quantum world, continually inviting us to explore the unseen mechanisms that shape our technological landscape, illuminating lives and redefining the possibilities of innovation in the modern era.

14.4. The Role of Quantum Mechanics in Quantum Tech

As we explore the role of quantum mechanics in quantum technology, it becomes apparent that quantum phenomena serve as the underpinnings for a broad spectrum of novel applications bridging the gap between theoretical concepts and real-world utility. The manipulability of quantum states—characterized by principles such as superposition, entanglement, and wave-particle duality—facilitates the development of cutting-edge technologies that challenge our traditional understanding of computation, communication, and measurement.

Quantum mechanics provides a fundamentally different approach to processing information compared to classical technology. Classical computers, based on bits that represent either a 0 or a 1, rely on a linear processing model. In contrast, quantum computers utilize qubits, which can coexist in multiple states simultaneously due to superposition. This allows quantum systems to perform complex calculations at an unprecedented speed, offering the potential to solve problems deemed intractable by classical means. Applications range from drug discovery and optimization problems to simulations of complex quantum systems, with transformative implications for fields such as finance, artificial intelligence, and materials science.

Moreover, quantum technology extends to the realm of secure communication through quantum cryptography, particularly through Quantum Key Distribution (QKD). By leveraging quantum mechanics' principles—the properties of entangled particles, for example —QKD establishes secure communication channels resistant to eavesdropping. The inherent characteristics of quantum states allow for the detection of any tampering or measurement attempts, resulting in an unprecedented level of security that far surpasses classical cryptographic standards. As digital communication becomes increasingly essential in contemporary society, the need for secure channels will only intensify, making quantum technologies vital in safeguarding sensitive information.

In the domain of measurement, quantum mechanics introduces quantum sensing, which enhances the capabilities of sensors beyond classical limitations. Quantum sensors exploit the concepts of superposition and entanglement to improve the precision and sensitivity of measurements, leading to advances in various applications, including medical diagnostics, environmental monitoring, and navigation systems. For instance, the exquisite sensitivity of quantum sensors can detect minute changes in physical quantities—such as gravitational waves or magnetic fields—enabling new avenues for scientific exploration and practical applications.

Furthermore, quantum mechanics offers insights into creating materials with unique properties through quantum engineering. By manipulating quantum states at the nanoscale, researchers can design and fabricate materials with tailored characteristics for applications in electronics, photonics, and renewable energy. Quantum dots, for example, have revolutionized display technologies and solar cells, while superconductors have applications in efficient energy transmission and magnetic resonance imaging.

The rapid advances in quantum technologies usher in both opportunities and challenges. As researchers continue to explore the implications of quantum mechanics, substantial efforts must be directed toward overcoming obstacles associated with error rates, decoherence, and material fabrication. The inherent complexity of quantum systems necessitates interdisciplinary collaboration across various fields, bridging the gaps between physics, engineering, materials science, and computer science.

The societal impact of these technologies cannot be overstated. Quantum innovations promise to reshape industries, enhance security, and improve our understanding of the natural world. However, ethical considerations regarding privacy, access, and potential disruptions to existing industries must also be part of the conversation as we venture into this new technological landscape. Public understanding of quantum technologies is crucial in promoting informed discussions about their role in society, as well as ensuring equitable access to their benefits.

In conclusion, the role of quantum mechanics in quantum technology exemplifies a remarkable fusion of scientific inquiry and practical application. As we harness the principles of quantum mechanics, we prepare to navigate a future filled with innovations that challenge our understanding of computation, communication, and measurement. This persistent journey toward realizing the potential of quantum technologies invites a celebration of curiosity and exploration, as we unlock the secrets embedded in the hidden quantum world, revealing a rich tapestry of possibilities that redefine our engagement with the universe. Through collaborative efforts and a commitment to responsible development, we can shape a future where the principles of quantum mechanics guide our advancements into uncharted territories, enriching our lives and our understanding of the cosmos.

14.5. Future Technologies Driven by Quantum Insights

As we traverse the vibrant landscape of future technologies driven by quantum insights, we encounter a realm rich with possibilities, marked by innovative advancements poised to redefine industries and reshape our understanding of the universe. The evolution of quantum mechanics from theoretical exploration to practical application encapsulates an extraordinary journey—one that intertwines scientific inquiry with the potential for transformative societal impacts.

At the heart of this exploration lies quantum computing, a frontier that promises to revolutionize how we process information. By harnessing the unique properties of quantum bits, or qubits, quantum computers can operate on multiple states simultaneously through superposition, enabling them to perform complex calculations that are effectively unattainable by classical computers. With the potential to address intricate problems in optimization, cryptography, and simulation—a wide range of applications encompassing logistics, drug development, and artificial intelligence—quantum computing stands as a catalyst for innovation. Research endeavors are already yielding advancements in quantum algorithms designed to exploit these capabilities, moving us closer to realizing practical quantum systems that significantly surpass the limitations of classical architectures.

Quantum communication represents another pivotal advancement driven by insights from quantum mechanics. By employing principles such as entanglement and the observer effect, quantum key distribution (QKD) is positioned as a secure method of transmitting sensitive information. The essential premise of QKD—that the act of eavesdropping will be detectable due to disturbances in quantum states —ensures a level of security and confidentiality that far exceeds traditional encryption methods. As the demand for secure communication channels grows in our digital age, quantum communication promises to redefine standards for privacy and security in government, finance, healthcare, and beyond.

Moreover, the burgeoning field of quantum sensing exemplifies how quantum mechanics can enhance measurement precision, extending capabilities beyond classical limitations. Quantum sensors leverage entangled states to detect minute variations and changes in physical quantities—opening avenues for advancements in medical diagnostics, environmental monitoring, and navigation technologies. The application of quantum sensing promises to elevate capabilities in detecting gravitational waves, elucidating our understanding of cosmic events, and providing more accurate and sensitive instruments tailored for real-world applications.

Yet, as we strive toward these advancements, the path forward is not without challenges. The inherent sensitivity of quantum systems to environmental factors poses obstacles in maintaining coherence and reliability. Quantum noise and decoherence, arising when quantum states interact with their surroundings, can disrupt operations, necessitating continual efforts to develop techniques for error correction, stability, and precision. Researchers are actively tackling these issues, investigating new materials capable of preserving quantum states and exploring innovative error-correcting codes to enhance reliability in practical quantum computing and communication systems.

The societal implications of these advancements invite comprehensive reflection. The integration of quantum technologies into daily life raises pertinent questions regarding access to technology, privacy rights, and ethical considerations surrounding data security. Ensuring equitable access to quantum solutions and addressing potential socioeconomic disparities that may arise from technological disparity requires collaboration among researchers, policymakers, and the public.

Additionally, as quantum insights reshape our understanding of various fields, including biology—a juncture known as quantum biology —new paradigms of knowledge emerge, fostering interdisciplinary dialogue. Innovations stemming from quantum dynamics trigger discussions surrounding the implications of consciousness, free will, and the philosophical ramifications of harnessing quantum insights for technological advancements.

In summary, exploring future technologies driven by quantum insights illuminates a dynamic intersection of innovation, theoretical exploration, and practical inquiry poised to redefine the fabric of existence. As we venture into this quantum future, the collective endeavor to harness these extraordinary principles will pave the way for advancements that challenge conventional paradigms and herald an era marked by transformative change across society. The uncharted territories of quantum technology invite curiosity—a testament to the hidden quantum world that lies beneath the surface of observable reality, waiting to be unveiled in its remarkable complexity and wonder. Embracing this journey beckons the promise of a future replete with astonishing capabilities, fresh paradigms, and deeper understandings of the universe and ourselves as we harness the quantum insights that lie ahead.

15. Experiments That Shaped Quantum Physics

15.1. The Double-Slit Experiment

Exploring the double-slit experiment, a pivotal demonstration in the realm of quantum physics, reveals the conflicting theories about the nature of light and particles and underscores the dramatic implications for our understanding of reality itself. When the classic setup of this experiment is utilized—where particles, such as electrons or photons, are directed through two closely spaced slits—its outcomes exemplify the strange and paradoxical behaviors that define the quantum world.

At a glance, the double-slit experiment may appear to be deceptively simple, yet its results elicit profound themes in the exploration of reality. The setup involves firing a stream of particles towards a barrier containing two slits, with a detection screen positioned behind the slits to observe where the particles land. Classical physics, which assumes that particles follow well-defined trajectories influenced by deterministic laws, would predict that each particle would pass through one slit or the other, resulting in two distinct bands of impact on the screen.

Surprisingly, the observed outcome diverges significantly from classical expectations. Instead of the expected two bands, a complex interference pattern emerges, indicative of wave-like behavior. This interference pattern implies that the particles behave like waves, interfering with each other and creating areas of constructive and destructive interference across the detection screen. Notably, this wave-like behavior occurs even when particles are sent through the slits one at a time, suggesting that each particle somehow traverses both slits simultaneously—a phenomenon that embodies the quantum principle of superposition.

The fundamental implications of this interference pattern lead to the integral question of what it means to observe and measure quantum phenomena. A remarkable feature of the double-slit experiment lies in the impact of measurement on outcomes. When detectors are introduced to ascertain which slit each particle passes through, the interference pattern vanishes, and particles revert to behaving like classical objects, resulting in two distinct bands corresponding to the two slits. The act of measurement collapses the wave function, manifesting a definite outcome in what can only be described as a striking demonstration of the observer effect—a concept suggesting that observation fundamentally alters the state of a quantum system.

These counterintuitive results shatter classical intuitions about reality, sparking profound philosophical inquiries. If the act of observation alters outcomes, what does this mean for the nature of reality? Are particles existing in a state of potentiality until observed? Does the universe depend on consciousness to define existence? The consequences of the double-slit experiment challenge foundational beliefs about objectivity, causality, and the role of consciousness in shaping reality.

Furthermore, the double-slit experiment has become a crucial touchstone within the debates surrounding different interpretations of quantum mechanics. The Copenhagen interpretation posits that quantum systems do not possess definite properties until they are measured, while the Many-Worlds theory suggests that all outcomes coexist in parallel realities, each branching from a quantum interaction. The double-slit experiment compels scientists and philosophers alike to grapple with the implications of these interpretations, exploring the intricate dynamics between observation, existence, and the very nature of reality.

The legacy of the double-slit experiment extends beyond theoretical contemplation—it represents a foundational visualization of quantum phenomena that influences ongoing research in various fields, including quantum computing, cryptography, and even quantum biology. It captures the imagination and curiosity of those seeking to uncover the hidden mechanisms that govern existence.

In conclusion, the double-slit experiment stands as a singular yet multifaceted exploration into the heart of quantum mechanics. It serves as a gateway into the complexities of reality, inviting us to ponder the nature of existence and the paradoxical behaviors of particles that lie beneath the surface of our perception. By unveiling the intricate dance between waves and particles, the double-slit experiment reveals the profound questions that intertwine the realms of physics, philosophy, and consciousness—inviting us to reconsider our understanding of the universe and our place within it.

15.2. Stern-Gerlach Experiment: Spinning Particles

The Stern-Gerlach experiment, conducted in 1922 by Otto Stern and Walther Gerlach, marked a significant milestone in the early exploration of quantum mechanics. This pivotal experiment provided compelling evidence for the quantization of angular momentum, demonstrating that particles like electrons possess intrinsic properties that lead to discrete measurable states. The findings of the Stern-Gerlach experiment not only served to validate key concepts of quantum theory but also raised deeper questions about the nature of measurement, quantum states, and particle behavior.

The experiment involved passing a beam of silver atoms through a non-uniform magnetic field. In classical physics, one would expect that particles with magnetic dipole moments would experience a continuous range of deflections due to their interaction with the magnetic field. However, what Stern and Gerlach observed was both surprising and transformative: instead of a continuous distribution, the beam split into distinct spots on a detection screen, indicating that the silver atoms were only deflected into specific angles corresponding to their intrinsic "spin" states.

In quantum physics, "spin" refers to the intrinsic angular momentum possessed by particles, akin to a bar magnet that can align with an external magnetic field in specific quantized directions. For the case of silver atoms, which possess one unpaired electron in their outer shell, the results revealed that each atom's spin can adopt only certain orientations relative to the magnetic field—specifically, spin-up or spin-down, corresponding to two discrete states.

Consequently, the Stern-Gerlach experiment not only provided empirical validation for the concept of quantized angular momentum but also prompted a deeper inquiry into the nature of measurement in quantum systems. The act of measuring a particle's spin necessitates the collapse of its wave function; prior to measurement, the particle exists in a superposition of states. The Stern-Gerlach experiment uniquely reaffirms this aspect, indicating that observation introduces an element of indeterminacy that fundamentally alters the quantum state.

The implications of the Stern-Gerlach experiment resonate beyond single-particle measurements. As quantum mechanics has evolved, researchers have turned their focus towards understanding the complexities of multi-particle systems, further probing the principles of entanglement, superposition, and quantum correlations. Entangled particles demonstrate that the measurement of one particle instantaneously affects its counterpart, regardless of the distance separating them—effectively showcasing the nonlocality inherent in quantum mechanics.

Moreover, the experiment has directly informed the development of various quantum technologies. For instance, magnetic resonance imaging (MRI) methods capitalize on similar principles of angular momentum and particle behavior in magnetic fields, allowing for sophisticated imaging in medical diagnostics. Ultimately, the insights gleaned from the Stern-Gerlach experiment have paved the way for a multitude of fields, including quantum computing, quantum cryptography, and quantum information science.

As we consider the broader narrative that the Stern-Gerlach experiment presents, we must recognize that it serves as a bridge between classical and quantum realms. The transitioning attitudes surrounding particles, observation, and measurement compel us to re-evaluate foundational assumptions about reality, encouraging rich discussions that continue to shape the field. This experiment stands not merely as a historical artifact of quantum exploration but as an active inspiration that invites ongoing inquiry into the intricacies of the quantum world.

In summary, the Stern-Gerlach experiment exemplifies a foundational inquiry that shaped the landscape of quantum mechanics. By revealing the quantization of angular momentum and demonstrating the role of measurement in determining quantum states, it prompts us to reflect upon the nature of reality, consciousness, and the interconnectedness of the quantum domain with observable phenomena. The legacy of the Stern-Gerlach experiment continues to influence scientific pursuits and philosophical discussions alike, urging us to explore the hidden quantum world that exists beneath the familiar mechanics of our daily lives.

15.3. Einstein-Podolsky-Rosen Experiment

In exploring the Einstein-Podolsky-Rosen (EPR) experiment, we delve into a significant moment in the history of quantum mechanics that sparked critical debates about the nature of reality, measurement, and the completeness of quantum theory. Proposed by Albert Einstein, Boris Podolsky, and Nathan Rosen in 1935, this thought experiment aimed to highlight what they perceived as the shortcomings of quantum mechanics, particularly its implications for locality and realism. The EPR experiment fundamentally challenges our understanding of quantum systems and lays the groundwork for discussions that persist in contemporary physics.

The crux of the EPR argument centers on the concept of quantum entanglement, a phenomenon that creates correlations between the properties of two or more quantum particles when they interact. According to the theory, once particles become entangled, their states are intertwined; the measurement of one particle is instantaneously reflected in the state of the other, even if they are spatially separated by significant distances. This nonlocal connection raised eyebrows among physicists, particularly Einstein, who famously dubbed it "spooky action at a distance."

The EPR paper outlined a scenario involving a pair of particles in an entangled state, demonstrating how measuring one particle's property (e.g., position or momentum) immediately defines the corresponding property of the second particle, irrespective of spatial separation. The intent was to argue that if quantum mechanics were complete, it must provide a description of all local hidden variables; otherwise, it would leave the interpretation of outcomes reliant on probabilistic measures that contradicted the deterministic nature of classical physics.

To encapsulate their reasoning, the EPR paper effectively proposed that if quantum mechanics could not describe the underlying "realities" of particles—those characteristics existing prior to measurement —it must be regarded as incomplete. Their critique encouraged physicists to reflect on the philosophical and conceptual foundations of quantum mechanics, igniting discussions about the nature of reality and the essential role of observers in shaping measurement outcomes.

This inquiry took on even greater significance with the advent of John Bell's theorem in the 1960s, which offered a framework for experimentally testing the implications of the EPR argument. Bell's theorem demonstrated that if local hidden variable theories existed, they would need to align with specific inequalities—known as Bell inequalities. Quantum mechanics, however, predicts correlations between entangled particles that violate these inequalities, suggesting that if the predictions of quantum mechanics hold, the concepts of locality and separability may need to be reevaluated.

In subsequent decades, numerous experimental tests have sought to validate Bell's theorem and the implications of the EPR experiment. These experiments have consistently confirmed the predictions of quantum mechanics, reaffirming the reality of entanglement and nonlocality. The results suggest that the universe operates in a fundamentally interconnected manner, challenging classical intuitions and inviting exploration into the philosophical ramifications of these findings.

The EPR experiment's enduring legacy lies not only in illuminating the complexities of quantum mechanics but also in prompting essential discussions about the nature of reality, locality, and the role of measurement. As physicists continue to explore entanglement and its implications in various fields—including quantum computing, cryptography, and foundational aspects of physics—understanding the EPR phenomenon remains critical to unlocking the hidden dimensions of the quantum realm.

In summary, the Einstein-Podolsky-Rosen experiment stands as a foundational inquiry in quantum mechanics, challenging traditional notions of reality and measurement while affirming the significance of entanglement in shaping our understanding of the universe. The legacy of EPR encourages ongoing exploration into the delicate interplay between quantum systems and the philosophical inquiries that arise as we strive to grapple with the nature of existence itself in a profoundly interconnected quantum world.

15.4. Bell Test Experiments: Nonlocality Confirmed

The late 20th century and early 21st century have witnessed groundbreaking research and development in quantum physics, culminating in a series of definitive experiments that have bolstered our understanding of quantum mechanics and its strange implications. Among these experiments, Bell test experiments stand out as pivotal demonstrations confirming the phenomenon of nonlocality, reshaping the landscape of quantum theory and challenging our classical intuitions regarding space, time, and reality.

To grasp the significance of Bell test experiments, we must first understand the historical context established by John Bell's theorem in 1964. Bell derived a set of inequalities, now known as Bell inequalities, which provide a mathematical framework to contrast the predictions of quantum mechanics with those of local hidden variable theories. In essence, local hidden variables suggest that particles possess predetermined properties before measurement, allowing them to follow deterministic paths in a manner consistent with classical physics. Conversely, quantum mechanics posits that particles do not exhibit definite properties until an observation occurs, leading to inherent uncertainties and nonlocal correlations between entangled particles.

Bell's theorem redefined the discourse surrounding the nature of reality in quantum systems. By proposing a method to empirically test the predictions arising from quantum mechanics versus local reality, Bell laid the groundwork for a series of experiments designed to discern which framework more accurately represented the behavior of entangled particles.

The first experimental tests of Bell's theorem emerged in the 1970s and 1980s, with physicists like Alain Aspect conducting pioneering experiments that explored the correlations predicted by quantum mechanics. In essence, these experiments involved creating pairs of entangled particles, such as photons, and measuring their properties (e.g., polarization or spin) at a distance from one another. When subjected to different measurement settings, the correlations observed consistently violated Bell inequalities, empirically supporting the predictions of quantum mechanics and, consequently, confirming the phenomenon of nonlocality.

These results catapulted science into a new era of understanding, as nonlocality challenges preconceived notions about separateness and locality that have dominated classical physics. If two particles can exhibit instantaneous correlations, regardless of distance, it raises profound questions about the nature of communication and causation in the universe. The implications of these observations stretch beyond the boundaries of physics into philosophy; they compel us to rethink concepts of time, space, and the fundamental structure of reality itself.

Further development of Bell test experiments has remained a vibrant field of inquiry, with researchers designing increasingly sophisticated setups to eliminate potential loopholes—where critics may argue that factors like local hidden variables could account for the observed correlations. Loophole-free experiments conducted in the latest years aim to address these concerns, providing even stronger support for the existence of nonlocality.

Importantly, these experiments do not exist in isolation; they resonate across multiple domains, influencing advancements in quantum technologies such as quantum cryptography and quantum computing. The acknowledgement of nonlocal properties inherently guides the development of secure communication methods that leverage entanglement and fundamentally changes the way we process information.

In conclusion, Bell test experiments epitomize a quantum revolution, confirming nonlocality, challenging classical intuitions, and inviting profound philosophical reflections on the nature of reality. As we navigate the implications of these findings, we remain poised on the threshold of a deeper understanding of the universe—a quest enriched by the subtleties of quantum mechanics, where traditional boundaries dissolve, inviting us to explore the intricate tapestry of existence that lies beneath our everyday experience. The unfolding narrative of quantum nonlocality compels us to embrace the mysteries of the quantum realm and recognize the profound interconnectedness that shapes our understanding of reality itself.

15.5. Recent Breakthroughs in Quantum Physics

Recent breakthroughs in quantum physics have ushered in an era characterized by unprecedented technological and theoretical advancements that challenge our understanding of reality and redefine the boundaries of human knowledge. These breakthroughs, rooted in the foundational principles of quantum mechanics, encompass a range of phenomena—from quantum computing and quantum entanglement to innovations in quantum cryptography and quantum sensing—each carrying profound implications for science, technology, and society as a whole.

One pivotal advancement in recent years centers around the development of quantum computers, which utilize qubits to perform calculations exponentially faster than classical computers. The realization of quantum supremacy has been marked by landmark demonstrations, such as Google's achievement with its Sycamore processor, which completed a specific problem in a fraction of the time it would take classical supercomputers. This triumph represents not just a feat of engineering but a testament to the practical applicability of quantum theory, showcasing how the manipulation of quantum states can yield results unattainable through classical means. Researchers continue to refine techniques in quantum computation, focusing on error rates and coherence times, ensuring that qubit performance mirrors the ambitious predictions of quantum computing's potential.

Another significant breakthrough lies in quantum entanglement, a phenomenon that has been further elucidated through experimental endeavors testing the predictions of nonlocality. Bell test experiments demonstrate that entangled particles exhibit correlations that defy classical intuitions, revealing the interconnectedness of quantum states regardless of distance. These findings have real-world applications, particularly in quantum cryptography, where secure communication protocols like Quantum Key Distribution (QKD) leverage the properties of entanglement to establish unbreakable encryption. The ongoing enhancements in QKD systems signal a growing emphasis on secure digital communication in an increasingly interconnected world, responding to the rising concerns over data security and privacy breaches.

In the realm of quantum sensing, breakthroughs exploiting quantum principles have yielded significant advancements in measurement precision. Quantum sensors harness entangled states to detect minute changes in physical quantities, leading to applications in medical diagnostics, environmental monitoring, and fundamental physics research. These sensors promise capabilities that far exceed classical counterparts, accentuating the transformative potential of quantum technology in our day-to-day lives.

Moreover, the integration of quantum principles into biological sciences has sparked a new frontier of research known as quantum biology. Investigations into quantum effects such as coherence and tunneling reveal how quantum phenomena might enhance critical biological processes, including photosynthesis and molecular transport. This burgeoning field not only provides insights into the mechanics of life but may also inspire innovations in technologies such as energy capture and delivery systems that mirror these natural processes.

While these breakthroughs are immensely promising, they also invite significant challenges, particularly regarding the ethical implications of deploying quantum technologies. As we leverage quantum advancements in communication and computation, concerns regarding privacy, data protection, and social equity must be addressed. The dialogues surrounding these ethical considerations will play a crucial role in shaping the acceptance and application of quantum technologies.

As we contemplate the future trajectory of quantum physics, an exciting landscape emerges—one marked by interdisciplinary collaboration among physicists, technologists, philosophers, and the public. The breakthroughs achieved so far provide a foundation for ongoing inquiry into the implications of quantum behavior on our understanding of reality, consciousness, and the nature of existence. By embracing the complexities of recent advancements and addressing the challenges they pose, we embark on a journey toward a future illuminated by quantum insights—a future where the mysteries of the universe continue to unfold, beckoning us to explore the hidden quantum world that lies beneath the surface of our perceived realities.

Through this engagement with quantum phenomena, we are not merely advancing our technological toolkit; we are forging pathways to profound philosophical questions, redefining our place within the cosmos, and ultimately enriching the human experience as we uncover the essence of life woven within the fabric of quantum mechanics.

16. Understanding Quantum Measurement

16.1. Measurement Problem: An Overview

In the vast universe of theoretical physics, few concepts evoke as much fascination and debate as the measurement problem. At its heart lies the struggle to understand how quantum systems transition from a state of potentiality to a definite outcome—the crux of what is known as quantum measurement. Understanding the measurement problem is integral to grasping the profound implications of quantum mechanics, as it challenges even our most basic intuitions about reality, observation, and existence.

The measurement problem emerges from the peculiar behaviors exhibited by quantum systems, particularly the wave function—a mathematical entity that encapsulates all possible states of a quantum system. Before measurement, a quantum system exists in a superposition, implying that it can occupy multiple states simultaneously. However, once an observation occurs, the wave function collapses to yield a single, definitive state. The nature of this collapse remains a contentious issue within the field of quantum mechanics and has led to various interpretations attempting to explain the underlying mechanisms.

One of the most prevalent interpretations of the measurement process is the Copenhagen interpretation, which posits that quantum systems do not possess definitive properties until observed. According to this view, the act of measurement fundamentally alters the system, leading to a unique outcome from previously existing probabilities. This notion invites philosophical inquiries surrounding the nature of reality and challenges the objective stance traditionally held in scientific inquiry.

In contrast, alternative interpretations such as the Many-Worlds Theory reject the idea of wave function collapse entirely. Instead, they propose that all possible outcomes of a quantum event occur, branching into parallel realities. While this interpretation elegantly resolves some paradoxes associated with measurement, it raises further questions about the nature of existence and the reality of the multiple universes posited.

Similarly, pilot-wave theory, or de Broglie-Bohm theory, introduces hidden variables to explain how particles possess definite trajectories guided by a wave function. This deterministic approach provides an alternative framework for understanding measurement that circumvents the apparent randomness of quantum mechanics. However, it has not gained the same level of acceptance as more mainstream interpretations.

Regardless of the interpretation adopted, the measurement problem underscores a fundamental insight: quantum mechanics challenges our conception of reality as an objective, observer-independent construct. The inherent role of the observer in determining outcomes poses deep philosophical inquiries about agency, reality, and the nature of consciousness.

Overcoming the measurement problem necessitates advances in technology that can probe and manipulate quantum states with greater precision. Recent developments in quantum technologies—such as quantum computing and quantum cryptography—have rejuvenated interest in understanding measurement processes, as they promise to unlock the full potential of quantum mechanics for practical applications.

Another crucial aspect of the measurement problem is quantum decoherence—an essential phenomenon where interactions between a quantum system and its environment lead to the apparent collapse of the wave function. Decoherence explains how classical behavior emerges from quantum systems, providing a bridge between quantum mechanics and everyday phenomena. By elucidating how environmental interactions affect quantum states, we gain insight into the transition from quantum superposition to classical reality.

Recent advances in quantum measurement techniques, including quantum-compatible technologies and real-time monitoring of quantum states, have also shed light on the measurement problem.

These innovative methods allow scientists to experimentally probe quantum systems while minimizing disturbances, fostering a deeper understanding of the complexities surrounding measurement.

In summary, the measurement problem encapsulates a profound challenge within quantum mechanics that invites rigorous inquiry and debate. The act of measurement transcends mere observation, compelling us to reconsider our standing notions of reality, existence, and human agency. As we navigate through the intricacies of quantum measurements and their implications, we find ourselves consistently drawn to the philosophical dimensions that accompany these scientific pursuits, leading us toward the hidden quantum realms beneath the surface of observable reality. Embracing this journey through the measurement problem not only enriches our scientific understanding but also prompts us to grapple with the deeper questions that define our existence in the cosmos.

As we advance in our quest to demystify the measurement problem and unravel quantum phenomena, we stand poised to unlock insights that will influence both our comprehension of the universe and our approach to future technologies that emerge from the quantum world. The unfolding narrative surrounding the measurement problem captures the spirit of scientific inquiry, exploring the intricate dance between observation, reality, and the quantum forces that lie beneath the surface of our perceived existence.

16.2. Wave Function Collapse: Myths and Facts

The exploration of wave function collapse reveals the intricacies of quantum mechanics, challenging our fundamental intuitions about reality and measurement. At its core, wave function collapse represents the transition of a quantum system from a superposition of multiple potential states to a single, definite state upon measurement. This profound phenomenon has spurred philosophical debate and inspired various interpretations of quantum mechanics, each seeking to elucidate the nature of reality, the role of the observer, and the implications of quantum behavior.

Historically, the concept of wave function collapse aligns closely with the Copenhagen interpretation, which asserts that quantum systems exist in a state of superposition until measured. According to this view, prior to measurement, a particle may occupy a myriad of states at once, encapsulated in its wave function. Once an observation occurs, the wave function collapses, resulting in a specific outcome that reflects one of the many possibilities. This interpretation underscores the idea that the observer influences the measurement process, raising questions about the implications of consciousness and perception on reality itself.

However, the notion of wave function collapse has not gone unchallenged. Various alternative interpretations, such as Many-Worlds Theory and pilot-wave theory, offer different perspectives on the nature of quantum states and the measurement process. Many-Worlds Theory posits that all potential outcomes coexist, creating a branching multiverse where every conceivable outcome is realized in its own parallel universe. This interpretation avoids the concept of wave function collapse altogether, suggesting that the true nature of reality encompasses a vast landscape of possibilities rather than a singular outcome determined by observation.

Conversely, pilot-wave theory asserts that particles possess definite trajectories at all times, guided by a wave function. This deterministic approach maintains that while quantum mechanics offers probabilistic predictions, the underlying behavior of particles is inherently predictable. By introducing hidden variables into the framework, pilot-wave theory provides a coherent narrative that reconciles wave behavior with classical intuitions.

The debate surrounding wave function collapse embodies philosophical inquiries about the nature of reality itself. If outcomes depend on measurement and observation, how do we define objective reality? What happens in the absence of an observer? These questions compel us to interrogate our assumptions about existence and the implications of quantum mechanics for our understanding of consciousness and agency.

Another critical aspect to consider is quantum decoherence—a process through which the interaction of a quantum system with its environment leads to the apparent collapse of the wave function. Decoherence illustrates how quantum behaviors give rise to classical phenomena, effectively bridging the gap between the quantum and classical realms. By understanding how decoherence operates, we can delineate the circumstances under which wave function collapse appears to occur, advancing our grasp of measurement and quantum state evolution.

Recent advances in quantum measurement technology also play a pivotal role in addressing the wave function collapse. New experimental methodologies are being developed to probe quantum systems' behavior and measurement processes without inducing significant disturbances. This has invigorated the quest to better understand wave function collapse and its implications for quantum mechanics, while also facilitating advancements in quantum technologies, including quantum computing and communication.

In summary, wave function collapse emerges as a focal point of inquiry in the quantum realm, capturing the interplay between measurement, observation, and reality itself. As we navigate the depths of quantum mechanics, the implications of wave function collapse prompt reflection on the nature of existence, the role of the observer, and the intricate dynamics of measurement. Engaging with the myths and facts of wave function collapse not only enriches our understanding of quantum mechanics but also invites us to explore the hidden realities that underlie our perceptions of the universe, urging us to embrace the complexities intrinsic to the quantum landscape. This journey into the quantum world paves the way for deeper insights into the nature of reality and the forces that govern our understanding of existence.

16.3. Role of the Observer in Measurements

In the field of quantum mechanics, the role of the observer in measurements stands as a compelling inquiry that intersects both scientific inquiry and philosophical discourse. This investigation is pivotal because it raises fundamental questions about the nature of reality, the process of measurement, and the relationship between the observer and the observed. As quantum mechanics challenges classical intuitions, understanding how observation influences quantum systems becomes essential to grasping the broader implications of quantum phenomena.

At the crux of this inquiry lies the concept of wave function collapse, which suggests that before measurement, a quantum system exists in a superposition of potential states. It is only upon measurement that the system's wave function collapses to yield a single observable outcome. This phenomenon highlights the active role of measurement in determining the properties of quantum systems, fundamentally at odds with classical physics, where measurements are seen as disconnected from the state of the systems being observed.

The implications of this observer effect prompt deep philosophical questions regarding the nature of reality. The conventional view posits that an objective reality exists independent of observation, where particles possess definite properties determined by physical laws. However, in quantum mechanics, this perspective becomes complicated, leading to interpretations that suggest reality may be contingent upon observation. The observer's presence can fundamentally alter the state of the system, inviting inquiries into whether objective reality can exist in the absence of observation.

Furthermore, this relationship between observation and quantum systems provokes discussions surrounding consciousness. Some interpretations of quantum mechanics propose that consciousness plays an integral role in shaping outcomes. If human observation influences quantum processes, what does this imply for our understanding of consciousness and the role it plays in the unfolding of reality? These questions stimulate rich debates within both scientific and philosophical communities, urging us to rethink the connection between the observer and the cosmos.

In addition to philosophical considerations, the technological implications of the observer's role are significant. Quantum technologies, including quantum cryptography and quantum computing, exploit the principles governing measurement and observation to develop secure and high-performance systems. For instance, in quantum key distribution (QKD), the security of communication relies on the detection of interference caused by any unauthorized observation. Understanding the intricacies surrounding the observer's role will be essential as we refine and integrate these technologies into practical applications.

The challenges of maintaining coherence in quantum states also highlight the importance of measurement techniques. Advances in quantum measurement technologies will allow for more precise and non-invasive probing of quantum systems, shedding light on the underlying mechanisms governing their behaviors while minimizing disturbances. Researchers continually strive to refine measurement strategies, working toward achieving the delicate balance between observation and the integrity of the quantum state.

As we contemplate the future trajectory of quantum mechanics, the inquiry into the role of the observer in measurements will undoubtedly remain central to advancements across theoretical and applied dimensions. Ongoing investigations will deepen our understanding of quantum phenomena while fostering discussions that bridge scientific inquiry with broader societal concerns. The interplay between measurement, reality, and the observer's influence invites us to explore the mysteries of the quantum world, where the hidden complexities beneath the surface may redefine our understanding of existence itself.

In conclusion, the role of the observer in quantum measurements encapsulates a rich tapestry of inquiry that challenges classical principles and expands our understanding of reality. By exploring the interplay between observation, quantum states, and the philosophical implications that arise, we engage with fundamental questions about existence, consciousness, and our place within the cosmos. The journey into understanding the observer's role in quantum mechanics invites us to embrace the complexities inherent in the quantum realm, paving the way for deeper insights and transformative advancements across both science and philosophy. As we navigate these uncharted territories, the truths we uncover will illuminate the hidden quantum world lying beneath the surface of our observed reality, guiding us toward an enriched understanding of the universe and our interaction with it.

16.4. Quantum Decoherence: The Process of Measuring

Quantum decoherence is a central element in understanding the measurement process in quantum mechanics, representing a transformative shift in how we grasp the interplay between quantum systems and their environments. As we delve into the intricacies of decoherence, we uncover insights into the behavior of quantum states, how they transition to classical realities, and the implications this has for measurement, observation, and our understanding of the nature of reality itself.

At its core, decoherence describes the phenomenon whereby a quantum system loses its quantum coherence due to interactions with its external environment. As a quantum system—such as a single particle or entangled particles—interacts with a surrounding environment composed of countless particles, the delicate wave function can become entangled with those environmental states. Consequently, the system becomes less purely quantum and more classical, leading to apparent wave function collapse in the context of measurement. In essence, decoherence reconciles the paradox between quantum mechanics and classical mechanics, elucidating how the classical world emerges from the quantum domain.

To illustrate this process, consider a quantum superposition—a state that describes a particle existing in multiple potential states simultaneously. When in isolation, the superposition can manifest as a delicate wave-like behavior. However, when exposed to environmental interactions, such as collisions with other particles or exposure to electromagnetic fields, the superposition begins to unravel. Information about the quantum state becomes increasingly distributed and entangled with the environment, leading to a loss of coherence. In practical terms, this means that, although the quantum system might still be in a superposed state, it appears classical to the observer as a singular outcome is measured.

The impact of decoherence on measurement is profoundly significant. Classical measurements are predicated on the assumption that systems possess definite properties prior to observation. In stark contrast, decoherence introduces a nuanced view: quantum systems exist in a superposition until perturbed by environmental interactions. Measurement, thus, becomes not merely a passive reflection of the system but an integral part of its dynamics. The act of measuring a quantum state inherently interacts with that state, collapsing the superposition into a definite outcome. This understanding redefines our perception of reality, challenging the classical notions of objectivity and prompting us to grapple with the philosophical implications surrounding the observer's role in shaping quantum states.

Decoherence also serves as a bridge linking quantum mechanics to classical physics, allowing scientists to illuminate the processes through which quantum behavior yields classical phenomena. Studies exploring the conditions under which coherence is lost provide invaluable insights, informing the design of experiments in quantum technology, such as quantum computing and quantum cryptography. Understanding how to manage decoherence, through techniques like error correction or controlled environments, remains an active area of research critical for realizing practical quantum devices.

Additionally, the consequences of decoherence extend into discussions about the fundamental nature of reality. If interactions with the environment cause quantum systems to lose their coherence, what does that imply about the fabric of existence? Does reality emerge from an intricate tapestry of quantum events, and where does the boundary lie between the quantum and classical worlds? The decentralized view of reality suggested by decoherence challenges traditional deterministic perspectives and invites philosophical inquiry into the nature of time, consciousness, and existence.

As we consider the future trajectory of quantum mechanics and the implications of decoherence, it becomes evident that interdisciplinary collaboration will be essential. Scientists from fields such as physics, philosophy, computer science, and cognitive studies must engage with one another to weave a cohesive understanding of quantum decoherence's role both theoretically and practically. By fostering such discourses, we pave the way for advancements that can illuminate the hidden dimensions of the quantum world—dimensions that lie beneath the surface of our conventional understandings of reality.

In summary, quantum decoherence stands as a pivotal concept that bridges quantum mechanics with measurement, shining light on the relationships between quantum systems and their environments. This phenomenon reveals the intricate dance of possibilities and how classical realities emerge from quantum potentials, leading us to richer inquiries about the nature of existence, observation, and the fabric of the universe itself. As we peel back the layers of decoherence, we unlock a deeper understanding of the hidden quantum world, inviting us to explore the profound dynamics that shape reality as we perceive it.

16.5. Recent Advances in Quantum Measurement

The exploration of recent advances in quantum measurement provides a window into the rapidly evolving landscape of quantum physics, a realm that continues to reshape our understanding of the universe and the nature of reality itself. Quantum measurement concepts form the backbone of quantum mechanics, impacting various fields from computing and cryptography to fundamental physics and cosmology.

At the center of these advances lies the measurement problem, which has long challenged the scientific community's perspective on how quantum systems behave. When observing quantum systems, one encounters the paradoxical situation where particles exist in superpositions of states, only to yield a definitive outcome upon measurement. This phenomenon has prompted various interpretations of quantum mechanics, each with its implications for understanding reality itself.

Recent experimental developments in quantum measurement aim to elucidate the nature of observation and the intricate mechanics involved in the act of measurement. These experiments include those that utilize advanced techniques to examine entangled particles and test the predictions of quantum mechanics against classical simulated behaviors. Innovations in measurement technology, such as quantum detectors and sensing devices capable of resolving fine quantum states, have opened new avenues for empirical research and potential applications.

One of the exciting recent advancements in quantum measurement is the emergence of "quantum tomography," a technique that enables scientists to reconstruct the quantum state of systems by collecting and analyzing measurement data. This process represents a significant leap in our ability to understand and manipulate quantum states, further refining our grasp of how measurement interacts with the quantum realm. Quantum tomography enhances our capacity to validate theoretical predictions, paving the way for future research that probes deeper into the quantum nature of reality.

Moreover, researchers have made strides in realizing quantum measurement techniques that minimize the observer effect—methods designed to achieve accurate measurements while preserving the delicate coherence of quantum systems. Such innovations include non-destructive measurement techniques, which allow for the exploration of quantum states without causing wave function collapse. These advances hold promise for improving quantum technologies, fostering the development of robust quantum systems that can operate effectively in practical applications.

As advances in quantum measurement continue to unfold, they raise crucial philosophical and practical questions about reality, perception, and the very nature of existence. The idea that observation alters the state of systems challenges our classical intuitions, compelling us to confront the intricate relationships between the observer and the observed. This interdependence encourages a rethinking of established scientific paradigms, prompting interdisciplinary discussions that seek to bridge the realms of physics, philosophy, and cognitive science.

Additionally, the implications of quantum measurement extend into the societal realm, as organizations increasingly look toward quantum technologies to enhance computing, secure communication, and improve data processing capabilities. The advent of quantum computing promises to revolutionize problem-solving across industries, as quantum measurement principles enhance the efficiency and performance of quantum algorithms.

However, the societal integration of these technologies also calls for deliberate ethical considerations as quantum measurement techniques come to influence data privacy, security, and access to information. As we explore the potential and challenges posed by these advances, ongoing dialogues around responsible development and proactive policy frameworks will be vital for navigating the implications of quantum technologies.

In summary, the recent advances in quantum measurement reflect a transformative phase in our understanding of quantum mechanics and its applications across various fields. By elucidating the intricacies surrounding measurement, researchers are forging connections between theory and practice that will shape the trajectory of quantum science and technology. As we continue to probe the depths of quantum measurement, we unlock profound insights into the fabric of reality—insights that encourage us to embrace the complexities of existence as we venture deeper into the hidden quantum world that permeates our understanding of the universe. By championing interdisciplinary dialogue and fostering collaboration across sectors, we can navigate the challenges and capture the opportunities afforded by advancements in quantum measurement, ultimately leading us to a richer comprehension of reality itself.

17. Quantum Reality and Human Perception

17.1. Reality: A Quantum Perspective

The understanding of reality, especially from a quantum perspective, brings forth a profound shift in our perceptions and metaphysical inquiries. Quantum mechanics fundamentally challenges classical notions through its inherent indeterminacies and the role of the observer in shaping outcomes. As we immerse ourselves in the quantum realm, concepts once held as absolute—such as objectivity, existence, and causality—transform into fluid constructs contingent on the measurement and interaction processes.

The essence of reality in quantum mechanics hinges upon pivotal phenomena, most notably superposition and entanglement. Quantum objects exist in a state of potentiality, where they can embody multiple configurations simultaneously until a measurement constrains them to a single outcome. This process raises questions about the relationship between consciousness and observation. If reality is influenced by the act of measurement, does consciousness itself play an integral role in determining states? This inquiry extends beyond mere scientific exploration; it intertwines with philosophical discourse regarding existence, the nature of being, and humanity's place within the cosmos.

Yet, the allure of quantum reality is tempered by its complexity, prompting reflections on the illusion of objectivity. Under classical physics, reality was perceived as an entity existing independently of human perception. However, in the quantum domain, we must acknowledge that what we observe is entirely contingent upon our methods of inquiry and measurement. This phenomenon not only invites skepticism about the nature of existence but also compels us to confront deeply philosophical questions about truth and understanding.

Further enriching our exploration is the connection between quantum mechanics, time, and its implications for how we comprehend temporal order. In classical physics, time holds a strict linearity, accompanied by predictable causality. Conversely, quantum mechanics introduces uncertainty into the temporal narrative, suggesting that our perception of time may not reflect a singular existence but rather a tapestry woven from possibilities influenced by quantum interactions.

The intersection of consciousness and quantum physics invigorates discussions centered on the nature and structure of the human mind. The hypothesis that consciousness could be informed by or even operate through quantum processes has spurred intrigue and skepticism alike, leading to profound investigations into the cognitive implications of quantum phenomena. Theoretically parsing out how mind and matter interrelate in quantum terms evokes challenging explorations of agency, self, and intellect.

As we synthesize knowledge about quantum reality, the philosophical discussions are essential. They probe the foundations of human understanding, juxtaposing scientific advancements alongside ethical and societal implications. Engaging in these dialogues is key for navigating not just the technical aspects of quantum mechanics but also their broader cultural impact.

The repercussions of quantum mechanics extend far beyond academic circles, as their implications influence education, scientific research, and societal perceptions of technology. Preparing future generations for a quantum future involves integrating quantum principles into curricula, enhancing public understanding, and fostering a society receptive to the transformative potential of quantum technologies.

In summary, exploring reality from a quantum perspective encompasses an intersection of science, philosophy, and consciousness. The revelations unearthed within quantum mechanics prompt us to confront our assumptions about existence, perception, and reality itself. The dialogue inspired by this framework engages us with the complexities of human experience—inviting continual exploration beneath the surface of observed phenomena, challenging our understanding of what it means to perceive, exist, and engage with the universe around us. As we advance in our inquiries, we do so with the understanding that hidden quantum realities not only shape the cosmos but also define our own paths toward knowledge, exploration, and existential inquiry.

17.2. The Illusion of Objectivity

In a world where perceptions of reality seem grounded in our intuitions and experiences, the quantum realm challenges this notion by introducing the idea that our understanding of objectivity may be illusory. The concept that the act of observation alters the nature of quantum systems invites an examination of how we define reality itself, provoking a reevaluation of the boundaries between the observer and the observed. In this chapter, we delve into the illusion of objectivity by exploring the principles of quantum mechanics that lead to this perception and the broader implications it has on our understanding of existence.

At the heart of quantum mechanics lies the phenomenon of wave function collapse. Until a measurement occurs, a quantum system exists in a state of superposition, embodying multiple potential outcomes simultaneously. The act of measurement forces the system to select a single outcome, thus collapsing the wave function. This unique behavior suggests that reality, at the quantum level, does not manifest independently of the observer; rather, it is contingent upon the act of observation itself. This raises profound questions about the nature of objectivity: Can reality truly exist without observation? Is the act of measuring an integral part of reality's fabric?

These questions evoke significant philosophical discourse surrounding the nature of consciousness and its interrelationship with quantum systems. Several interpretations of quantum mechanics arise in response to the observer's role, each grappling with the implications of measurement on reality. The Copenhagen interpretation posits that quantum systems do not possess definite states until measured, thus rendering observer-dependent realities for each individual. In contrast, Many-Worlds Theory suggests that all potential outcomes coexist within a multiverse, negating the need for wave function collapse. Both interpretations highlight the contextual nature of reality, emphasizing that our understanding of existence is not fixed but rather shaped by observation and interpretation.

The illusion of objectivity also permeates discussions related to free will and determinism. Classical physics grapples with deterministic laws that suggest every event follows a clear chain of causation. Quantum mechanics, on the other hand, introduces uncertainties and probabilities that alter how we understand choice and agency. If quantum events operate under probabilistic principles, do we possess genuine free will, or are our actions simply manifestations of indeterminate quantum events? This dynamic interplay encourages a reevaluation of the role of consciousness in decision-making and reinforces the intricate relationship between the observer and reality.

Recognizing the implications of quantum mechanics on our understanding of objectivity compels us to consider broader societal and ethical questions. As we advance in quantum technologies, the foundations of security, privacy, and personal freedom may be redefined. The integration of quantum principles into communication technologies and data security necessitates that we critically examine how these advancements influence our perceptions of privacy and human agency. Furthermore, fostering public understanding of quantum principles and their implications can facilitate informed discussions about the ethical considerations surrounding quantum technologies.

As we navigate through the complexities of quantum mechanics and the illusion of objectivity, interdisciplinary collaboration will prove vital. The merging of insights from physics, philosophy, neuroscience, and other fields can yield a holistic understanding of the implications of quantum principles, enriching our comprehension and awareness of reality. By fostering these dialogues, we can address the subtleties of existence and encourage a broader discourse surrounding the nature of consciousness, perception, and knowledge.

The journey into understanding the illusion of objectivity reflects a conscious effort to embrace the complexities inherent in quantum mechanics. By engaging with these themes, we broaden our perspectives and deepen our inquiry into the hidden quantum world, revealing the remarkable intricacies shaping our understanding of reality. As we grapple with the implications of the observer's role in measurement, we stand at the interface of science and philosophy, exploring the profound questions that define existence and shape the essence of our journey through the cosmos.

17.3. Quantum Mechanics and the Nature of Time

Quantum mechanics has profoundly challenged and reshaped our understanding of the fundamental nature of reality, particularly in relation to the concept of time. This enigmatic field invites us to reconsider our perceptions, as classical intuitions about the flow of time break down in the quantum realm. In this exploration, we delve into how quantum phenomena inform our understanding of time, leading to significant implications not only for physics but also for philosophy and our day-to-day experiences.

At its core, time in classical physics is often depicted as linear and absolute—a continuous progression from past to present to future. This linear view allows for clear cause-and-effect relationships, where events can be predicted based on preceding states. However, quantum mechanics introduces a much more complex picture. The uncertainty principle, woven into the fabric of quantum theory, suggests that the precise simultaneity of measurements becomes murky. When measuring quantum particles, one is confronted with a set of possible outcomes rather than definitive states, distorting traditional notions of temporality.

The concept of superposition, critical in quantum mechanics, allows particles to exist in multiple states simultaneously, further complicating our understanding of time. For instance, the behavior of particles in quantum systems does not follow classical time progression but occurs within a probabilistic framework—where events may manifest at different rates and in different sequences. This fluidity suggests that time itself might operate differently within the quantum context, challenging our traditional, sequential understanding of past, present, and future.

Entanglement, another hallmark of quantum mechanics, deepens this inquiry. When two particles become entangled, measuring one particle instantaneously influences the state of the other, irrespective of the distance separating them. This nonlocal correlation raises thought-provoking questions about the nature of causality and temporal order. If events can influence one another beyond classical limits, does this imply a redefinition of temporal relationships? Could it suggest that time operates differently at quantum levels, perhaps influencing how we understand its unidirectionality at macroscopic scales?

Additionally, the implications of quantum mechanics for the concept of time extend into gravitational contexts, where theories such as quantum gravity seek to reconcile quantum mechanics with general relativity. The complexity of time in this framework leads to intriguing discussions about the nature of space-time, the potential for time dilation, and the existence of singularities, such as black holes. Here, quantum effects interplay with gravitational forces, prompting further reflection on the implications and underpinnings of both time and existence within the universe.

Philosophical reflections on quantum mechanics and the nature of time raise profound inquiries about human experience. If quantum phenomena distort traditional timelines and challenge our perceptions of causality, does this influence the nature of consciousness? How do our cognitive processes engage with time, and what role does perception play in shaping our understanding of reality? These questions evoke interdisciplinary dialogues that traverse physics, philosophy, psychology, and neuroscience, inviting deeper consideration of how we comprehend time and its intersections with the human experience.

As research continues to push the boundaries of quantum mechanics, our understanding of time will likely evolve. Innovations in technology, driven by quantum principles, propose new methodologies for measuring and experiencing time, from advanced quantum clocks to systems that utilize entangled states for synchronization. This shift will undoubtedly influence how we navigate our daily lives and shape the societal structures surrounding time, information, and communication.

In conclusion, the relationship between quantum mechanics and the nature of time invites us to reconsider long-standing assumptions about reality. The fluidity of time in the quantum domain challenges classical notions of causality, forcing us to engage with profound questions about existence and perception. As we continue to unravel these complexities, we stand at the intersection of science and philosophy—an exciting frontier that beckons us to explore the hidden quantum world beneath the surface of our everyday realities. Embracing this journey into the enigmatic relationship between quantum mechanics and time will undoubtedly enrich our understanding of the universe and our place within it, as we probe the intricacies of existence and seek to comprehend the mechanisms that govern the tapestry of reality.

17.4. Consciousness and Quantum Physics

In the realm of quantum physics, the relationship between consciousness and quantum mechanics has sparked significant interest and debate among scientists, philosophers, and psychologists alike. At the heart of this exploration lies the question of whether quantum principles can elucidate the nature of consciousness, and if so, how this interplay between the quantum realm and human cognition might reshape our understanding of both mind and reality.

Quantum consciousness is a theoretical concept that posits that quantum mechanics may play a fundamental role in the processes underlying consciousness and cognition. Proponents of this perspective suggest that certain features of quantum mechanics—such as superposition, entanglement, and coherence—can provide insights into phenomena like decision-making, awareness, and the subjective experience of being. For instance, some theories propose that the brain's neural processes may exhibit quantum states, allowing for unique forms of information processing and interconnectedness that classical models cannot adequately explain.

Key figures in the quantum consciousness discourse, such as physicist Roger Penrose and neuroscientist Stuart Hameroff, have developed frameworks that suggest that consciousness arises from non-algorithmic processes grounded in quantum mechanical phenomena. Penrose's Orch-OR (Orchestrated Objective Reduction) theory proposes that consciousness results from orchestrated events in the brain at the quantum level, wherein microtubules—structural components of neurons—exhibit quantum behavior. If true, this concept would mean that consciousness is not merely the product of classical neurobiological processes but is intricately woven into the quantum fabric of the universe.

The implications of these theories are profound, leading us to reconsider the traditional notions of the mind-body connection. If consciousness entails quantum processes, the relationship between mental states and physical actions may be more complex than previously understood. The classical idea of a detached mind influencing an independent body becomes less tenable; instead, we may need to explore a synergistic interaction governed by quantum dynamics, wherein thought and action are interdependent.

Moreover, quantum decision-making emerges as a captivating area for exploration, as the unpredictability inherent in quantum mechanics could inform our understanding of human choice. If decision-making involves a probabilistic process reliant on quantum superposition, we may glean new insights into how we navigate complex choices and engage with uncertainties. This perspective echoes notions from behavioral economics that view human decisions as often diverging from classical rationality, instead influenced by a myriad of factors that might encompass quantum effects.

As we delve deeper into the psychological implications of quantum theory, we confront profound questions regarding identity, awareness, and the nature of subjective experience. How does the awareness of our quantum nature influence our perception of existence? To what extent does our understanding of consciousness evolve as we incorporate quantum mechanics into our narrative? These inquiries resonate throughout various disciplines, urging an interdisciplinary dialogue that encompasses findings from physics, neuroscience, psychology, and philosophy.

Furthermore, the intersection of quantum mechanics and consciousness raises ethical questions as our understanding advances. As we explore the potential implications of quantum consciousness and its interaction with cognition, we must grapple with the societal consequences of manipulating these principles. Ethical considerations surrounding cognitive enhancement, autonomy, and the nature of consciousness itself must be addressed as society navigates the implications of these discoveries.

In summary, quantum consciousness presents a fascinating and complex exploration that intertwines quantum mechanics with our understanding of the human mind. The theoretical foundations suggest that the very nature of consciousness may be deeply interconnected with quantum phenomena, challenging traditional views of separation between mind and matter. As this field of inquiry continues to evolve, the interplay between quantum mechanics and consciousness invites significant philosophical reflection, broadening our perspectives on existence and our relationship with the universe. Ultimately, as we seek to understand the hidden dimensions of consciousness through the lens of quantum mechanics, we embark on a transformative journey toward discovering the nature of reality itself and the profound mysteries inherent in the fabric of existence.

17.5. Philosophical Discussions on Quantum Reality

Philosophical Discussions on Quantum Reality serves as a space where the profound implications of quantum mechanics collide with enduring questions about existence, observation, and the nature of the universe. As a scientific framework, quantum mechanics challenges classical intuitions, propelling us toward reconsiderations of reality itself.

At the heart of these discussions lies the observer effect, a phenomenon that suggests the act of measurement plays an integral role in the behavior of quantum systems. In classical physics, reality is often viewed as an objective reality existing independently of our observations. In contrast, quantum mechanics introduces the notion that particles exist in superposition—a state where they can embody multiple outcomes—until measurement forces a collapse of these possibilities into a single outcome. This brings forth profound questions: If observation influences reality, can we truly claim to understand the universe independently of our perceptions? What does this mean for the nature of consciousness and its role in shaping existence?

The implications reach into discussions surrounding determinism and free will. Classical deterministic frameworks propose a universe governed by strict laws where every event follows cause-and-effect sequences. However, quantum mechanics introduces non-locality and probabilistic behaviors that complicate this view. The interconnectedness of entangled particles, for instance, implies outcomes can be correlated across distances, highlighting a collective dimension of interaction that transcends classical expectations. Herein lies the potential for a redefined understanding of free will—if outcomes of quantum events can influence our actions, do we possess agency in a fundamentally unpredictable universe?

Explorations of quantum mechanics also delve into the relationship between reality and perception, particularly concerning consciousness. The proposition that consciousness interacts with quantum systems calls into question pre-existing paradigms of mind and matter. Can consciousness itself be understood through a quantum lens? Investigations into topics such as quantum cognition suggest profound connections between cognitive processes and quantum phenomena, leading us to ponder the very nature of decision-making, awareness, and subjective experience.

Philosophically, the intersection of quantum mechanics and reality invites broader discussions about the role of knowledge and interpretation in our understanding of the universe. The quest to grasp the quantum realm intertwines scientific rigor with philosophical inquiry, revealing layers of complexity that compel us to reckon with the limitations of our cognitive frameworks. It calls upon us to discern how we construct knowledge within a probabilistic context, igniting conversations about social constructs surrounding reality and the philosophical implications therein.

As society grapples with the advances of quantum technologies —from quantum computing to quantum cryptography—ethics and societal impacts become paramount considerations. The accessibility and implications of quantum technologies prompt questions about equity, privacy, and the responsibility of scientists and technologists in shaping a future where quantum principles are integrated into daily life. How do we ensure that the benefits of quantum advancements are equitable? What ethical frameworks must guide the implementation of such transformative technologies?

The path forward is undeniably complex yet exciting. It demands interdisciplinary collaboration across physics, philosophy, cognitive science, and social studies to foster a holistic understanding of the implications raised by quantum mechanics. Engaging in these dialogues will enable us to navigate the changing terrain where quantum reality intersects with human experience, ultimately leading to enriched perspectives on existence and our role within the cosmos.

In summary, the philosophical discussions surrounding quantum reality illuminate profound inquiries into existence, observation, and the interconnectedness of all things. As quantum mechanics challenges traditional notions, we are invited to reflect on the nature of consciousness, free will, and the quest for knowledge itself. These inquiries enrich the discourse at the intersection of science and philosophy, encouraging deeper explorations into the hidden quantum world that lies beneath the surface of our perceived realities. The journey into quantum reality urges us to embrace the complexities inherent in existence and the enigmatic nature of the universe, paving the way for a greater appreciation of the intricacies that define our experience of the cosmos.

18. Quantum Mechanics and the Human Mind

18.1. Quantum Consciousness: Theoretical Foundations

As we delve into the theoretical foundations of quantum consciousness, we enter a complex and nuanced interplay between quantum mechanics and our understanding of the mind. At its essence, quantum consciousness posits that quantum processes may play a significant role in the workings of consciousness itself, offering fresh perspectives on fundamental philosophical questions about the nature of awareness, perception, and existence.

Historically, the exploration of consciousness has predominantly resided within the realms of philosophy and neuroscience, often approached from a classical standpoint that aligns with deterministic and mechanistic views of the universe. However, the advent of quantum mechanics has opened new avenues for inquiry, compelling us to examine how principles such as superposition and entanglement may influence cognitive processes and subjective experience.

Central to the discussion of quantum consciousness is the concept of the observer effect, which suggests that the act of observation alters the state of the observed quantum system. This raises profound questions about the role of the mind in interpreting and shaping reality. Are consciousness and measurement intertwined in a way that impacts the very fabric of existence? If so, how does this interplay inform our understanding of self-awareness and decision-making processes?

Theoretical frameworks proposed by physicists such as Roger Penrose and neuroscientist Stuart Hameroff offer intriguing models that connect quantum phenomena with consciousness. Penrose's orchestrated objective reduction (Orch-OR) theory posits that consciousness arises from quantum computations occurring in microtubules—structural components within neurons. This theory implies that quantum processes are essential for consciousness, framing the mind as an emergent phenomenon resulting from the orchestration of quantum events rather than merely classical neural processes.

While the theory raises exciting possibilities, it also confronts significant skepticism. Critics point out that empirical evidence linking quantum mechanics directly to consciousness is limited, stressing that much of the current discourse is speculative. The challenge remains to devise experimental frameworks capable of validating these theories in practical contexts, bridging the divide between quantum physics and cognitive sciences.

Additionally, integrating quantum mechanics into our understanding of human decision-making introduces another layer of complexity. Quantum decision-making models propose that agents do not always allocate probabilities according to classical logic. Instead, individuals may experience choices influenced by the unique characteristics of quantum phenomena. The probabilistic nature of quantum mechanics offers a novel frame for examining how decisions unfold and the potential that these processes might not follow traditional deterministic pathways.

The psychological implications of quantum theory extend into trauma, memory, and existential inquiry. If consciousness embodies quantum processes, it raises questions about the nature of human experience—how do we reconcile the subjective with the objective? How might understanding consciousness through a quantum lens inform therapeutic practices, aid in processing trauma, or enhance our understanding of cognitive distortions? These inquiries converge at the intersection of psychology, neuroscience, and quantum mechanics, fostering dynamic conversations that extend beyond traditional boundaries.

The philosophical discourse surrounding quantum consciousness invites further scrutiny regarding ethics, agency, and human experience. As our understanding deepens, implications extend into fields such as artificial intelligence, mental health, and the ethical implications of cognitive enhancements derived from quantum insights.

Rigorous interdisciplinary dialogue will be essential, as we align scientific exploration with the ethical considerations inherent in advancing technologies informed by quantum principles.

In summary, the theoretical foundations of quantum consciousness represent a multifaceted inquiry that intertwines quantum mechanics with the essence of human thought and experience. The interplay between quantum phenomena, consciousness, and perception invites profound questions about existence, self-awareness, and the complexities of decision-making processes. As researchers continue to investigate these connections, the quest for knowledge beckons us to explore the relationships that define the human experience and the nature of reality itself. Quantum consciousness holds the potential to enrich our understanding of the mind and the universe, ultimately guiding us toward deeper insights into the mysteries that lie beneath the surface of observable existence.

As we advance in our exploration of quantum consciousness, it becomes increasingly important to foster interdisciplinary collaboration among physicists, philosophers, neuroscientists, and psychologists. This dialogue will serve to illuminate the pathways that intertwine quantum mechanics and consciousness, ultimately leading us toward a richer, fuller understanding of existence and the profound intricacies of the universe we inhabit. Through continued inquiry, reflection, and openness to the possibilities presented by the intersection of quantum phenomena and human cognition, we embark on an exciting journey that promises to reveal the hidden depths of reality and consciousness beneath the surface of our everyday experiences.

18.2. The Mind-Body Connection in Quantum Terms

The relationship between the mind and body has long fascinated thinkers in philosophy, psychology, and neuroscience. When viewed through the lens of quantum mechanics, this inquiry takes on new dimensions, revealing potential interconnections between consciousness and quantum phenomena that have the power to reshape our understanding of human experience and reality itself.

In traditional philosophical discussions, the mind-body problem centers around the relationship between conscious experience and physical existence. Many theories, such as dualism and physicalism, seek to explain how mental states relate to physical brain states and bodily actions. Yet, as we explore the effects of quantum mechanics on cognition and perception, particularly through concepts such as entanglement and superposition, we encounter new possibilities that challenge classical views.

In quantum terms, consciousness may not simply be a product of neural activity but rather a complex interplay of quantum processes. Some theorists propose that the operations of consciousness involve superposition of thoughts or potential decisions—where multiple possibilities coexist within the brain until a conscious choice directs thought along a particular path. This view suggests that our decision-making processes may be inherently influenced by the probabilistic nature of quantum mechanics, allowing for a more nuanced understanding of free will.

Moreover, entanglement may play a role in establishing connections between individuals. The seemingly instantaneous correlations between entangled particles echo the dynamics of human relationships, invoking questions about shared consciousness and interconnected experiences. As researchers explore how entangled states may manifest in cognitive processes, we may begin to grasp the underlying threads that bind human interactions and cognition together and shape our collective experiences.

Some have speculated about the possibilities of quantum effects facilitating a greater interconnectedness between minds, alluding to concepts of collective consciousness. This notion—while largely theoretical—raises significant philosophical inquiries about individuality, agency, and how our thoughts and actions intertwine within a broader context of consciousness.

As we further examine the psychological implications of quantum mechanics, it becomes essential to engage with the ethical considerations surrounding these ideas. If quantum processes truly influence our thoughts and behaviors, the implications for concepts such as autonomy, responsibility, and personal integrity warrant critical reflection. Additionally, the integration of quantum cognition concepts into therapeutic practices has potential, offering new pathways for addressing mental health conditions grounded in quantum perspectives.

In the realm of education, integrating quantum principles into curricula could evolve our understanding of mind and consciousness. Teaching students about the quantum underpinnings of cognition encourages them to develop a nuanced perspective on themselves, others, and their interactions with the world. Such educational paradigms serve to enrich the discourse about human potential and the intricacies of existence.

As we continue to navigate the intersections of quantum mechanics, consciousness, and human experience, collaboration across disciplines—be it physics, philosophy, neuroscience, or psychology—will be pivotal. Engaging with these fields allows us to tackle some of the most pressing questions pertaining to the nature of reality and consciousness itself.

In summary, the mind-body connection in quantum terms invites us to explore the exhilarating possibility that consciousness may extend into the quantum realm, where quantum phenomena shape and inform our perceptions, decisions, and interactions. This perspective challenges us to reassess long-standing assumptions about reality, agency, and the essence of existence. Moving forward, this inquiry serves as a bridge between science and philosophy, fostering deeper understanding while inviting thoughtful exploration of the profound mysteries that lie beneath the surface of our conscious experience.

18.3. Quantum Decision-Making

In the realm of decision-making, the application of quantum principles opens exciting avenues for exploring how we make choices and how probabilities influence our actions. Quantum decision-making derives inspiration from the unique features of quantum mechanics, particularly superposition and entanglement, to propose that human decisions may not conform to the deterministic models traditionally employed in psychology and behavioral economics. Instead, quantum decision-making posits that our cognitive processes exhibit a more nuanced interplay of possibilities, reflecting the probabilistic nature of quantum systems.

At the core of quantum decision-making is the acknowledgment that human cognition can be influenced by multiple, competing outcomes that exist in a superposition of states until a specific decision is made. This framework suggests that instead of paths followed strictly by rationality, the decision-making process may embrace elements of indeterminacy. When faced with a choice, a person might weigh numerous probabilities simultaneously, reminiscent of quantum systems that traverse multiple states before collapsing into a definitive outcome. This perspective inspires a richer understanding of how free will operates within a realm governed by both uncertainty and possibility.

The implications of quantum decision-making extend to the insights it provides into cognitive biases and heuristics—psychological shortcuts that influence our decisions. Classical models often assume that human decisions align with rational expectations; however, quantum decision theory reclaims the subtlety and randomness associated with real-life choices. It incorporates probabilistic behaviors, reflecting how individuals may not always act strictly rationally but are influenced by their circumstances, preferences, and contextual factors. This quantum paradigm provides a more comprehensive understanding of human behavior, recognizing that decisions are not merely a product of deterministic formulas but are infused with complexities akin to quantum interactions.

Moreover, experimental research has begun to investigate how quantum models can successfully predict decision outcomes in various contexts, illuminating the potential for enhanced predictive power. For instance, if a quantum model can yield insights into preference reversals or paradoxes of choice, it may bolster the integration of quantum principles into behavioral sciences, further validating their applicability beyond physics.

The exploration of quantum decision-making may also have significant implications for artificial intelligence (AI). Incorporating quantum principles into decision-making algorithms could encourage more adaptable and nuanced systems that mirror human behaviors, effectively enhancing AI capabilities. This cross-disciplinary exploration inspires new directions in both cognitive science and computer science, urging us to think beyond the confines of traditional modeling.

However, the engagement with quantum decision-making raises philosophical inquiries about human agency, responsibility, and the nature of choice itself. If we concede that our decisions are influenced by quantum probabilities, how does this interact with our cultural assumptions about determinism and accountability? This inquiry invites us to reflect on our positions concerning morality, free will, and how we understand the essence of choice.

As research progresses toward a deeper understanding of quantum decision-making, interdisciplinary collaboration remains paramount. Bringing together experts across physics, psychology, economics, and philosophy can bridge gaps between theory and practical applications, enriching discussions that seek to expand our knowledge of both quantum systems and human cognition.

In summary, the exploration of quantum decision-making illuminates how quantum principles can reshape our understanding of choice, preference, and human behavior. By applying insights from quantum mechanics to decision theory, we open up new avenues for understanding the complexities of cognition, providing a framework that incorporates both probability and indeterminacy. As we seek to unlock the mysteries of decision-making through the lens of quantum mechanics, the journey invites profound reflections on free will, agency, and the underlying principles that define our existence. This intersection of physics and psychology promises to foster a richer dialogue, enabling us to embrace the intricate landscape of human choice in an exciting new quantum light.

18.4. Psychological Implications of Quantum Theory

The study of quantum mechanics often leads us to profound questions that extend beyond the realm of physics and touch upon philosophy, psychology, and the very fabric of societal constructs. The psychological implications of quantum theory suggest that the quantum world not only alters our understanding of physical reality but also influences our perceptions and interpretations of life itself. This section explores the intersections of quantum mechanics with human cognition, consciousness, and social dynamics, illuminating how scientific advancements can reverberate through our psychological frameworks and societal structures.

Quantum mechanics challenges classical determinism, introducing a probabilistic framework in which outcomes are not guaranteed but rather exist within a spectrum of possibilities. This probabilistic nature can have psychological implications, particularly regarding decision-making processes. If human behavior is influenced by quantifiable probabilistic outcomes, it suggests that our choices may not always stem from entirely rational or deterministic motivations. Rather, we may navigate through complexities where unpredictability and chance are intrinsic to the decision-making framework. This shift in understanding could lead to a reevaluation of concepts such as free will, personal agency, and moral responsibility. In light of quantum insights, we may be prompted to reconceptualize human agency as one that embraces certain uncertainties, fostering a richer understanding of choice and action.

Moreover, the philosophical questions surrounding consciousness are closely intertwined with the implications of quantum mechanics. The observer effect—a phenomenon that suggests the act of measurement influences quantum systems—invites profound reflections on the role of human perception in shaping reality. Many theorists and philosophers propose that consciousness itself may have a fundamentally quantum nature, suggesting that cognitive processes could be informed by quantum mechanisms. If true, this perspective would initiate a transformative dialogue surrounding cognition, identity, and our place within the cosmological narrative. The relationship between knowledge, consciousness, and quantum phenomena could ultimately redefine our approach to understanding the mind, opening avenues for research that integrate quantum theory with cognitive and neurosciences.

In addition to these philosophical inquiries, the impact of quantum mechanics on society cannot be understated. Quantum technologies —like quantum computing, sensing, and cryptography—hold the promise of revolutionizing industries ranging from communication and finance to healthcare. However, as these technologies become more integrated into the fabric of society, ethical considerations regarding privacy, equity, and accessibility must accompany their development. As quantum capabilities expand, fostering public discourse about their implications is vital to ensure that the benefits of quantum advancements are equitably distributed and that societal concerns regarding security and ethics are addressed thoughtfully.

Furthermore, the psychological implications of quantum theory extend into education and public perceptions of science. Engaging students in quantum mechanics from an early age can empower them to grapple with the complexities of quantum phenomena and its real-world applications. By integrating quantum principles into curricula, educators can foster critical thinking skills and encourage students to approach scientific inquiries with an openness to uncertainty and complexity. Public engagement initiatives that enhance understanding of quantum concepts can demystify quantum science and foster a more informed society prepared to navigate the challenges and opportunities presented by quantum advancements.

As we consider the future trajectory of quantum mechanics, it becomes apparent that interdisciplinary collaboration will be instrumental in realizing its full potential. Bridging the gap between physicists, psychologists, philosophers, and educators will promote innovative perspectives that resonate across diverse fields of study. By embracing these collaborative efforts, we can enhance our understanding of the psychological and societal implications of quantum mechanics, ultimately shaping a future where quantum principles inform and inspire new horizons of understanding and technological advancement.

In conclusion, the psychological implications of quantum theory extend far beyond the realm of physics, impacting our understanding of consciousness, agency, and societal dynamics. As quantum mechanics reshapes our perceptions of reality, we must navigate the complexities, uncertainties, and ethical considerations that accompany these advancements. By fostering interdisciplinary dialogue and engaging the public in the wonders of quantum science, we can illuminate the profound connections between quantum mechanics and the human experience, creating pathways for deeper understanding and richer existences as we explore the hidden quantum world that lies beneath the surface of our observed reality.

18.5. Where Science Meets Philosophy: Quantum and Mind

The intersection of science and philosophy regarding quantum mechanics and the mind reveals complex and profound implications that challenge our understanding of reality, consciousness, and human experience. Quantum mechanics has fundamentally altered our perception of the universe, introducing elements of indeterminacy, duality, and interconnectedness that invite scrutiny into the nature of existence itself. Within this context, the way we perceive our own consciousness and how it interacts with the quantum realm opens new avenues for inquiry and debate.

At the heart of this exploration is the acknowledgment that quantum mechanics defies classical interpretations of determinism. In the quantum realm, the act of observation plays a critical role in shaping the outcomes of events. Quantum systems exist in superpositions of states until measured, leading to the collapse of the wave function and the realization of a specific result. This raises profound questions about the observer's influence—does the conscious mind play a role in determining outcomes? Are our perceptions of reality fundamentally contingent upon our observations? These questions forge a connection between quantum phenomena and theories of consciousness, compelling us to reevaluate the nature of knowledge and the relationship between mind and matter.

Philosophical discussions of quantum consciousness have drawn attention to the relationship between quantum events and cognitive processes. Some theorists, such as Roger Penrose, propose that the workings of consciousness may be intrinsically linked to quantum processes occurring in the brain. This speculation invites a host of inquiries surrounding the essence of consciousness and our capacity to understand it through a quantum lens. If quantum mechanics underpins cognitive processes, does that illuminate the nature of human thought, creativity, and decision-making in ways classical neuroscience cannot fully capture? The notion that consciousness might reflect quantum properties encourages a reexamination of how we approach the study of the mind, yielding interdisciplinary dialogues that embrace insights from physics, philosophy, psychology, and neuroscience.

Moreover, the relationship between quantum mechanics and philosophical inquiries about existence and agency becomes poignant within the framework of free will. Classical views often portray human action as deterministic, where the future is shaped by a predictable chain of causation. However, quantum mechanics suggests that the universe is probabilistic, leading to the notion that human decision-making is intertwined with uncertainty. This interplay challenges long-standing assumptions about autonomy and agency, provoking philosophical debates around moral responsibility and our understanding of human identity.

The implications of quantum mechanics extend into societal contexts as well. The encroachment of quantum technologies—such as quantum computing, cryptography, and sensing—demands careful ethical considerations regarding privacy, security, and access. As advancements unfold, questions arise about who has access to quantum technologies and how these innovations may shape societal structures. Public understanding and engagement with quantum concepts will be vital as we prepare for a future entangled with quantum technologies, urging us to ensure equitable benefits and mitigate potential harms.

As we navigate these uncharted territories, collaboration becomes essential. Scientists, philosophers, ethicists, and educators must come together to engage in thoughtful dialogue that considers the ethical implications, societal responsibilities, and cognitive dimensions of quantum phenomena. Educational initiatives that incorporate quantum ideas can foster curiosity and inspire future generations to grapple with these profound questions, equipping them to understand the complexities that lie at the intersection of science and philosophy.

In summary, the dialogue surrounding quantum mechanics and the mind invites us to investigate the intricacies of existence, consciousness, and perception. By probing the relationships between quantum phenomena and human cognition, we find ourselves in a landscape filled with both uncertainties and revelations. As we explore these connections, we engage with fundamental philosophical inquiries that drive our understanding of reality while preparing us for the transformative impact of quantum advancements on society. The journey into the quantum world encourages curiosity, openness, and interconnectivity, as we uncover the hidden dimensions of existence that lie beneath the surface of our observed realities.

The ongoing exploration of quantum theory's impact on the human mind propels us to embrace the complexities inherent in existence, ultimately guiding our inquiry into the mysteries of consciousness and reality itself. As we delve deeper into these quantum questions, we unlock insights that may transform our understanding of both the cosmos and the intricacies of our own lives, encouraging continual investigation into the enigmatic quantum realm where science meets philosophy.

19. Impact of Quantum Mechanics on Society

19.1. Quantum Mechanics in Education

Within the field of education, the implications of quantum mechanics resonate deeply, driving a transformative shift in how scientific knowledge is imparted and understood. As quantum theories increasingly permeate various disciplines—from physics to biology and information technology—the importance of equipping students with a robust understanding of quantum principles becomes paramount. Education in quantum mechanics not only fosters critical thinking skills but also encourages curiosity and engagement with the complexities that define our universe.

At the core of integrating quantum mechanics into educational curricula is the necessity for accessibility. Traditional views of quantum physics may present barriers to students due to its abstract nature and counterintuitive principles. Consequently, educators must strive to present quantum concepts in a multifaceted manner. Utilizing analogies, visual tools (such as Feynman diagrams), and interactive learning experiences can help demystify quantum phenomena while making them relatable to students. By bridging the gap between complex theory and practical understanding, educators can spark interest and intrigue among learners, stimulating a desire to explore the quantum realm further.

In addition to enhancing understanding, education in quantum mechanics prepares students for careers within a rapidly evolving technological landscape. Quantum technology—encompassing fields such as quantum computing, quantum cryptography, and quantum sensing—represents a burgeoning sector with the potential to reshape industries. By instilling an appreciation for quantum principles at an early age, education empowers students to pursue careers in quantum research and technology, ensuring a skilled workforce prepared to tackle the challenges and opportunities of the future.

Moreover, interdisciplinary approaches to quantum education can foster dialogues that transcend traditional disciplinary boundaries. Integrating insights from philosophy, ethics, and societal implications reinforces critical discussions about the implications of quantum technologies, urging students to engage with both the scientific and ethical dimensions of their work. Such holistic frameworks allow for a more comprehensive understanding of how quantum mechanics influences not only scientific inquiry but also societal structures, equity, and individual agency.

As students venture into higher education, specialized programs focused on quantum mechanics become increasingly relevant. Graduate programs and research initiatives centered around quantum technologies can cultivate expertise, fostering innovation among future physicists, engineers, and technologists. Collaborations with industry and research institutions can enhance practical experiences, equipping students with real-world applications that reinforce the relevance of their studies and deepen their understanding of quantum systems.

Beyond the classroom, public engagement in quantum science is essential to dispel misconceptions and raise awareness about the significance of quantum advancements. Science communicators, educators, and researchers should collaboratively develop outreach programs aimed at demystifying quantum mechanics for the public —from workshops and lectures to interactive exhibits and online platforms. Empowering individuals with knowledge fosters a scientifically literate society capable of critically evaluating the implications of emerging quantum technologies, thus ensuring informed discourse that shapes policy decisions.

As we advance into an era defined by quantum discoveries, the emphasis on quantum mechanics within education serves as an opportunity to empower generations of thinkers, innovators, and leaders. By nurturing a foundation of understanding that embraces the complexities and possibilities embedded in quantum phenomena, we equip future generations to navigate and contribute to a world that increasingly relies on quantum principles.

In conclusion, the role of quantum mechanics in education represents a transformative force capable of shaping scientific literacy and preparing individuals to engage with the realities of a quantum-driven future. By focusing on accessibility, interdisciplinary approaches, and public engagement, we open the door to a rich exploration of the quantum realm, fostering a generation of individuals ready to unravel the hidden mysteries beneath the surface of reality itself. As we embrace this journey, we cultivate not only scientific inquiry but also the potential to shape a sustainable, equitable, and informed world driven by the wonders of quantum mechanics. The exploration of quantum mechanics in education is not simply an academic pursuit; it is a vital investment in the future of society as we delve deeper into the intricate dance between the quantum world and our understanding of existence.

19.2. The Quantum Leap in Scientific Research

The Quantum Leap in Scientific Research marks a period of unprecedented advancement in our understanding of fundamental science powered by the insights derived from quantum mechanics. This leap encompasses not only breakthroughs in theoretical frameworks but also transformative applications that ripple across diverse fields—from computing and cryptography to biology and materials science. As quantum concepts ground innovative methodologies, the implications for scientific research expand significantly, reshaping the trajectory of discovery and inquiry in the 21st century.

The impact of quantum mechanics on scientific research can be traced back to its foundational principles, which challenge classical paradigms and encourage new approaches to understanding the universe. Quantum phenomena such as superposition, uncertainty, and entanglement dismantle deterministic views, revealing a world that operates probabilistically. This shift compels researchers to explore the boundaries of knowledge through techniques that embrace quantum behavior, enabling a vast array of experimental investigations.

A key advancement is seen in the realm of quantum computing, which has the potential to redefine the parameters of computation itself. By employing qubits that thrive on quantum principles, researchers can explore complex calculations across vast datasets, elucidating solutions that classical computers struggle to achieve. This capability extends to multiple disciplines, including physics, chemistry, and artificial intelligence, where simulations of quantum systems promise to enhance our understanding of fundamental interactions and material properties. The development of quantum algorithms, tailored to exploit the unique capabilities of quantum computers, represents an exciting frontier for scientific research, pushing the boundaries of computational efficiency and precision.

Moreover, the advent of quantum cryptography introduces new methodologies for secure communication grounded in the principles of quantum mechanics. Quantum Key Distribution (QKD) exemplifies a crucial application where the security of communication hinges upon the inviolable nature of quantum states. This advancement empowers researchers to engage with complex problems surrounding data security, privacy, and integrity, signaling a departure from classical security protocols that are increasingly vulnerable.

The connection between quantum mechanics and biological research also presents compelling opportunities for discovery. Investigations into quantum phenomena in biological systems, such as photosynthesis and avian navigation, urge researchers to reevaluate the underlying mechanisms of life. The emergence of quantum biology inspires novel approaches that can bridge the gap between physical sciences and the life sciences, enabling breakthroughs that enrich our understanding of biological processes and lead to innovative applications in medicine and biotechnology.

Nevertheless, as we embrace the transformative potential of quantum mechanics in scientific research, we must also confront the accompanying challenges. The inherent complexity of quantum systems poses barriers to practical implementation—particularly related to maintaining coherence, error rates, and environmental interactions.

Overcoming these obstacles requires interdisciplinary collaboration, where physicists, engineers, computer scientists, and material scientists converge to devise solutions that harness the power of quantum technologies effectively.

Furthermore, as quantum mechanics increasingly becomes integrated into the social and economic fabric, understanding the implications on society is paramount. Discussions regarding access to quantum technologies, the implications for personal privacy, and potential disparities emerging from technological advancements demand careful consideration. Engaging the public in conversations about quantum research fosters awareness, aiding in dispelling misconceptions surrounding quantum phenomena and their practical applications.

As we look ahead, the future of quantum mechanics in scientific research is poised for a revolution. The quest for deeper insights into the quantum realm drives us to envision a future where quantum principles redefine our technologies, enhance our understanding of nature, and inspire the next generation of scientific inquiry. This vision includes collaborative efforts that transcend traditional disciplines, fostering a culture of inquiry that embraces complexity, curiosity, and innovation.

In conclusion, the quantum leap in scientific research signals a transformative chapter in our understanding of the universe, where quantum mechanics serves as an integral foundation for advancements across diverse fields. As we navigate the challenges, opportunities, and innovations fostered by quantum research, we embrace a future rich with potential that continuously unravels the mysteries hidden beneath the surface of reality. The ongoing exploration of quantum phenomena invites us to broaden our perspectives and expand the frontiers of knowledge as we advance into an era defined by the extraordinary capabilities of quantum science.

19.3. Social Implications of Quantum Technologies

The exploration of the social implications of quantum technologies invites us to reflect on how advancements in quantum mechanics not only transform scientific inquiry but also reshape societal inter-actions, governance, and the ethical considerations surrounding technology. As quantum principles begin to permeate various sectors —ranging from computing and communication to healthcare and environmental monitoring—understanding the societal consequences of these innovations becomes increasingly crucial.

At the forefront of these implications is the evolution of quantum computing, which promises to revolutionize our ability to process information and solve complex problems that are beyond the capa-bilities of classical computers. Industries such as finance, logistics, and pharmaceuticals stand to benefit enormously from the speed and efficiency of quantum algorithms. However, this power also raises significant concerns regarding data privacy and security. Quantum computers pose a potential threat to traditional encryption methods, underscoring an imperative to develop quantum-resistant crypto-graphic systems and mechanisms that protect sensitive information from the vulnerabilities exposed by quantum advancements.

Furthermore, quantum key distribution (QKD) presents a transforma-tive approach to secure communication, leveraging the principles of quantum mechanics to ensure unbreakable encryption. As organiza-tions adopt QKD, this paradigm shift reinforces the importance of secure communication in an era of escalating cyber threats. Never-theless, specific challenges must be addressed, including the practical implementation of quantum communication infrastructures and en-suring accessibility of these technologies across various societal sectors.

Beyond the realm of security, the deployment of quantum technolo-gies will also influence labor markets and economic opportunities. As quantum advancements redefine industries, there is a pressing need for education and training programs that prepare the workforce for emerging roles in quantum computing, communications, and engi-neering. Developing a skilled workforce will ensure that individuals and communities can participate in and reap the benefits of the quantum revolution, preventing the widening of existing socio-economic disparities.

The implications of quantum technologies extend into the realm of ethics and societal responsibility. As the development and deployment of quantum innovations progress, conversations surrounding fairness, accountability, and public good must guide decision-making processes. As quantum technologies become an integral part of daily life, engaging stakeholders—including scientists, policymakers, and the public—in thoughtful deliberations surrounding ethical standards will be essential.

Public perception of quantum science plays a critical role in shaping societal engagement with these technologies. As quantum principles are often counterintuitive and abstract, building public understanding and awareness becomes paramount. Effective science communication strategies can foster curiosity and interest in quantum mechanics while promoting informed discourse about the implications of these advancements. As society grapples with the social consequences of quantum technologies, fostering dialogue rooted in accessibility and understanding will be essential for developing public trust and acceptance.

Preparing for a quantum future also invites explorations of interdisciplinary collaboration, where scientists from physics, computer science, biology, philosophy, and social sciences unite to navigate the complexities introduced by quantum principles. This collaborative environment fosters a reciprocal exchange of ideas, enhancing our understanding of the implications of quantum advancements and leading to the holistic development of technologies that prioritize societal welfare.

In conclusion, the social implications of quantum technologies reflect a multifaceted landscape encapsulating security, economic viability, ethics, and public perception. As we navigate this uncharted territory, acknowledging the interconnections among these elements is essential in shaping a future where quantum advances benefit the collective. By fostering interdisciplinary collaboration and engaging in thoughtful dialogues with the public, we can unravel the hidden potential of quantum technologies while addressing the ethical and societal responsibilities that accompany such profound transformations. Through this reflective journey, we prepare to embrace a quantum future woven into the fabric of society, illuminating the vast possibilities that lie beneath the surface of our current understanding.

As we move forward, let us be guided by curiosity, openness to new ideas, and a commitment to ensuring that the benefits of quantum advancements are shared equitably, fostering a society enriched by the insights drawn from the hidden quantum world that shapes our reality.

19.4. Public Perception of Quantum Science

In contemplating the public perception of quantum science, we must first acknowledge that quantum mechanics presents concepts and phenomena that are often counterintuitive to everyday experiences and classical intuitions. While the foundational principles underlying quantum theory have been established over a century, the complexities and oddities of the quantum realm continue to evoke a range of reactions, from awe and fascination to confusion and skepticism among the general populace. Understanding how individuals perceive quantum science is crucial for fostering a productive dialogue surrounding its implications, applications, and the collective vision for a quantum future.

One significant hurdle in shaping public perception is the inherent complexity of quantum mechanics. Concepts such as superposition, entanglement, and wave-particle duality can challenge even the most astute minds, creating barriers to understanding. Scientific terminology, abstract formulations, and the probabilistic nature of quantum phenomena can alienate those without specialized training. Therefore, effective science communication becomes essential. By employing visual aids, analogies, and relatable examples, educators and communicators can translate quantum complexities into accessible narratives that resonate with broader audiences.

Furthermore, popular representations of quantum mechanics in media often exacerbate misconceptions. Fictional portrayals that sensationalize quantum phenomena or present them through fantastical lenses can mislead the public into oversimplifying or misunderstanding these concepts. While creative narratives can serve to intrigue and engage, they may inadvertently contribute to confusion if disconnected from scientific reality. It is vital for scientists and educators to engage with the media to ensure accurate representations of quantum science and to clarify the implications of these concepts to the public.

The public's perception of quantum science is also influenced by emerging technologies that stem from quantum principles. Innovations in areas such as quantum computing, quantum entanglement in secure communication, and quantum sensing are tangible applications that capture public interest. By emphasizing the real-world benefits of quantum advancements, such as enhanced computational capabilities or improved security measures through Quantum Key Distribution (QKD), scientists can foster enthusiasm and optimism about the potential of quantum technologies to address pressing global challenges.

However, these advancements must be accompanied by discussions about the ethical implications and societal consequences of quantum technologies. Public concerns regarding privacy, security, and access to emerging technologies necessitate thoughtful conversations and community engagement. Ensuring that the benefits of quantum advancements are equitably distributed, and addressing potential vulnerabilities regarding classical and quantum cybersecurity, must be paramount in shaping a holistic understanding of quantum mechanics.

Moreover, there is an opportunity for interdisciplinary collaborations that promote the integration of quantum science with various social sciences, humanities, and policy-making processes. Engaging experts from diverse fields can foster a richer public dialogue about the implications of quantum mechanics and its technologies, bridging the gap between scientific inquiry and societal engagement. These collaborations can provide broader perspectives on how quantum advancements resonate within the fabric of daily life and individual experiences.

As we prepare for a quantum future, addressing public perception is integral to ensuring a collective understanding of quantum science. Initiatives that promote quantum literacy—from educational initiatives to public outreach programs—can foster a society that is equipped to engage with quantum concepts thoughtfully. By instilling curiosity, openness to new ideas, and a commitment to responsible innovation, we can nurture a landscape where public perception aligns with scientific realities, illuminating the hidden quantum world that lies beneath the surface of observed phenomena.

In summary, the public perception of quantum science poses both challenges and opportunities. By prioritizing accessible communication, clarifying misconceptions, emphasizing practical applications, and engaging in ethical discussions, we can foster a more informed public dialogue around quantum science. Engaging interdisciplinary collaborations may further enhance public understanding, securing a unified vision for a future enriched by the insights drawn from the quantum realm. As we navigate this landscape, the potential to uncover the mysteries of the universe and the essence of existence through quantum mechanics invites exploration and inquiry, empowering us to unravel the layers of complexity that lie beneath the observed surface of our reality.

19.5. Preparing for a Quantum Future

Preparing for a Quantum Future involves not only understanding the current landscape of quantum mechanics but also envisioning the profound shifts that these principles will bring to society, technology, and our understanding of reality itself. As we stand on the brink of potentially revolutionary advancements in quantum technology, we must carefully consider the implications of these developments and strategize on how to harness them for the greater good.

At the forefront of this preparation is the acknowledgment of the challenges that accompany the integration of quantum technologies into existing systems. Quantum systems exhibit unique behaviors, such as sensitivity to external stimuli, which introduces complexities that classical systems do not face. Decoherence, where a quantum system loses its coherent properties due to interactions with the environment, poses significant obstacles in the development of practical quantum computing and communication systems. Researchers are actively engaged in finding methods to mitigate these issues, including error correction protocols, innovative qubit designs, and the cultivation of materials that enhance coherence times.

Quantum technologies also present formidable barriers related to scalability and practical implementation. The ambition to develop large-scale quantum computers or to deploy quantum networks necessitates substantial advances in engineering and architecture that can effectively manage quantum states and preserve their delicate properties. Moreover, as quantum systems become operational, addressing the potential for unforeseen vulnerabilities—such as new forms of cyber threats—becomes paramount. Developing comprehensive frameworks for security and ethical use will be essential in preparing for a future where quantum technologies are woven into the fabric of society.

However, alongside these challenges lie boundless opportunities. The advancements in quantum computing, cryptography, and sensing already promise tools that can solve intricate problems far beyond our current reach. The capacity for quantum computers to process information at astonishing speeds opens avenues for breakthroughs in medicine, materials science, and artificial intelligence. Innovations inspired by quantum mechanics may yield solutions to pressing global challenges, including climate change, energy sustainability, and complex logistical systems.

Furthermore, as we cultivate our understanding of quantum mechanics, interdisciplinary collaboration will be crucial in maximizing the potential of quantum technologies. Engaging experts from various fields—such as physics, computer science, biology, philosophy, and ethics—enables us to address the multifaceted implications of quantum advancements holistically. This collaborative approach will ensure that quantum innovations are designed with an awareness of societal needs, ethical considerations, and environmental sustainability.

Preparing for a quantum future entails not just technological readiness but also public education and engagement. As quantum mechanics can seem abstract and counterintuitive, fostering a public understanding of its principles is vital. Education initiatives that address quantum literacy and outreach programs aimed at demystifying quantum principles can cultivate a scientifically informed public, enabling informed discussions about future quantum technologies and their implications.

In summary, preparing for a quantum future requires a multifaceted approach that encompasses addressing challenges and seizing opportunities within the realm of quantum mechanics. By embracing interdisciplinary collaboration, fostering public understanding, and emphasizing ethical considerations, we can effectively navigate the complexities of quantum advancements. The journey toward a quantum future invites us to explore the depths of possibility nestled within the hidden quantum world—a future where the technologies we develop will reshape our society and continually enhance our understanding of existence itself. As we prepare for the next quantum revolution, let us remain open to the transformative potential embedded within quantum principles and the new realities they will unveil in our ongoing quest for knowledge and understanding.

20. The Future of Quantum Mechanics

20.1. Challenges for the Quantum Field

In the context of quantum mechanics, various challenges exist that hinder the full realization of its potential, both in theoretical constructs and practical applications. The exploration of these challenges reveals the intricacies inherent in quantizing our understanding of the universe, prompting researchers to engage with complex phenomena that defy classical intuitions.

A primary challenge in the quantum field is the issue of decoherence, which affects quantum systems' ability to maintain superposition and entanglement. Quantum systems are inherently delicate; interactions with the surrounding environment can inadvertently collapse their wave functions, leading to the loss of coherence vital for quantum computation and communication. Researchers are actively pursuing techniques that can stabilize quantum states and extend coherence times, but these endeavors require innovative materials and experimental setups capable of minimizing environmental disturbances.

The scalability of quantum technologies also presents significant hurdles. While small-scale quantum systems have yielded promising results, developing larger, practical quantum computers and communication networks poses engineering and design challenges. The need for precise control mechanisms, the effective integration of qubits, and the management of errors in quantum operations create a dynamic landscape in which theoretical advancements must be matched by engineering breakthroughs. Addressing these scalability challenges is paramount to realizing the full capabilities of quantum technologies.

Additionally, the rapid evolution of quantum computing and quantum cryptography engenders societal and ethical considerations that necessitate scrutiny. As quantum computers threaten traditional cryptographic methods, there is an urgent need to transition to quantum-resistant algorithms to safeguard sensitive data effectively. The deployment of quantum communication systems like Quantum Key

Distribution (QKD) must also grapple with questions surrounding privacy, data security, and access to technology. Policymakers and researchers must engage in thoughtful dialogues to establish robust regulations and standards that ensure equitable access and address potential disparities resulting from technological advancements.

The philosophical implications of quantum mechanics further complicate the challenges faced by researchers. Concepts such as wave function collapse, the role of the observer, and nonlocality raise fundamental questions about the nature of reality and our understanding of consciousness. While these challenges incite profound inquiries and deepen philosophical discourse, they also demand interdisciplinary collaboration across fields such as physics, philosophy, psychology, and social sciences. Addressing the various dimensions of these challenges requires a holistic approach that embraces the synergy between scientific inquiry and philosophical reflection.

While challenges abound, opportunities within the quantum field are equally vast. The pursuit of quantum computing can yield transformative advancements in fields like machine learning, optimization problems, and materials science. Quantum sensing technologies promise significant improvements in measurement precision, leading to applications in medical diagnostics, environmental monitoring, and navigation. The intersection of quantum mechanics and biology opens up new avenues for understanding complex biological systems and could lead to innovations in medicine and renewable energy.

As we anticipate future developments in quantum mechanics, fostering interdisciplinary collaboration will be paramount. Researchers from various backgrounds must unite to explore the multifaceted challenges and opportunities presented by quantum technologies. By building bridges between disciplines, we can create a robust knowledge base that addresses both the theoretical and practical implications of quantum physics, ultimately enhancing our understanding of the universe.

In summary, the challenges within the quantum field underscore the intricacies that define our understanding of quantum mechanics and its applications. Addressing issues like decoherence, scalability, ethical considerations, and philosophical inquiries will forge a path toward realizing the transformative potential of quantum technologies in our world. By embracing interdisciplinary collaboration, we can navigate these complexities, revealing the opportunities inherent in the hidden quantum world that awaits our exploration. As we confront challenges and embrace the possibilities, we are positioned to shape a quantum future that enriches our comprehension of reality and enhances our engagement with the cosmos.

20.2. Opportunities and Innovations

Opportunities and Innovations

The field of quantum mechanics is at the forefront of scientific revolution, heralding an era of remarkable opportunities and innovations that promise to reshape technology, deepen our understanding of reality, and alter the societal landscape in profound ways. As researchers continue to unveil the intricate principles underlying quantum systems, the translation of theoretical concepts into real-world applications is becoming increasingly feasible. This momentum not only enhances existing technologies but also inspires entirely new domains of inquiry and exploration.

Central to these opportunities is quantum computing, which has the potential to dramatically outperform classical computing in solving complex problems. As the capabilities of quantum computers advance —exemplified by significant breakthroughs in error correction, qubit coherence times, and scalable architectures—numerous industries stand to benefit. Whether it's drug discovery through better molecular simulations, optimizing supply chains, or developing advanced materials, the implications of harnessing quantum computing for practical solutions are staggering. The pursuit of quantum supremacy not merely represents a computational milestone; it symbolizes a shift in our ability to tackle problems once deemed insurmountable.

In addition to quantum computing, quantum communication presents equally thrilling opportunities, particularly through the lens of quantum key distribution (QKD). By employing quantum principles to establish unbreakable encryption, organizations can enhance cybersecurity, protecting sensitive information against the rising threats of malicious actors. QKD, which ensures that any interference in the communication channel is immediately detectable, offers a secure framework for future communications across government, finance, and personal data exchanges. The advancement of quantum communication networks can foster a new era of secure global communication infrastructure.

Quantum sensing technologies offer yet another frontier, enabling unprecedented measurement precision in various applications. Leveraging entangled states and the principles of quantum mechanics, quantum sensors can detect subtle changes in physical quantities such as magnetic fields, temperature, and gravitational waves. The potential applications span medical diagnostics, where quantum sensors can enhance imaging techniques, to environmental monitoring, where they can detect pollutants with remarkable sensitivity. The continual refinement of quantum sensors positions them at the cutting edge of scientific investigation and practical utility.

However, as we embrace the momentum of quantum opportunities, it is paramount to address the challenges intertwined with these innovations. Quantum technologies often face hurdles related to stability, scalability, and resource requirements, necessitating a deep commitment to research and development. The journey to practical implementations involves navigating complex questions surrounding error reduction, maintaining coherence, and ensuring the physical realization of quantum devices that can operate effectively within existing infrastructures.

Additionally, as quantum technologies evolve, so do ethical considerations. The interplay of data security, privacy, and equitable access to advancements requires that we carefully contemplate the deployment of quantum systems in society. Engaging diverse stakeholders

—including scientists, policymakers, industry leaders, and the general public—in discussions surrounding the ethical implications of quantum achievements can help foster a more equitable landscape and ensure that the benefits of quantum innovations are widely accessible.

Interdisciplinary collaboration will be vital as we move forward into the quantum age. Integration among physicists, engineers, computer scientists, biologists, and social scientists fosters a holistic approach to exploring quantum phenomena and developing applications that may address multifaceted problems. Such collaborations can catalyze innovations that draw on diverse perspectives, ultimately enhancing our capabilities to harness the full potential of quantum mechanics.

In conclusion, the opportunities and innovations presented by quantum mechanics signify a transformative leap into a future where technology fundamentally redefines our engagement with the world. The convergence of quantum computing, communication, and sensing illustrates the ever-expanding dimensions of possibility as we navigate these complexities. By embracing interdisciplinary collaboration, addressing challenges, and fostering ethical discourse, we can unlock the hidden potential embedded within quantum principles, shaping a future enriched by the marvels of the quantum world. This journey invites us not only to explore the scientific frontiers but also to engage with the broader implications of quantum advancements as we redefine our place within the universe and the intricate fabric of existence that surrounds us.

20.3. The Next Quantum Revolution

In the next quantum revolution, we stand at the brink of a transformative era that promises to redefine our technological landscape, enhance our understanding of reality, and reshape society in profound ways. The strides made in quantum mechanics over the last century have laid the groundwork for pivotal advancements across various fields, ushering in new applications that extend far beyond traditional physics. As we move forward, we anticipate a wave of innovations that challenges our perceptions, informs our ethics, and captivates our curiosity about the hidden quantum world.

The potential for quantum technology spans an array of industries —from healthcare and communication to computing and environmental monitoring. Quantum computing envisions systems capable of solving complex problems at unprecedented speeds, revolutionizing data analysis in fields such as artificial intelligence, materials science, and drug development. As researchers continue to refine qubit architectures, develop error correction protocols, and enhance coherence times, the practical realization of quantum computing becomes increasingly feasible. This technological leap not only augments computational capabilities but also permits explorations of previously inaccessible realms of understanding, expanding the horizons of scientific inquiry and innovation.

The domain of quantum communication is equally poised for expansion, primarily through advancements in quantum key distribution (QKD) and secure communication protocols. The principles of quantum entanglement and the observer effect guarantee unbreakable encryption methods that protect sensitive data in an age dominated by cyber threats. As organizations adopt these quantum security protocols, we can expect a marked improvement in the integrity and confidentiality of information shared across digital platforms.

Quantum sensing technologies are also set to transform scientific research and practical applications. These sophisticated devices leverage quantum principles to achieve unprecedented measurement precision—holding promise in medical diagnostics, where they can enhance imaging techniques, and in environmental monitoring, where they can detect pollutants at tiny concentrations. As these technologies mature, they will likely bolster our capabilities in fundamental physics research, unlocking deeper insights into cosmic phenomena, gravity, and other unexplored realms.

While these opportunities abound, realizing the next quantum revolution comes with formidable challenges. The integration of quantum technologies into existing infrastructures poses technical hurdles related to scalability, environmental resilience, and operational consistency. Researchers must develop effective methods to manage decoherence while ensuring stability in quantum systems, enabling effective quantum technology deployment across diverse applications.

Moreover, ethical considerations surrounding quantum technologies must be at the forefront of our discussions. As we embrace the advancements offered by quantum mechanics, we must address issues related to privacy, equitable access, and societal implications. Engaging a broader spectrum of stakeholders—including policymakers, researchers, business leaders, and the general public—in dialogues about the ethical dimensions of quantum developments will ensure we consider diverse perspectives and responsibly address potential vulnerabilities introduced by new technologies.

Interdisciplinary collaboration will be paramount as we navigate the complexities of the next quantum revolution. Merging insights from physics, engineering, computer science, biology, and social sciences fosters holistic approaches in addressing intricate challenges. By working together, researchers can devise solutions that not only advance quantum technologies but also hold societal value. This integration of knowledge across disciplines will empower transformative applications capable of addressing pressing global challenges, such as climate change, health disparities, and data security.

As we envision the role of quantum mechanics in the next century, a vision emerges where the wonders of quantum technologies serve to enhance everyday life. The synergy between quantum innovation and societal needs promises to redefine our interactions with technology, promoting transparency, security, and efficiency in various domains. A future empowered by quantum mechanics beckons us to explore the hidden dimensions of existence, illuminating pathways to a deeper understanding of reality while unlocking the potential for unprecedented advancement.

In conclusion, the next quantum revolution stands poised to redefine our understanding of the universe and our position within it. Through collaborative efforts, ethical considerations, and a commitment to responsible innovation, we are equipped to harness the transformative potential of quantum mechanics. As we embark on this exhilarating journey, we invite inquiry and exploration into the mysteries that lie below the surface, guiding us toward a future filled with promise, possibility, and discovery in the realms of science and technology. The unfolding narrative of the hidden quantum world challenges us to embrace its complexities and engage with the wonders that lie ahead.

20.4. Interdisciplinary Collaboration in Quantum Research

Interdisciplinary collaboration is essential to the advancement of quantum research, as the complexities and nuances inherent in quantum mechanics demand expertise from multiple fields. The challenges and opportunities presented by quantum phenomena extend beyond the boundaries of traditional scientific disciplines, urging physicists, engineers, computer scientists, and even philosophers to come together to unravel the mysteries of the quantum realm.

At the forefront of interdisciplinary collaboration in quantum research is the recognition that quantum mechanics permeates various domains. For instance, quantum computing not only involves physicists but also requires collaboration with computer scientists to develop efficient algorithms that take advantage of quantum superposition and entanglement. This collaboration fosters a synergistic relationship that enhances our understanding and application of quantum principles to solve complex problems.

Similarly, as quantum technologies such as quantum key distribution (QKD) continue to evolve, interdisciplinary cooperation becomes paramount for addressing the practical implementation of secure communication systems. Understanding the cryptographic needs of different industries—such as finance, government, and healthcare—demands input from not only quantum physicists but also cybersecurity experts and legal professionals who can navigate the implications for privacy and security.

Collaboration can also extend into the realm of biology, where quantum phenomena might play significant roles in processes such as photosynthesis or avian navigation. Engaging researchers from biology, chemistry, and physics to study these interactions promotes a holistic understanding that can lead to discoveries with real-world implications—an approach that aligns closely with the burgeoning field of quantum biology.

Education plays a critical role in facilitating interdisciplinary collaboration. Promoting quantum literacy through curricula that integrate physics, philosophy, ethics, and technology prepares the next generation of scientists and researchers with a versatile understanding of quantum mechanics. This foundation allows students to appreciate the interconnectedness of various disciplines and empowers them to formulate innovative approaches to challenges in quantum research.

As quantum research expands, societal engagement becomes increasingly relevant. Engaging the public in discussions about quantum mechanics, its potential applications, and its implications for daily life nurtures an informed population capable of critically evaluating emerging technologies. Moreover, involving diverse perspectives in these discussions can help address ethical concerns and promote equitable access to quantum advancements.

Interdisciplinary collaborative frameworks can also extend to industry partnerships, where businesses work alongside researchers to translate quantum discoveries into marketable technologies. By fostering partnerships between academia and industry, researchers can refine their theories and technologies while ensuring that innovations remain grounded in real-world applications—leading to faster transitions from laboratory to practical use.

In summary, interdisciplinary collaboration is fundamental to the advancement of quantum research, enhancing our ability to understand, apply, and innovate across diverse fields. The complexities inherent in quantum mechanics invite physicists, engineers, computer scientists, biologists, and policymakers to join forces, unraveling the intricacies of the hidden quantum world. As we forge ahead, fostering a culture of collaboration that emphasizes knowledge-sharing and respect for diverse expertise will be essential in fully realizing the potential of quantum mechanics for scientific exploration, technological advancement, and societal progress. By embracing this collaborative spirit, we open the door to groundbreaking discoveries that can reshape our understanding of reality and enhance our future in the quantum age.

20.5. Vision for Quantum Mechanics in the Next Century

As we gaze into the future of quantum mechanics over the next century, we find ourselves at the precipice of a transformative era marked by unprecedented advancements in technology, philosophical inquiry, and scientific understanding. The intricate tapestry of quantum phenomena, interwoven with everyday experiences, beckons a deeper exploration of realities previously hidden from view. This vision for quantum mechanics emphasizes the exciting possibilities, societal implications, and challenges that lay ahead, as we forge new pathways in the quantum realm.

The progression of quantum technologies promises to revolutionize multiple fields, from computing to communication, healthcare to materials science. As researchers harness the extraordinary capabilities of quantum systems, we anticipate a new wave of innovations characterized by enhanced computational power through quantum computing, secure communication through quantum cryptography, and remarkable precision in sensing technologies. These advancements have the potential to address complex problems and create solutions that reshape industries, enhance efficiencies, and revolutionize our approach to societal challenges.

In quantum computing, the exploration of qubits will lead to the refinement of algorithms that exploit the properties of superposition and entanglement, enabling researchers to solve problems far beyond the capabilities of classical systems. As we march toward practical quantum computers, interdisciplinary collaborations will be essential in overcoming challenges related to error rates and coherence. This synergy will cultivate a vibrant community dedicated to unlocking the full potential of quantum computing, positioning it as a cornerstone of future scientific inquiry and technological innovation.

Simultaneously, quantum communication will reinforce the frameworks for secure digital exchanges, protecting sensitive information in an era increasingly fraught with cybersecurity threats. The feasibility of quantum key distribution systems expanded across telecommunications infrastructure presents an opportunity to enhance privacy and security, ingraining trust in digital interactions. However, careful consideration of ethical implications will be vital to ensuring equitable access to quantum communication technologies across diverse societal sectors.

Quantum sensing technologies are poised to redefine measurement capabilities, enabling unprecedented accuracy in detecting environmental changes, biological signals, and even gravitational phenomena. As these sensors advance, they will enhance our understanding of physical processes while paving the way for solutions to urgent challenges such as climate change monitoring, medical diagnostics, and fundamental physics experiments.

The philosophical inquiries ignited by quantum phenomena will inevitably influence discourses surrounding reality, consciousness, and the nature of knowledge itself. Your anticipation of addressing the complexities inherent in these discussions will be crucial as quantum mechanics increasingly informs our understanding of existence. The notions of free will, the observer's role, and the interconnectedness of reality will remain at the forefront, driving interdisciplinary dialogues that bridge science and philosophy.

As we prepare for the quantum future, the necessity for education and public engagement will become increasingly apparent. Instilling quantum literacy within curricula across educational institutions will empower future generations to critically assess the implications of emerging technologies and engage with the challenges presented by quantum advancements. Promoting awareness and understanding within society will foster informed discussions, ultimately guiding public policies that reflect ethical standards, accessibility, and equity.

While the possibilities associated with quantum mechanics in the next century are tantalizing, we must remain cognizant of the challenges that lie within. Overcoming technical hurdles, addressing ethical dilemmas, and promoting collaboration will be paramount as we navigate this intricate landscape. The journey toward realizing the vision of quantum mechanics will require an unwavering commitment, curiosity, and an openness to exploring uncharted territories that challenge our current understanding.

In conclusion, the vision for quantum mechanics in the next century embodies an exhilarating narrative accompanied by transformative possibilities, profound philosophical inquiries, and significant societal implications. As we embrace this unfolding journey into the quantum realm, the truths hidden beneath the surface will illuminate our understanding of reality, enrich our perspectives on existence, and inspire innovations that redefine the fabric of our society. The next century will undoubtedly herald an era in which quantum mechanics not only enhances technology but also reshapes our understanding of the universe and our place within it, inviting us to explore the boundless intricacies woven into the quantum tapestry of existence.